Praise for *Above Quota Performance*

"Whether you wish to run a world-changing global company or make enough money to be comfortable for generations, you need to know how to sell and how to motivate those that sell with you. There is no more difficult role in a company than that of a salesperson. In order to succeed you need to approach the journey with curiosity, diligence, and practice. Steve Weinberg's, *Above Quota Performance*, is a great place to start your understanding of the true complexity of the science of selling. This work is a treasure trove of wisdom: understanding that objections are golden opportunities to understand the motivation of a buyer, articulating a meaningful value proposition that excites (or irritates) a prospect toward an action, and realizing that price is perhaps the least important element of a deal are only some of the lessons contained. I urge you to read with a notebook handy. You will want to refer back to those notes frequently as you embrace your selling education."

—Hugh M Jones IV is the Chief Executive Officer of RX (Reed Exhibitions) in Richmond, England, UK. He was formerly the CEO Of Accuity, a RELX Company, and has successfully sold several companies.

"Steve Weinberg brings decades of selling and management experience to the topic of enterprise sales, and he knows the research. *Above Quota Performance* is smart, timely, and clear about myths versus realities in this area of business. If you're a seller, the book is worth it for the practical checklists alone. And if you're a sales manager, his discussion about the characteristics of high performers and the implications of new buying processes for value propositions, effective sales presentation, and responding to RFPs are essential reading."

—**Frank Cespedes, Ph. D.** is a senior lecturer at the Harvard Business School and subject matter expert specializing in aligning sales and strategy. He is the author of: *Sales Management That Works: How to Sell in a World That Never Stops Changing, Aligning Strategy and Sales: The Choices, Systems*, and *Behaviors That Drive Effective Selling* and five other books.

"*Above Quota Performance* is a book written by a practitioner for practitioners. It's a book that could only be written by a one who has learned their craft over a lifetime. If you are looking for answers to the question, "How do I achieve above quota performance," let this book be your guide."

—**Anthony Iannarino** is the author of *Elite Sales Strategies: A Guide to Being One-Up, Creating Value,* and *Becoming Truly Consultative.*

"This is a terrific book for all salespeople. It addresses all critical performance challenges that salespeople face in this rapidly changing world. It is a fast read and it contains many golden nuggets that salespeople can use to close more sales and hit their quota."

—**Gerhard Gschwandtner** is the CEO of Selling Power magazine (www.sellingpower.com.) He is the CEO of the Sales 3.0 Conference and has over 15,000 followers on LinkedIn.com. He is the founder of MindSet Science, a founding member of the Sales Enablement Society, and an Advisor to DocuSign.

"A ton of actionable ideas for salespeople and sales managers. A MUST for your sales library."

— **Dr. Tony Alessandra** is the founder of Assessments 24x7 and the author of *The Platinum Rule for DISC Sales Mastery & People Smart in Business, Non-Manipulative Sales* and *The Platinum Rule for Sales Mastery*.

"*Above Quote Performance* has an approach to sales success that brings to mind the same techniques professional athletes utilize: the baseball player who says the game comes into focus and slows down to the point they can see the seams on the ball before they hit it; or the champion golfer who visualizes their putt go in before they even take their swing. If you want to be a professional salesperson of any kind, this is a must-read book."

— **Warren Weiss** is the Managing Partner at WestWave Capital and General Partner at Foundation Capital, leading venture capital firms, in Menlo Park, CA. He's a four-time CEO of venture backed companies and worked with Steve Jobs at NeXT.

"*Above Quota Performance* is a definitive 'how-to' book for Sales Executives, Sales Managers and Salespeople determined to create success in this post-Covid-19 world of complex B2B sales."

— **Bill Hoffman** is the principal Professional Sales Consultant and Training Facilitator at Sales Dynamics in Atlanta, GA. He has trained thousands of salespeople at hundreds of companies.

"*Above Quota Performance* shows you how to create a sustainable competitive sales edge. It's filled with actionable advice on maximizing every opportunity in today's ever-changing business environment."

—**Jill Konrath**, author of *SNAP Selling, Selling to Big Companies, More Sales Less Time* and *Agile Selling*

"This book is the answer key to finding prospects, setting up meetings, and then closing the deals. I can't wait to share this with my network and encourage everyone to stay the course to a winning formula!"

—**Chad Coe is a highly respected recognized expert in wealth management strategies and the CEO of Coe Management Group. He is the author of *The Auctioneer's Apprentice a Parable for Living an Abundant Life, The Power of Peopletizing: Networking Your Way To An Abundant Life* and *The Confident Leader.***

"I have been a professional sales trainer and speaker for over 20 years in the business of helping service professionals become rainmakers. I very much enjoyed reading this book. It is very informative and it will be valuable to all salespeople—those struggling and those that are already successful. I especially liked the chapter on objections. Steve is an excellent writer."

—**Gary Pines trains and coaches non-salespeople to change behaviors so they can increase their sales. He primarily works with management consultants, actuaries, accountants, financial consultants, recruiters, and lawyers.**

"Sales is no longer a linear process where sellers can simply 'check the box' and rely on the old tried-and-true processes that worked for the previous generation. In *Above Quota Performance*, Steve Weinberg shares how to get past the tired and false and to move forward into the next generation of selling and into what really works for sellers who want to help their customers—and increase their quota performance."

—Phil Gerbyshak is a sales enablement consultant and trainer, and sales rep of 20+ years. He has 14,000 followers on LinkedIn.com.

"Above Quota Performance is an excellent read for anyone who considers themselves to be a sales professional. Going well beyond most sales training material, Steve Weinberg offers insights that will take the reader to a new level of understanding and capability for successfully navigating the sales process. Anyone involved in revenue generation (sales) will gain from reading but the reader who has truly embraced the sales profession and desires to continually improve is the ideal target reader."

—Thomas Herman
Managing Director
CRO Executive RoundTable

"I like the way *Above Quote Performance* transitions from one chapter to the next. It makes the reader eager to move forward in anticipation of new information. I'm learning many new terms and concepts and keys to behavior, motivation, and sales analytics."

—Lee Sundholm, PhD is a Professor of Economics at North Park University, where he has taught for 55 years.

ABOVE
QUOTA
PERFORMANCE

ARMINLEAR

Above Quota Performance
Copyright © 2022 by Steve Weinberg
All rights reserved under the Pan-American and International Copyright
Conventions. This book may not be reproduced in whole or in part, except for
brief quotations embodied in critical articles or reviews, in any form or by any
means, electronic or mechanical, including photocopying, recording, or by any
information storage and retrieval system now known or hereinafter invented,
without written permission of the publisher, Armin Lear Press.

Library of Congress Control Number: 2022938042

ISBN (paperback): 978-1-956450-27-9
(eBook): 978-1-956450-28-6

Armin Lear Press Inc
215 W Riverside Drive, #4362
Estes Park, CO 80517

ABOVE QUOTA PERFORMANCE

Steve Weinberg

ARMINLEAR

To John,

Good luck in your sales efforts. I hope this book provides you with a few new tips.

Steve Weinberg
12/2022

"Everyone lives by selling something"[1]

---

1   "Robert Louis Stevenson Quote," Treasure Quotes, accessed April 24, 2022, https://www.treasurequotes.com/quotes/everyone-lives-by-selling-something.

This book is dedicated to my wife, Phyllis, my late parents, Ruth and Lawrence Weinberg, and my children, Genevieve and Joel.

"When all the dust is settled and all the crowds are gone, the things that matter are faith, family, and friends."
—Barbara Bush

Contents

PREFACE
The Paradox of Selling: Why is it so difficult?

Many people think selling is extremely difficult. They view sales as an arena-type profession where gladiators fight to an almost fatal finish, culminating in either private or public humiliation. Over the years, when I have told people my profession, many have responded "I could never do that."

The *Wall Street Journal* recently featured the article "The Pay Is High and the Jobs Are Plentiful, but Few Want to Go into Sales," and in it, the author, Patrick Thomas, noted that "Demand for sales roles has shot up as companies emerging from the pandemic switch to growth mode, but recruiters say they struggle to convince people to make sales a career."[2] In addition, many college graduates shun entry-level sales jobs. "Images of glad-handing car salesmen or 'Mad Men'-style account representatives are hard to shake."[3] Keith Wolf, a recruiter quoted in that article noted that "many young workers

---

2   Patrick Thomas, "The Pay Is High and Jobs Are Plentiful, but Few Want to Go into Sales," The Wall Street Journal (Dow Jones & Company, July 14, 2021), https://www.wsj.com/articles/the-pay-is-high-and-jobs-are-plentiful-but-few-want-to-go-into-sales-11626255001.
3   Ibid.

assume that sales work means convincing customers to buy with high-pressure tactics and are turned off."[4] But success in sales no longer results from such tactics. Today, sales is far more about problem-solving on behalf of your client.

Sales admittedly does involve speaking in front of groups of people, often by yourself, and it can be a little scary at first. When I ask people why they are so anxious about public speaking, they often say they are uncomfortable speaking in front of strangers and do not have the "gift of gab." They lack the self-confidence or perhaps the gravitas needed to risk possible disapproval. Most people worry about what others will think of them and if they will embarrass themselves. Several people have told me they would rather skydive than speak in public.

In fact, according to biologist Dr. Glenn Croston, in *Psychology Today,* public speaking is universally one of the most common fears in people today. Surveys routinely show fear of public speaking at the top of the list. Our fear of standing up in front of a group and talking is so great that some fear it more than death, in surveys at least. On one hand I understand, having sweated myself about getting up in front of a group. On the other hand, it seems odd that we're so afraid—what are we afraid of, anyway? What do we think will happen to us? We're unlikely to suffer any real or lasting harm—or are we?[5]

Jerry Seinfeld, the comedian, and star of the long-running television show *Seinfeld* once stated: "According to most studies, people's number one fear is public speaking. Number two is death. Death is number two. Does that sound right? This means to the average person, if you go to a funeral, you're better off in the casket than doing the eulogy."[6]

---

4   Ibid.
5   Glenn Croston, "The Thing We Fear More Than Death," Psychology Today (Sussex Publishers, November 29, 2012), https://www.psychologytoday.com/us/blog/the-real-story-risk/201211/the-thing-we-fear-more-death.
6   Susan Adams, "Why Public Speaking Scares You and How to Overcome Your

Billionaire investor Warren Buffett was so terrified about public speaking that he signed up for a Dale Carnegie speaking course to overcome his fear. Now he regularly speaks in front of thousands of people at the Berkshire Hathaway shareholders meetings. Buffett would later tell a class of business students "effective public-speaking raises a person's value by 50% instantly."[7]

Sounds crazy, doesn't it? I would hazard a guess this fear has a lot to do with the fear of embarrassment or not being able to properly express oneself. Or perhaps it may have to do with personal vanity or of being judged by the audience.

After reading this book, it is my hope that you can apply the lessons I discuss to acquire confidence in your communication skills and public speaking will become easier. Included throughout this book are sixty "takeaways" that highlight certain important facts, points, or ideas. A list of all the takeaways is included in the appendix.

One of the most frequent problems that many sales managers have now is that of inadequate pipeline creation. The concern is that pipelines are not robust enough to support their sales quotas. This book is largely focused on how to resolve that problem by using the tips and techniques that worked well for me and the sales pros I managed.

It is my intention, in this book, to help sales pros improve their effectiveness and decrease the chances of being fooled during the sales process. My goal is to have fewer greyhounds chasing the rabbits they can never catch. The sales profession offers a lot of individual freedom and creativity, merit

---

Fear," Forbes (Forbes Magazine, May 7, 2012), https://www.forbes.com/sites/susanadams/2012/03/07/why-public-speaking-scares-you-and-how-to-overcome-your-fears/#3a5854792c86.

7   Carmine Gallo, "Warren Buffett Was 'Terrified' of Public Speaking and Took 3 Steps to Conquer His Fear," Inc.com (Inc., February 27, 2018), https://www.inc.com/carmine-gallo/3-steps-to-overcome-stage-fright-that-worked-for-warren-buffett.html.

advancement, travel, opportunities to meet new people, and it can be financially rewarding. But I have also seen the ugly consequences of low sales performance on marriages, families, and employers, and it's time to change the status quo.

SECTION 1

Despite spending millions of dollars on training, corporations have not been able to solve the pervasive problem of low sales quota achievement. Companies often hire outside consultants to conduct training at annual and semi-annual sales meetings, only to see the training or new methodologies ignored by both sales managers and sales pros, who immediately return to their prior practices during the remainder of the year.

The latest solution is to focus on investing in sales enablement, a new function within the salesforce. "The foundation of sales enablement strategy is to provide sales-people with what they need to successfully engage the buyer throughout the buying process."[8] I expect that this will help improve sales success. But it is not enough. Sales professionals of all levels need to question the sales practices that have been employed for decades because technology, better-informed buyers, and the Millennial generation have made many of those practices obsolete. Due to the pandemic, virtual selling, rather

---

8   Gartner, Inc, "The Who, What, How and Why of Sales Enablement," Gartner, Inc., August 28, 2018, https://www.gartner.com/en/articles/the-who-what-how-and-why-of-sales-enablement.

than meeting in-person, has become the new norm. Changes had to be made, and many will become permanent as we move forward into the future.

One thing that hasn't changed is that turnover, primarily due to under-performance, continues to be a challenge for sales managers. Managers spend a large portion of their time on counseling underperformers, terminating them, and then recruiting and training new sales pros. This is time that could be spent assisting the salesforce in building pipelines and closing business, their area of competence and greatest value.

Under-quota performance also takes a toll on the personal lives of sales pros. In addition to the loss of income due to unemployment, sales pros question their competence, their confidence can be shaken, and their families can often be severely impacted as a result of the stress. In Section 1, I review the statistics on under-quota performance, explain that the sales cycle is no longer a linear process as it once was, and list some of the common reasons for sales failure. In these chapters, the reader will also learn how to find and use "The Edge" to your benefit, how to ask for feedback from your prospect throughout the sales cycle, and finally, I will explain why a lot of what sales pros have been taught, and are still being taught, is either out-of-date or just plain *wrong*.

ONE

More Than 50 percent Of Sales Pros Do Not Achieve Their Sales Quotas

From managing more than one thousand sales pros over my career, to researching the topic of achieving sales quotas, I have been intrigued by the fact that a large percentage of all sales pros regularly do not achieve their sales goals. Research by CSO Insights in 2015 concluded that "only 54.6 percent of sales professionals produce enough revenue to meet quota.".[9] Software firm Salesforce.com's third annual "State of Sales" report found that of all sales pros "57 percent expect to miss their quotas this year (2019)."[10]

This alarming lack of sales success should receive greater attention from corporate and sales executives, but it does not. There is no other profession where this pattern of low-performance success is tolerated. Corporations have invested generously in training, but it does not seem to be effective. Sales quota performance has remained stable at the 50 – 60 percent

9   William MacDonald, "What's the Number One Reason Salespeople Miss Quota?," Pleinaire Strategies, accessed April 25, 2022, https://pleinairestrategies.com/2016/01/whats-the-number-one-reason-salespe ople-miss-quota/#:~:text=A%20whopping%2045.4%20percent%20 of,enough%20revenue %20to%20meet%20quota.
10 Tiffani Bova, "26 Sales Statistics That Prove Selling Is Changing," The 360 Blog from Salesforce, January 25, 2019, https://www.salesforce.com/blog/2017/11/15-sales-statistics.html.

level for the past ten years.[11] This has resulted in both sales managers and sales pros looking for other answers.

Not reaching a sales quota normally results in a sales pro being classified as a "marginal performer." No one wants that label. Most sales pros desire to be high-achievers, receive recognition, win awards, and earn an above-average income. However, the typical consequence of not reaching a quota is that they are put on a performance plan, often resulting in involuntary separation. This can frequently cause cascading catastrophic effects on one's mental health, family, relationships, and economic status. And it is not just the employee who suffers. Their employer incurs the costs of high employee turnover, which can exceed $100,000 per person!

This is a no-win situation for all involved and more needs to be done to address it. There is more that companies can do to support their sales professionals, and more the sales pros can do to understand the hurdles they will face and how to address these issues *before* they become a permanent problem.

Sales Is No Longer a Linear Process

Compounding those difficulties, sales is no longer a simple linear process. McKinsey & Company noted the following trends that have resulted in more complicated sales cycles:

» Complexity of offering
» Multiple decision-makers
» Longer buying processes
» Multi-touchpoint usage
» Unpredictability of demand.[12]

---

11   CSO Insights, "2016 Sales Performance Optimization Study" (MHI Global, 2016), http://www.critical-moments.com/wp-content/uploads/2016/05/2016-Sales-Performance-Optimization-Study-Key.pdf.
12   Homayoun Hatami et al., "Sales Incentives That Boost Growth," McKinsey & Company (McKinsey & Company, October 19, 2018), https://www.mckinsey.com/business-functions/marketing-and-sales/our-insights/sales-incentives-that-boost-growth#.

There are no simple solutions to the problem of under-achieving sales quotas; there are only incremental changes that can help "move the needle" in the right direction. One answer is that sales managers and sales pros need to adapt to the changes in sales practices that have resulted from the new digital marketplace and understand that some of the sales practices previously taught are now obsolete. They also need to recognize that many buyers have become much more educated and discerning and have limited interactions with sellers. All these things factor in to taking small steps in the right direction.

Reasons for Sales Failure

Commonly cited reasons for sales pro failures are:

- » Insufficient or unproductive prospecting.
- » Not thoroughly qualifying leads.
- » Deficient preparation for calls and meetings.
- » Inadequate communication with the prospects.
- » Lack of a compelling value proposition
- » Poor follow-up skills.
- » Did not communicate with the key decision-maker.

Sales pros will also tell you that they do not receive enough leadership and coaching from their sales manager, despite the company's investments. In many cases onboarding consists of one or two days of training on internal procedures, products, marketing, and completing company forms—all of which is insufficient. Companies do own a large part of the problem.

Do You Need Help Closing Sales?

How do you know whether you really need assistance in closing more sales? Perhaps you have been questioning your abilities or are suffering from advice fatigue. I suggest that you take this quick, seven-question self-assessment.

☐ Did you fail to reach your sales quota last year? Or, in two of the past three years?

☐ Did you have opportunities that you forecasted would close, but that did not?

☐ Were you unable to reach or have conversations with the key decision-maker in several of your opportunities?

☐ Did you find that you frequently competed based solely on price?

☐ Did you have difficulty effectively articulating the value of your company's proposition at critical times?

☐ Did you prepare responses to requests for proposals but were not invited in to present?

☐ Did your company fail to provide you with enough leads?

Now score the results. If you answered "yes" to at least four of the seven questions, you did not achieve your sales goal because you have been deploying sub-optimal or obsolete sales skills.

The bottom line is that you own your success or failure. If you are not getting the help you need from your manager, marketing department, or company, it is on you to take the necessary actions to turn your sales deficit around. Whether you like it or not, you may need to make some changes to add new skillsets to fill in the gap between your current and desired results. This should include increasing activities to add qualified leads from higher probability prospects, improving your questioning of prospects, handling objections without being manipulative, providing clear and concise value propositions, understanding when to respond to a request for a proposal, delivering more memorable presentations, working your prospects effectively through the sales funnel, taking greater control of your selling time, and closing sales more efficiently.

The good news is it is not hopeless if you are willing to be open-minded to fresh ideas and make some changes. The chapters that follow contain proven sales tips and techniques that have worked for me and people that I have trained. And they will work for you as well.

Your sales results will not get any better without taking significant action. You can ask for more sales training, personal coaching, sales tools, and to tag-along with other over-quota colleagues to observe how they operate and close sales. All of that will be helpful.

You may be reluctant to turn to your manager because you do not want them to know you are having difficulty or need assistance. Or you may be afraid that if your manager senses your uncertainty, coupled with your below-average sales performance, you will lose your job. I can assure you that your manager already knows you need help but may not know what to do about it.

Goal for This Book

This book is not intended to be a sales primer on basic sales skills for beginners—it is not "Sales 101." There are many excellent books that provide tips on the fundamentals of sales and specific areas. They will cover topics such as cold calling, conducting meetings and presentations, and negotiation. This book should instead be considered an augmentation of others on the market, not a replacement. It is for sales pros who are either struggling to achieve their sales goals, or who are meeting them but still want to improve their performance. As billionaire investor Warren Buffett stated ". . . it is not necessary to do extraordinary things to get extraordinary results."[13]

This book is also for sales managers who are exasperated because they do not know how to help their sales pros achieve their sales quotas. This book is intended to be prescriptive. The adoption of the concepts discussed in this book will result in more sales pros exceeding their sales quotas. The ideas, principles, and tips included were developed over the course of my career and have worked well for me. *They can work for you, too.*

13 Benjamin Snyder, "7 Insights from Legendary Investor Warren Buffett," CNBC (CNBC, May 1, 2017), https://www.cnbc.com/2017/05/01/7-insights-from-legendary-investor-warren-buffett.html.

TWO
What Is "The Edge" And How Do I Get It?

To be successful in today's highly competitive and highly connected global marketplace, sellers need to have *The Edge* to win the sale . . . This is the "point of the spear"—the sharp tip that allows you to penetrate or puncture the hunted object, and it can be the difference between closing or losing a sale. *The Edge* is intangible—it is information about the buyer, who the decision-maker is, their short-term and long-term priorities, what has worked or not worked for them in the past, their current pain points, their personality types, or the role of the procurement person in the decision. It could also be an outstanding offering, great service, twenty-four-hour support, quick delivery, lower price, better geographical coverage, multi-language capabilities, better logistical and delivery options—and they are not mutually exclusive, as there can be several "edges" and they can change at any time.

The Edge is not something that the buyer readily identifies for the sales pro, but successful sales pros will find it through multiple conversations with the prospective buyer. It will be found through probing questions as well as non-verbal cues.

The latter are called "tells" in poker: an unconscious change in a person's behavior or demeanor that may be observed by another person. Finding *The Edge* may also take a lot of outside research: reviewing annual reports, news media releases, periodicals, and internet web searches. We may think of it as a clue, but it is more substantial. Sales pros need to discover and positively relate the prospect's needs to their offering–even if the prospect does not know how to properly articulate them, so that the business case of making a purchase is apparent to the decision maker. To win without *The Edge* is analogous to the extremely nearsighted Mr. Magoo crossing the street without being hit by a car. It can happen, but I would rather not count on it. Knowing *The Edge* can also shorten the sales cycle or even eliminate competition.

The Secret to Sales?

People frequently ask me what the secret to sales is—as if there were a single concept that will perpetually lead to repeated success. My answer is that sales is more complex than a single simple secret could provide, and yet it is simpler than many people believe possible.

Frank Bettger, the author of the classic, inspirational sales book, *How I Raised Myself from Failure to Success in Selling,* met one of the leading sales pros of his era, Clayton Hunsicker, at a sales convention. Hunsicker told Bettger "The most important secret of salesmanship is to find out what the other fellow wants, then help him find the best way to get it."[14] Simple, but accurate. Bettger rephrases this as "When you show a man what he wants, he'll move heaven and earth to get it."[15] In

---

14 Frank Bettger, *How I Raised Myself from Failure to Success in Selling* (New York, NY: Fireside, 1992), 36.
15 Bettger, p. 43.

other words, a motivated person will try to accomplish their goals. Sometimes a person needs to be prodded or incentivized to be motivated, but it is almost impossible to motivate a non-motivated person.

I frequently use analogies, especially when teaching, and some of my co-workers have poked fun of my frequent use of them throughout my career. One of my favorites is that the sales process is often like a football game. In the sport of American football, the objective of each offensive play is to earn a "first down" by advancing the ball at least ten yards, eventually gaining up to a hundred yards and a "touchdown."

The sales cycle is comparable to the process of getting the next down in football. It is best to achieve small successes (short wins) and keep moving toward the goal of closing the sale. Sales do not result from a first effort. Your objective, each time you speak or interact with the buyer is not to achieve an immediate touchdown, which is probably unrealistic, but to keep "moving the ball" toward a touchdown by achieving small successes throughout the process. Success can be holding a productive conversation, or a meeting, or even conducting a presentation. On the contrary, progress can be halted or could be moved backward, what's known as a "sack" in football. This can happen if the buyer goes on a visit to see a competitor's customer or if the sales pro cannot provide a feature or function that the buyer feels is necessary for their operation. Like football, you should not try to win dramatically by using a desperate "Hail Mary" pass that rarely works. Instead, you should keep moving positively toward the goal of fulfilling the buyer's needs with your solution.

Buyers often do not know what they want or may not be aware of a problem or pain point or recognize an opportunity to improve the current process. Some buyers are not on top of the latest developments or changes in technology in their industry. It's your job to make them aware and help them be proactive problem solvers. They will then be "heroes" at their company and with their managers, and you will likely have a friend for life, and a repeat customer.

Bettger also quotes his friend and contemporary Dale Carnegie, the famous American motivational writer and lecturer, on what it takes to motivate people:

"There is only one way under high heaven to get anybody to do anything. Did you ever stop to think of that? Yes, just one way. And that is by making the other person *want* to do it. Remember, there is no other way."[16]

It sounds simple, but it is not. You must find qualified and motivated buyers. Most of the time they are not easy to find. You also must be able to effectively communicate a story to buyers that makes them *know* you understand their needs and will put those needs first when developing a solution. By putting the buyers' needs first, you will demonstrate your integrity. Done consistently, it will lead to success in sales.

Takeaway 1: Closing Should Be a Natural Progression—If You Have Prepared For It

Consistently succeeding in sales is a result of finding qualified buyers, moving sequentially through the sales cycle, asking relevant questions to the proper people, drawing out and properly addressing all objections, while providing guidance and consultation to achieve a better solution for the buyer. You must also articulate a vision that gives the buyer confidence in your

---

16 Bettger, 41.

company's ability to deliver to the buyer's complete satisfaction. If this process is performed properly, asking for the order becomes a natural step in the sales process and comfortable for both parties. Closing should be natural and anticlimactic because you have properly performed all the "heavy lifting" by that point in the sales cycle. Closing is the next step in the progression of events. There should be no need for a hard close or the use of any gimmicks. Whenever I felt that a prospect was ready to buy, I would ask them if I should begin preparing the paperwork in a very non-threatening manner.

Is Sales an Art or a Science?

While this is up for some debate, I believe it is both—art and science. Think of it like music. There is absolutely a large amount of artistry involved, but the underlying elements to music are grounded in mathematics. The perfect combination. Selling is an art because it involves imagination and creativity and allows each person to be successful with their own, unique styles, tactics, and strategies. How to influence or persuade people is considered by some to be an art, but I, along with many others, consider it to be more of a science. Selling is also a science because a sales pro needs to understand social psychology and human behavior, product knowledge, basic mathematics, and statistics, while also exhibiting exceptional listening and, speaking skills, and time management abilities.

Succeeding in sales is not formulaic. There is not a single pattern that will work every time. Each sales opportunity is unique and has its own challenges. The people, culture, needs, sense of urgency, and budget will be different for each sales opportunity. It rarely runs the course that you may have predicted at the onset. The approach that worked well in your last sale may backfire on you on the next opportunity. But you can increase your odds of closing more sales by utilizing the simple tips and techniques that are included in this book.

THREE
If You're Not Winning, You're Losing

This sounds like a perfectly obvious statement. Isn't it a binary condition—it is either one or the other? And isn't the reverse then true, too?

No, not really. It also could be neither.

It is not always obvious. How do you know whether you are winning or losing? Who should you ask? The buyer? They're not always truthful. Your competition? They definitely can't be trusted to be honest. Your sales manager? This is probably your best option, but do you really want them to know that you have no idea of whether you are winning or losing an opportunity?

Takeaway 2: If You Are Winning You Should Be Receiving Continuous Feedback

Are you receiving positive or negative buying signals throughout the entire sales cycle? These signals might include questions, requests for additional information, objections, and feedback from your contacts. The feedback could be verbal or even non-verbal, (for instance, if they suddenly start "ghosting" you). Buyers will rarely tell you that you are winning or losing the sale, or why. If you are not receiving feedback or questions, then ask the buyers whether there is sufficient interest before proceeding further. If they are not returning your calls in a reasonable amount of time, then it is likely you are not in the final few being considered. A long period of continued silence by the buyer is normally very bad news.

You may go through a period of days or weeks without contact from a prospect and then they re-engage you for further information. When that happens, it is possible they were going in another direction and then found something that they did not like with the alternative and circled back to you. Optimally, you should be continuously in contact with several people in the corporation and will be providing them information—and gaining more information for yourself—throughout the sales cycle. When they go quiet on you, it could be that they are busy or between phases, or it could be they are avoiding you because they are uncomfortable telling you they have gone another way (or are about to do so). Most people try to avoid confrontation and do not enjoy giving bad news, especially one-on-one. They do not want to get into an argument with you about why you were not selected. Sometimes they give you reason to hope, or mixed messages, and then cut off communication. It is your job to uncover the truth so that you can either try to change the decision or cut your losses.

You Thought the Deal Was Going Well—Surprise!

"Everything was going well. We had a very good presentation. Everybody was engaged and active." When asked, the buyer responded, "Yes, your product is a possible solution," and seemed genuinely interested. Then the sales pro could not reach anyone for several days or weeks. When you finally reached somebody, the person seemed cold, indifferent, and in a hurry to get off the phone. You told your sales manager, "When I asked the prospect what the next step was, they told me they did not know and was not sure when I should contact them again." What went wrong?

The prospect has now obliquely told you that they are no longer interested in your offering, but you did not understand their message. You were not tuned in. You were on the AM radio band, and they were on FM. If there was a button the buyer had on their desk that delivered a "Sorry, but you were not selected" message, they would have used it. Instead, they go on with their business and avoid speaking with you. *If you are not winning*—by actively conversing and working with the buyer on a solution—*you are losing* or are in danger of losing the sale. You have already won or lost at that point—you just don't know it yet. The sales pro is always the last person to know whether you have won or lost.

Perhaps, you have been following the instruction of your contact to not communicate with anybody else at their company during the evaluation. Guess what? Your competitor may have ignored the contact's instruction and may secure the sale. I am not advising you to ignore the instructions, but rather to be aware that not contacting all the buying influences, including the key decision-maker, can cost you the sale. Some suggestions to not alienate your contact are to ask permission from your contact to call others, explaining that it is required as part of your process; invite the contact to attend the calls or meetings; have your sales manager contact others, or you can blame it on your manager—tell the contact that your manager insists that you do so. Completing ignoring the contact's instructions is not advised.

The "But" Call

In my opinion, these calls are the worst. Prospects will sometimes start a call by telling you how much they have enjoyed working with you on the project for the past several months. They may tell you what a nice person you are. Then the "but" comes. Instead of being direct, they waste your time with niceties. For example, "We have enjoyed working with you and you did a terrific job in getting back to us when we had questions, *BUT* . . . We decided we could go with either you or your competitor. Either one would do the job for us." Translated: You have lost the decision. They have decided to go with your competitor, and they do not want to hurt your feelings. Then they tell you that either solution will work, *but* they decided to go with the other one. The sales pro may hear everything up to the "but" statement, then nothing afterward. It is like the buyer hit a mute button after they said "but." It would be better if they were just direct about it, but customers rarely are.

One way to avoid this call is to determine if your value proposition is resonating with the buyer by asking them what they perceive to be the benefits or value of your solution, especially as compared to the alternatives, *during* the sales cycle, not at the end. It is a good sign if they can articulate the benefits as they see them, or at least some of them. It may be a cautionary sign if they cannot do so. If that happens, you can offer to help them by discussing it further and reviewing the calculations or assumptions that were developed. If they decline, it is probably the time to move on to the next opportunity.

Sales pros often ask me how frequently they should ask the buyer whether they are winning or losing. The answer is not often ... *if* you are receiving periodic requests for information, holding meetings, and speaking with all the people involved in the sales process. If that is not happening, you are probably already losing. It is best to find out as early as possible so you can either put a plan in place to turn the decision around or exit from the opportunity before investing additional time and resources. You should be regularly qualifying the opportunity throughout the sales cycle. Qualifying is not a one-time event; it should be a continuous effort throughout the entire sales cycle. You should always be on alert for buying signs—or the lack of them.

Weak sales pros are often reluctant to put the buyer "on the spot" by asking for a commitment. If a sales pro is not willing to do this, he or she belongs in another profession. It may sound harsh, but it's very true. The sales profession isn't for everyone, and it's best to get out now if you can't commit to this. And if the buyer is evasive, then they're giving you negative buying signals and you need to ask for confirmation of where the buyer is in the process. It is best to find this out as early as possible in the sales process; once they have made a buying decision, it is usually too late to turn the decision around.

FOUR
Why Sales Trainers Are Often Wrong

Maybe "wrong" is not the correct word—perhaps "obsolete" is more appropriate.

Sales fundamentals never change, but how they are applied to our new technology-driven market does change. Sales pros who were once successful but are now failing to keep up with the times will be left wondering why they no longer have the skills or talent to close sales that once came easy to them. They will be depressed, like Willy Loman, the fictional protagonist in Arthur Miller's *Death of a Salesman*, a sales pro who is no longer successful in the modern world of 1949 and ultimately commits suicide.[17] You can't allow yourself to be left behind. It is important to cultivate the mentality of staying current with the market and new trends and technology.

Some Sales Trainers Have Not Updated Their Advice

As with many things in life, we have all had the experience of learning what was good/healthy/etc. only to learn that new research has proved the old information wrong. My father was

---

17   Arthur Miller, *Death of a Salesman* (New York, NY: Penguin Books, 1949).

told by U.S. military instructors during WWII that cigarette smoking was healthy. (I still do not know whether it is "safe" to drink coffee, or whole milk, or eat white bread.) This same phenomenon can be found with some of the "established" sales training practices, mostly due to the greater market education of buyers and the availability of more information from the internet. Buyers are also now wary of the old devious sales tactics—often attributed to "Used Car Sales" techniques in pop culture.

Takeaway 3: Some Sales Advice Is Obsolete and May Be Harmful

Here are fourteen sales training concepts that are now obsolete. Some are foolish, others are downright insulting:

1. "Tell them what you are going to tell them, then tell them what you're here to tell them, then tell them what you told them." The purpose of this is to reinforce your message. However, buyers will likely recognize what you are doing, and they may believe that you are trying to manipulate or trick them. It is also redundant and condescending. One alternative is to include the major topics in the meeting agenda and explain what you plan to discuss at the beginning of the meeting and then at the conclusion ask them if you have adequately covered the agenda. Do not ask the attendees if they understood you. They will not admit it publicly if they did not.

2. "Buyer's objections are bad and must be shot down." Or objections should at least be nullified by using

several well-known techniques (like those in the following bullet points). Sales pros have been trained that they should not lose to objections and will win by overcoming them. They are wrong! Objections are GOOD and should be welcomed. They are your "roadmap" to a sale and are the clues to determining what information the buyer needs. Often, they can help you shorten the sales cycle, as opposed to lengthening it. We'll discuss this in more depth in Section 2.

3. There are many specialized sales closes that are commonly used to manipulate an unwilling or uncertain prospect into buying. These include:

  » "Ben Franklin," a.k.a. the pro-con close and named in honor of Franklin's love of pro-con lists.[18]
  » the direct close, "Can you sign the order today?"
  » the alternative close, "Which of our three products works best for you?"
  » the trial close, "If we can show you how our product can handle your requirement to complete the process in thirty minutes or less, do we have a deal?"
  » the deadline close, "discounted price only good today," or "the last one available at this price."
  » the assumptive close, where you fill out the order sheet and hand it to them for signature.
  » the summary close, where you hand them a list of what you have agreed upon.
  » the "sharp-angle" close which is in response to a request from a buyer, "we will include that if you will . . ."

---

18 Cody Cameron, "Closing Technique of the Week: The Ben Franklin Close," Medium (The Startup, September 19, 2018), https://medium.com/swlh/closing-technique-of-the-week-the-ben-franklin-close-2bda69c87b6.

» the "How many do you need?" close.

» and the puppy dog close, where you tell them to take it home for a trial, (nobody ever returns a puppy).

"Trick" closes, such as these, should be retired (or confined to the used car lot) as they are offensive and ineffective. Closing should be a natural, non-threatening, concluding step of your sales process if you have earned the trust of your qualified prospect, have worked with them to demonstrate that your product, service, or solution will bring value to them, have addressed their concerns, and if they have a sense of urgency.

4. "A, B, C: Always Be Closing," a saying popularized by the David Mamet play and the later movie *Glengarry Glen Ross*, is the notion that you must be (trial) closing throughout your conversations which may offend the prospect so much that they may show you the door, close off the videoconference, or hang up the telephone. Instead, it is important to follow your sales process and recognize buying signals that indicate that they are ready to move forward with you, or if you must address additional concerns. Some sales trainers will advise you to always ask for the order at each meeting with the buyer, especially at the end. The idea behind this is that by asking for the order you may be lucky enough that the buyer might say "yes," or it will draw out an objection, such as "we think your price is too high." But is it appropriate to ask for an order at your first meeting? I do not think so.

5. Some trainers advise changing your style and your posture to mimic that of the buyer. If they are aggressive, then you act aggressively. If they talk fast, then you do so as well. This advice is sales malpractice. You are what you are, and if you believe that being a sales pro means acting like a chameleon or mynah bird, you will find that buyers will detect your lack of authenticity and you will likely lose the sale. They will also detect fake enthusiasm. Instead, just cultivate an air of confidence and sincerity.

6. "Keep using the buyer's first name." In your conversation with buyers, keep addressing them by their first names repeatedly. For example:

» You: "How are you today, *Jane?*"
» Jane: "I am fine."
» You: "*Jane,* I would like to discuss your excessive finished goods inventory problem with you."
» Jane: "Yes, that is a problem for us."
» You: "*Jane,* we have provided a solution that has helped XYZ Corp solve this problem by reducing their inventory by 25 percent. Does that sound like something you would like more information on, *Jane?*"

This is a distortion of the teachings of Dale Carnegie, who advised people to use first names in conversations because most people like to hear their names spoken. "A person's name is to that person, the sweetest, most important sound in any language."[19] Allegedly, people "tune in" when they hear their names, and it perhaps

---

19 "Remembering Names," Remembering Names | Dale Carnegie, accessed April 18, 2022, https://www.dalecarnegie.com/en/courses-v2/3741.

makes the buyer feel more important. However, I find this practice archaic, condescending, and offensive. It is a trick that has had its day and should be rested.

7. "When closing or negotiating, present your proposal and do not speak. The first person that speaks loses, even if that means sitting for several minutes of silence." So if the buyer does not respond, are you supposed to sit indefinitely and wait for them to speak? If you have been working with the buyer throughout the sales process, discussed their needs and how your value proposition meets or exceeds their expectations, your proposal should not be a surprise to the buyer. When the proposal is presented, allow time for review, and then ask if there are any questions about the specifics. Then I would ask them how much time is needed to formally respond. Sitting in front of them in silence is awkward and can come across as a "mind-game."

8. "Show up and throw up" or "spray and pray." Tell the buyers everything that you think they need to know about your product and solution: How many of this it has, how many of that, what is the maximum it can handle, what the last company that bought it liked, and then hope that something sticks. The notion is that by providing the buyer with this information about your solution they will be so overwhelmed they will decide to purchase it. This may have worked when selling copying machines in the 1960s and 1970s, but it does not work now. It is all about them, not you! They are buying a solution to their problem,

an opportunity to improve their current processes or profitability.

9. "Sell the sizzle, not the steak." This is an old sales proverb that is often misunderstood. The point is to sell benefits, not features. But it is often important to sell both, depending on the circumstance. My advice is to focus instead on the buyer's needs and wants and try to match them to your value proposition. Remember: It's all about problem-solving.

10. "Exert great pressure on the buyer to get a commitment." Some believe that when you are in a situation where the buyer does not seem interested, the sales pro should use extraordinary persuasion techniques to convince them to commit to buy your products—*now*. This can include tricks to overcome their objections and wear down their resistance. Selling is no longer trying to wear down the buyer's resistance as the characters did in the play and movie *Glengarry Glen Ross*. This might work with selling used cars or real estate, but it does not work in business to business (B2B) sales today.

11. "If you are winning, try to get a quicker decision and close the sale as fast as you are able. If you are losing, try to delay the decision." Or accelerate or stall your opportunity, depending on whether you are winning or losing. Delay could include postponing meetings, not providing timely responses, introducing issues that the buyer may not be aware of to create F.U.D. (fear, uncertainty, and doubt.) During the delay, you can try to convince the buyer that the solution they selected is

inferior in value or functionality to the one you offer. Most buyers will see through your stall techniques and will react negatively to them.

12. "Cold calling is dead." Some sales trainers assert that cold calling (defined as calling contacts that have not expressed an interest in your product or service, often from a list) is not worthwhile and is a waste of time. While I still have not yet met one sales pro that enjoys calling prospects from a list, I recognize that there are two reasons why cold calling may still be necessary:

» Most sales pros do not receive enough quality leads from their company.

» Many do not have enough qualified prospects in their pipeline to reach their sales goal.

A good guideline to use is that a pipeline equivalent to *at least* three times your target or quota of opportunities is necessary to achieve your quota. So to be successful, you own the task of filling the gap between your existing pipeline and the quantity necessary to achieve your sales goals this year. A personal marketing program, which consists of emails and cold calls is often necessary to augment the lack of leads.

13. "Sell only to the highest probability prospects." Of course, we want to sell to only the best prospects. But how does that happen? Many trainers emphasize seeking only the most qualified prospects, rather than trying to sell to the whole marketplace. They often have a methodology to help qualify the prospects, such as a questionnaire or a checklist. The result is that sales pros often spend a lot of time and resources trying to sell to a prospect that passes a basic, high-level qualification test, but may be less than optimal. For example, they may have a need, a project team, and a budget, but no real sense of urgency. Or, perhaps your product is not the best fit for their needs. And what do you do if you do not have enough high-probability prospects? The reality is that it is better to focus on prospects that are in the *Sweet Spot* where the buyer's needs, your value proposition, and your product's strength are aligned. If you do not have enough prospects, you should deploy marketing campaigns to replenish your pipeline. (This will be discussed further in Chapter 15.)

14. Do whatever is necessary to be the final presenter when the buyer is reviewing several suppliers. Many trainers say it is to your advantage to present last. The thinking is that the buyer will remember what was most recently presented to them when they make their decision. This strategy has an element of validity because buyers may forget the key points that you pointed out during your meeting, especially if there has been either a lapse in time or worse if they scheduled several on the same day.

However, I always prefer to be the first presenter so I can set the bar that the others have to meet and set the competitors up (without mentioning them by name) by emphasizing our strengths and their weaknesses—weaknesses those competitors then have to overcome in their own presentations after mine. Another reason to be first is that buyers will often choose their first or strongest choice to present before the others.

I call my strategy "the Secretariat" approach, after the Thoroughbred horse that won the Triple Crown in 1973. Secretariat usually sprinted to the lead at the outset and never gave it up.

However, I advise avoiding getting stuck in the middle of presenters if you can (for example, second of three), as the buyer will usually remember and be influenced more by the first or last presenter. One note of caution: be careful not to present *too* early in the process or you will have given it your best shot before the buyer was prepared to receive it.

Takeaway 4: Formal Sales Training Is Still Worthwhile

I am not suggesting that your company should abandon formal sales training. On the contrary, I strongly recommend it. I have attended many sales training classes and have learned a lot from various sales trainers over the years. What I am suggesting is that many of the older practices are now out-of-date and ineffective in the present marketplace and need to be replaced.

If you have worked the sales cycle properly by simply addressing the prospects' needs, demonstrated why your proposal or value proposition meets their needs better than the status quo and your competitors' proposals, then it will not be necessary to rely on hard closes or manipulation. If the buyer does not believe that your proposed solution is superior to the others, it is essential for you to gain a better understanding of their perspective and why they have come to that conclusion. You can then put a plan in action to present information, to the right people, that will change their minds.

Sales pros who do not emphasize continually building relationships with multiple levels of people in a buyers' organization (which are often not stressed in the old sales models) will not achieve their sales quotas. Today's highly competitive marketplace is analogous to the mass-extinction event that killed off all the dinosaurs. To be very successful in over-achieving your sales targets, the next generation of sales pros must focus on providing their buyers with ideas and solutions that improve their business operations and that help executives and project managers achieve their personal and business goals, resolve any known (or unknown) issues and pain points, and bring greater value to them by improving efficiency, increasing revenue, or decreasing costs.

Why Objections Are Good!

Given the choice of going into a meeting with a qualified prospect where you are certain to receive as many as ten objections versus a room with a dozen smiling faces and no objections, most sales pros would choose the latter. Not me! I love objections. Why? Because they clarify what I need to do to close the sale and what I have not done well in the sales process. The smiling faces tell me that they may have had a nice breakfast or lunch, are happy to be away from their desk, or that they have a friendly disposition. All of that is nice, but it doesn't help me close the sale.

Most sales training classes include at least one session on "objection handling." We are taught that objections are obstacles to sales and need to be neutralized. The purpose of the training is to prepare the sales pro to better handle objections that inevitably come up during the sales process, such as "Your price is too high." The sales pro needs to be able to handle the objection swiftly or maneuver around it, like hurdles in a track race, and proceed with closing the business. The class prepares the sales pro for objection "Jiu-Jitsu."

Objection Jiu Jitsu

Objections should not be a battle—or be contentious. They are the opening of a dialogue. They provide you with actionable information and will lead to valuable insights on what is holding the buyer back from purchasing your product.

Some people are very good at verbal sparring and are quick with a response to overcome each objection, such as "too expensive compared to what?" I have found that challenging objections in this manner may be considered evasive or insulting by the buyer—and often results in them being more convinced of the validity of the objection, rather than being eased by the response. Unaddressed or avoided objections remain in the mind of the buyer and grow like cancer during the evaluation.

Takeaway 5: Objections Should Be Welcomed

I offer a radical departure from the above notion. Objections are truly good—and they should be welcomed! Indeed, they should be sought. They are a roadmap telling you how to get the sale, giving you the route on how you can get from where you are to the destination—closing the sale. If you are receiving or seeking objections, it is easier to read the buyer's minds. It is all out in the open—right in front of you.

There is an old Cherokee proverb that says, "Listen to the whispers and you won't have to hear the screams."[20] Some sales pros are not tuned in when prospects make comments, or objections, which are clues to what they are thinking. These should be followed up on, either during the call or meeting or afterward, one on one with the person who stated them. For example: "Jane, during our meeting you mentioned that you did not see any availability of I.T. resources before January of next year. How does that impact your decision, and is it something I should be concerned about?" It is important to be aware that many of the comments are "red flags."[21]

Some sales pros have told me that they felt very optimistic about closing the sale because there were no objections raised during their meeting with the prospect. They assumed silence meant agreement. I have found that the opposite is often true. Silence frequently means that they do not agree with you but have chosen not to argue with you—or they have already made up their mind. Or they did not understand your solution and its value proposition and did not bother to ask any questions. You will find out later in a letter or e-mail that they dismissed you as a potential supplier. Do you wonder what has happened since the meeting or sales call? Why did the buyer deceive you? The truth is that you deceived yourself.

Let's look at a real-world example. I once conducted an account review with our Southeast sales team in Atlanta and one of our top sales pros, Ted, explained that he was having a

20 "Cherokee Proverb," Education Project Management, March 9, 2005, https://educationprojects.blogs.it.umich.edu/post/79068639172/listen-to-the-whispers-and-you-wont-have-to-hear.
21 Robert B. Miller, Stephen E. Heiman, and Tad Tuleja, *The New Strategic Selling: The Unique Sales System Proven Successful by the World's Best Companies* (New York, NY: Grand Central Publishing, 2005), 69-70.

lot of trouble closing a deal with one of the regional fast-food chains. He was convinced that our company was losing to a competitor because our price was too high. It just so happened that I had previously worked for the man who became the CEO of this chain. So I called for a break and telephoned the CEO, Carl. He confirmed that he was aware of the situation and informed me that we had already lost to our competitor. I asked Carl if our price was too high relative to our competitors, as Ted had stated. Carl told me that our prices were comparable, but our team had never explained to his team how our solution could handle their difficult account coding requirement. That was a disqualifier, and we were not considered further. I went back into the account review meeting and Ted said they brought up the account coding issue just once during his several meetings with the team, but that it was never mentioned again. Perhaps Ted lost because he did not follow up on this comment to find out how important the concern was to their decision.

If You Do Not Receive Objections, Ask for Them!

Being proactive and bringing up potential objections if you do not receive any is one of the best techniques you can learn. You are not trying to sabotage your own sales opportunity; on the contrary, you are just trying to openly deal with the objections before you are ambushed with them later. For example, "Does our proposal meet your price expectations?" or "Does the functionality that we demonstrated meet your needs?" The reason is that if you deal with these (sometimes hidden) objections early in the sales cycle, there is a lower likelihood that they will come up later, or even worse, never come up until it is too late for you to do anything about them.

Other than being told you have been chosen as the supplier,

the best information that you can receive in the meeting is to be told what their concerns are with your proposal, such as:

- » "We need more information before we make our decision."
- » "Your price is too high."
- » "Your delivery date is unacceptable."
- » "We are skeptical that you can deliver the solution on time."
- » "We are not ready to buy at this time. Call us next quarter."
- » "We do not see much difference between your solution and your competitors."
- » "We do not currently have funds for this in our budget."
- » "We need to get approval from our Managing Director, before proceeding."
- » "I like your proposal, but I am not the decision-maker."

Many objections, such as "your price is too high," should be anticipated. Once you receive an objection, thank the prospect for voicing it. Validate, and do not attack, their opinion. Also do not ignore or disparage the person that brought up the objection.

Make sure that you understand the context and real reason for the objections. Often, the way they state something may be misinterpreted. You can do this by saying something like "I understand your concern." Then restate the objection in your own words to make sure you understood it correctly and receive clarification if you did not. For example, "You have expressed a concern that you are unfamiliar with our company.

I understand that you may be worried about our ability to service your account or how long we will be around. Let's discuss how we can alleviate your concern." Listen carefully to their response. Never interrupt the prospect when they are explaining the objection to you.

If the buyer had not voiced these objections, you would not have had the opportunity to properly respond. You would have wallowed in ignorance and only been able to close the sale through blind luck, not salesmanship.

Perhaps It Is Not a Real Objection

Sometimes a voiced objection is not a real objection or a reason why they would not buy from you. However, you must treat it as though it is and evaluate its worth later. If you do not react defensively, the buyer may even provide additional, valuable, information (such as which person on the team raised the issue, the issue's importance to the decision, and any relevant company politics or quirks). There are probably other objections that are not being vocalized, at least not to you, and it is the sales pro's job to uncover as many of those as possible.

Do Not Over-React to Objections

By that I mean that when a prospect informs you that your solution is missing a feature, you should not automatically go to your product managers and urge them to commit to adding it. It is important to find out what problem they are trying to solve with that specific feature and how important it is to their evaluation. Will they purchase a solution without it? Perhaps it could be handled with an alternative (and maybe even better) approach that you already have. Or maybe there is an adequate work-around. If your product engineers did commit to adding the feature it would probably take six months to two years, and the prospect will not wait that long if another competitor already has it. If confronted with an objection for a feature that you do not have, will never have, or do not have a work-around, it is on you to shift the prospect's focus to areas of greater importance to them.

One traditional objection handling technique is called "feel, felt, and found." When the prospect voices an objection, first empathize with them so they *feel* you understand their concern. You can then follow that up with how others that purchased have *felt* similarly. Finally, explain the positive experience other clients have *found* by purchasing your product. For example: "I understand, Jennifer, that you feel our price is too high. Other prospects have felt the same way. However, after they purchased our product (or service) they experienced a 250 percent return on their investment and a reduction in customer complaints." While this technique is better than trying to counter the objection, it still does not encourage the prospect to be more forthcoming with their objections so you can determine the best strategy going forward. It is also too formulaic and will soon be revealed when potential buyers provide more than one objection.

Let's look at my "Quick Guide to Overcoming Objections." Something like this guide should be prepared by each seller's sales operations, marketing, or sales-enablement department for each of its products or solutions and discussed with all new sales pros during onboarding and refreshed at quarterly and annual sales meetings. Ideally, it should be role-played so that each person is comfortable providing an optimal response. Be sure that your response does not challenge the person who voiced the objections, but rather begins a friendly conversation.

STEVE WEINBERG'S
QUICK GUIDE TO OVERCOMING OBJECTIONS

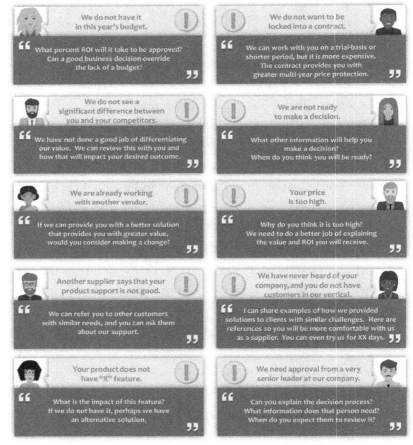

We do not have it in this year's budget.

What percent ROI will it take to be approved? Can a good business decision override the lack of a budget?

We do not want to be locked into a contract.

We can work with you on a trial-basis or shorter period, but it is more expensive. The contract provides you with greater multi-year price protection.

We do not see a significant difference between you and your competitors.

We have not done a good job of differentiating our value. We can review this with you and how that will impact your desired outcome.

We are not ready to make a decision.

What other information will help you make a decision? When do you think you will be ready?

We are already working with another vendor.

If we can provide you with a better solution that provides you with greater value, would you consider making a change?

Your price is too high.

Why do you think it is too high? We need to do a better job of explaining the value and ROI you will receive.

Another supplier says that your product support is not good.

We can refer you to other customers with similar needs, and you can ask them about our support.

We have never heard of your company, and you do not have customers in our vertical.

I can share examples of how we provided solutions to clients with similar challenges. Here are references so you will be more comfortable with us as a supplier. You can even try us for XX days.

Your product does not have "X" feature.

What is the impact of this feature? If we do not have it, perhaps we have an alternative solution.

We need approval from a very senior leader at our company.

Can you explain the decision process? What information does that person need? When do you expect them to review it?

STEVE'S SUCCESSFUL SALES STRATEGIES
WWW.STEVEWEINBERGSALES.COM

©2020 Steve Weinberg, All Rights Reserved

SECTION 2

The buyer's experience is an essential—and often neglected—aspect of the sales process. First, we will review the common steps to follow in the enterprise sales process. My term for one of these steps is "solutioning." It involves working with the prospect to determine the best solution for your customer's needs. This step is key because it should be a collaborative exercise with the buyer, and it is a step not usually identified by most sales trainers and authors. After learning those steps, we will review the typical buyer's roles and how to best work with them throughout the sales cycle.

After building the foundation of the sales process, we will look at that same process from the viewpoint of the buyers, including the procurement staff. Most sales pros are trained on how they should work the sales cycle, but they are not trained to appreciate the buyers' corresponding activities. The buying process, once mostly linear like the sales cycle, has become almost completely nonlinear and no longer follows a more predictable pattern. The buyer's staff now encompasses many more people—even compared to just ten years ago—in the evaluation and decision-making processes, and they are now better able to educate themselves on more aspects of products, services, and your competition. You need to prepare for that. So in Chapter 8, we discuss the real "why" behind many purchasing decisions, which is the reason not often disclosed to the seller, and then go on to describe who your real competitor is in most sales cycles. It is not the competing company that you often see in the marketplace, which many sales trainers and sales tip books focus on. But rather, it is the "do nothing" decision that is the toughest challenge for most sales pros.

Finally, we will close this section by discussing some reasons why your contracts *didn't* close and solutions for the common dilemmas that cause losing a contract despite positive feedback.

FIVE
Mastering the Enterprise Sales Process

The enterprise sales specialty is concerned with selling to medium to large corporations.

These sales tend to be very complex, consist of many stages, and often take many months to close, in contrast to other forms of sales. In addition, enterprise sales are usually sold by companies that employ anywhere from 25 to 2,500 sales pros. Start-ups, governments, not-for-profits, and smaller organizations have unique challenges that require a different sales approach and skill set. This chapter is aimed at improving your sales results in the enterprise sales marketplace.

There are several steps in the enterprise sales process where even minor improvements can yield dramatic results by removing unnecessary friction from your sales cycle. The most obvious are more rigorous qualification of leads, more thorough surveys/discoveries, active solutioning, building trust, and making closing a more natural process. Below are ideas that worked well for me in moving prospects through the sales cycle to a positive conclusion:

Qualifying the Lead—Make a Go/No-Go Decision

The objective of qualifying a lead is to determine whether you should continue to pursue the opportunity. In other words, deciding whether trying to sell to that company is a waste of your valuable time. This decision is made regardless of whether you developed the lead through your marketing program, calling, or an in-bound lead, such as a web inquiry. You are validating the interest of the buyer or looking for reasons to disqualify the lead or dismiss it as a real buyer in this step. A mistake that both competent and incompetent sales pros make is investing a lot of time on leads or prospects that turn out to be unqualified or unlikely buyers.

IBM developed a qualification process many years ago with an acronym, BANT, which stands for Budget, Authority, Need, and Timeline.[22] This process has had widespread adoption, and I recommend it as a basic sales tool for the initial qualification. You need to verify that there is an existing budget for the expenditure or a willingness to consider a favorable return on investment (a return greater than your expenditure), that there is an executive sponsor with the authority to purchase, and a defined need and project timeline. It is important to remember that qualification is not a one-time step; it is a continuous process throughout every single step of the sales process.

Survey & Discovery

Survey and discovery is an important information-gathering step. This consists of conducting a detailed survey in which

---

22 "Bant Opportunity Identification Criteria," IBM, accessed April 18, 2022, https://www-2000.ibm.com/partnerworld/flashmovies/html_bp_013113/html_bp_013113/bant_opportunity_identification_criteria.html.

you question members of the prospect's organization, preferably one-on-one, to learn as much as possible about them and the company. This includes learning the strategic and tactical business plans and objectives of the company and the people that you are calling on (including who the decision makers are), their industry and market forces including their competition, their key products, the company politics, financial condition, and the interest level in making changes. You cannot learn too much! The information you gather will help you later to determine areas for improvement and where there may be an opportunity for your product, service, or solution to fit the company's needs, and to formulate a sales strategy. It is a best practice to complete a prepared standard survey form, which can be referred to throughout the sales process. An example is included in the appendix.

This is often the initial time the prospect has encountered you professionally, and it is important to make a good impression regarding your subject matter expertise and your interest in not wasting their time.

Some sales pros ask the buyer: "What are your pain points?" as if they were reading a script. The question itself is trite and shifts the burden on the buyer when it belongs to the seller. It also transfers the control of the conversation to the buyer. The buyer will sometimes look at the sales pro and not know what to say. Maybe they do not have any they consider pains. Or perhaps, and more likely, they do not want to share them with you at this point because you have not established trust with them, or they are embarrassed. Perhaps they caused a problem or inefficient process to be put in place that they do not want to highlight. Artfully wording the right questions to acquire the necessary information will get you what you need while still building trust with your buyer. The understanding, linkage, and articulation of the pain points to your solution will be the backbone of your proposal and will help provide a quantification of the return on investment that the buyer will need as they build their business case so that they can receive internal approval to make a purchase. Included in Chapter 18 are many sample questions that will assist you in uncovering the pain points or needs of the buyer.

If there is an existing evaluation in process, will the prospect share their decision criteria? It could be a checklist or a vendor grading form. If you ask, and if they have established criteria, they will often share the ungraded form. You can then measure how well a fit your product is. This is also further evidence for you that they intend to make a purchase. When this process is completed, you will make a second go/no-go decision on whether you will continue to invest sales resources on this prospect.

Sometimes the prospect is not sure what they want and may not even know if they have a current problem. If that is the case, it is an opportunity for you to provide your expertise. For example, if they were not aware that they are wasting time or money on an inefficient process, it is a good idea to suggest that there might be a better way to accomplish a task. It is important to identify the costs or implications of doing nothing—of remaining with the status quo—*as that is what all change needs to be measured against.*

Your objective is always to get to the next call. This is not the time to introduce any of your solutions, even if it seems that they may be interested in hearing about them. The next call could be for additional survey and discovery/information gathering, follow-up to questions they ask, or to schedule the next step, your sales presentation.

Sales Presentation

The sales presentation, often with or succeeded by a product demonstration, will normally occur after the prospect is satisfied that you have a potential solution to an existing issue or resulting from interest you have created. It is still the most effective B2B selling tool. Product demonstrations, direct interaction, and references have the greatest likelihood of influencing a purchasing decision, according to a recent study by Cespedes and Bova.[23] However, these last two years, sales pros have had to adjust for limited contact and utilize video meetings during the coronavirus pandemic. Although some of these changes will likely stay, nothing will completely replace the traditional presentation and demonstration. I provide suggestions on how to optimize the presentation meeting in Chapters 18 and 19.

Solutioning

Some have termed this sales cycle phase as investigation or diagnosis. I prefer the term "solutioning." It is the ideal next step when the prospect is interested. In this important process, the prospect explores alternatives with you, or by themselves, that may solve their current and future problems, pains, or issues, in an interactive workshop environment. This process may be completed either before or after the presentation, but my preference is the latter. This is where they envision your product or solution in their environment and discuss issues or obstacles that may arise and how they may be solved amongst themselves. The goal is to determine if the solution being considered is a good fit and to identify any issues or hurdles. Solutioning is a good buying signal that indicates the prospect is interested in buying, but they need to resolve obstacles. For

---

23 Frank V. Cespedes, *Sales Management That Works: How to Sell in a World That Never Stops Changing* (Boston, MA: Harvard Business Review Press, 2021), 7.

example: "If we purchase this product, we will need to add staff and move this department to another area," or "It may cause Project B to be delayed due to the resources being assigned."

Prospects often will want to investigate alternatives that may include solutions that you do not offer, but you should still be involved in this process. If you are not participating in or observing this process, please be assured that the prospect will do this without you being present or involved. Or, even worse, your competitor may be involved in the process—and you are not. It is here you begin to demonstrate to the prospect that you can provide value to them.

My preference is to do a solutioning workshop in a scheduled meeting (plan for a minimum of ninety minutes) with the proper participants, using an erasable whiteboard, a chalkboard, or a flip chart. I would try to have a representative from many functional areas attend this workshop, and ideally the executive sponsor should attend as well. During the meeting, you can consider several alternatives and explore the assumed positive outcomes and negative risks (or costs and benefits) of each.

Solutioning might go something like this:

Joe: *What if we replace the current interface with one that allows integration with the back office?*

Mary: *If we do that, we will need to bump something else from our already tight schedule.*

Al: *I think the whole idea stinks.*

Joe: *How would you prefer to handle it?*

Al: *I would replace the entire application with one written in Java to avoid the interface problems we usually encounter.*

And so on.

Takeaway 6: Solutioning Should Never Be Interrupted!

You can learn a lot of important information about a prospect's people and their processes through quiet observation. By solutioning during the meeting, they are indicating that they are serious about your product, service, or solution, and are trying to determine the best ways to deploy it or are discussing what obstacles need to be overcome, such as resource issues or company politics. *Never* interrupt the team or try to insert yourself into their conversation when they are solutioning in your presence. Not only is it impolite, but it is also stupid. Sit there, be quiet, listen, and observe. Everything they are discussing is far more important to them, and you, than anything you can say. Be as unobtrusive as possible. Be silent unless they call on you for advice or for more information. Do not excuse yourself and leave the room. Instead, wait until they come back to you with a question or comment. You can learn a lot about what they view as the pros and cons of your solutions, plus any potential internal hurdles. You should also observe who seems to have the most power during their conversation. Ride that wave. Interrupting prospects when they are solutioning is sales malpractice.

The outcome of the solutioning should be a stacked rank of best and worst alternatives, which may or may not include your solution or product. Never argue with them about their conclusion, but it is fine to question whether it will achieve the desired outcome. If it does not, you will not book a sale, but you will enhance your credibility as a potential solution provider in the future. It is better to be in this position than to try to force fit your solution into a situation. The most likely outcome is that your solution will not be selected and then it is a lose/lose case—you will likely have cost yourself a better opportunity in the future. This step must be taken seriously, and you can't take it personally or get defensive. Getting the immediate sale isn't always your only goal.

Building Trust

It has been said that people will buy from people they like. It is much more complicated than that now. The project team may like the sales pro of each of the potential suppliers, (or none of them). That will not separate you from the pack, but the reverse will. If they find you to be difficult to work with, it may result in being eliminated from consideration.

Takeaway 7: People Buy From Sellers They Trust, Not Just the Ones They Like

The paradigm today is that people buy from sellers they trust. According to a recent study, the Edelman Trust Barometer, trust is the overwhelming reason for choosing a supplier. "[Eighty] percent of respondents chose to buy a particular product or service because they trusted the company behind it. Sixty-three percent said they refused to purchase a product or service because they distrusted a particular company."[24] Trust is showing the buyer or customer that meeting their needs with integrity is your highest priority—not closing the sale tomorrow. Buyers will trust sales pros who have their best interests in mind—and demonstrate it through their words and actions. It may mean recommending another solution or even

---

24 Brenda van Camp, "Lessons from Volkswagen: Branding Is Not Just a Marketing Tool, Trust Matters, And the Possibility of Combining Profit and The Common Good," LinkedIn (LinkedIn, September 27, 2015), https://www.linkedin.com/pulse/lessons-from-volkswagen-branding-just-marketing-tool-trust-van-camp/.

withdrawing from the opportunity. Buyers can like sales pros that they do not buy from. Being liked is not enough.

It is important that you begin building trust with the buyer from the first moment you approach the buyer, be it on the telephone, email, letter, at the trade show booth, or an in-person meeting. Always treat the buyer respectfully, especially concerning their time and working toward helping them achieve their business (and personal) goals. Optimally, you will have gained an understanding of the customer's current situation, desired future state, obstacles that prevent success, areas of potential improvement, and company politics because of the discovery process. It is important that you have complete mastery of your company's products, services, and solutions and how they can apply to the buyer's environment, as well as extensive knowledge of what other companies have done successfully and unsuccessfully, the current trends (such as blockchain, bitcoin, e-commerce, identity theft), and that this information is shared with the buyer. Trust is built when you show sincere interest in learning about their company, by asking general questions about the management, facilities, operations, culture, market and customers, and competition, (even if you have already researched these topics; you will learn more from them than you did on the internet, plus it shows them that you really are interested in their company). I often asked for a tour of the plant if they were a manufacturer.

Trust will also be built when you provide accurate information to the buyer during question-and-answer sessions or solutioning workshops, even if this information is not what the prospect or customer wants to hear. Telling them "No, we cannot do that," or "We do not think that is a good idea," with an explanation or a suggested alternative, enhances your credibility. Perhaps your company has an alternative solution that you can explain, along with its benefits to the buyer. On the flip side, an easy way to destroy trust is to be deceptive or lie to the buyer about the solution's functionality. There is a high likelihood that this deception will be discovered, either before or after the close of the sale and then your credibility and trust is reduced to zero. It takes a long time to build trust, but just a short amount of time to destroy any you have built.

Trust is also built when you follow through on all commitments, especially being on time. If you promise to have an answer to them by next Tuesday, then that commitment must be met, or you must inform them that you still do not have an answer but are working on it. The project team may be working on a timetable, and you need to keep them informed. Stay in contact with the customer after the sale and ensure that all your comopany's commitments are met, and that the client is satisfied. This includes contacting the executive sponsor to ensure that the positive value they are receiving exceeds the risk that she took by buying your solution. Not only is it your ethical obligation, it also may result in a later sale or referral from your satisfied customer.

Let's look at a real-life example from my own experience:

About twenty years ago, I was in the process of selling software to a large not-for-profit organization, but after I found out the database software his team had chosen, I informed the decision maker that the chosen database was sub-optimal for our solution and that I advised not utilizing our software on that platform. The team later reconsidered their decision regarding the database, chose a different one that would work better, and chose our solution. The decision maker and I became very good personal friends and still are in frequent contact with each other to this day. I established trust with him and his organization because I gave them the best advice I knew, even at the risk of not closing a sale.

I have other examples throughout my career as well, including some about my competition who failed to do this. Like this one: I often competed against a company that had sales pros who would exaggerate their solution's functional capabilities to buyers. When customers discovered this (sometimes with my help), I would ask them if they were comfortable doing business with a company that had representatives lie to them about important information that could be very impactful later on. Often, they responded that they would not do business with such a person or firm. At that point, I knew that I would likely win the opportunity and said nothing further about it.

Your Value Proposition

We touched a little on value propositions in Section 1 and the topic will be discussed further in Chapter 11. As a quick recap, the value proposition is the unique, positive business value that your solution brings to the prospect. It represents your competitive advantage. It is essential to demonstrate or explain how your product brings value to the prospect. Without proving a valid, measurable, and quantifiable value proposition it is highly unlikely that the buyer will proceed with a major purchase. What is in it for them if they proceed? Co-develop the value proposition with the buyer's team to ensure its veracity and their "buy-in." The members of the project team will need to present their case for the expenditure to executive management for approval. It is important that they are able to justify the expenditure with a full assessment on your solution's return on investment, cost of ownership, or improvement of customer relations. You are the best resource to help them prepare for this. Take that on willingly and give it careful consideration.

Present Your Proposal

After the solutioning phase is complete, it is incumbent on you to research alternative solutions, organize your data, and present your findings to your prospect. If you have determined that you can provide a solution that will provide substantial benefits to them, it is time to explain your proposal to the prospect's evaluation team. This is normally done in a face-to-face, or via a virtual meeting, ideally attended by the Economic Buyer and the other buying influences.

Asking for Buyer Commitment: The Natural Close

Once you have discussed, quantified, and agreed upon the value proposition, you can ask the buyer for a commitment. Not before. For example, "Now that we have agreed that our solution meets your needs and provides your company with exceptional value, will you purchase it from us?" If the prospect does not provide a commitment or positive response, you should take it as a red flag, but also know that it does mean that you have lost the sale. If they are unwilling to commit to purchasing, find out the reasons for their reluctance. It could be that they just have not reached the point in the process where they are ready to decide. Sometimes there are timing and scheduling issues, and the buyers are unable to meet for a while. There are vacations, illnesses, funerals, and other unanticipated events. If they seem to be stuck at one benchmark, ask what further information they need to make their decision. Or, they may have decided on or are leaning toward an alternative solution, which includes maintaining the status quo. Often, silence or the inability to reach your contacts indicates that this is the case. If so, it is important to confirm this information so that you can prepare your next steps, which includes determining their level of interest in buying, identification of issues that may be holding up their decision or finding the persons that support or that may be blocking the purchase of your solution.

It is essential to have a thorough understanding of the typical roles of each of the players that are involved in the purchase decision to bring your proposal to a successful close. And it is undesirable to treat the evaluation team as a single monolith, as it is made up of different roles, personalities, needs and agendas. The best way to understand the responsibilities of each person in the decision process, and to build a winning sales strategy, is to classify the team into four different roles. In the next chapter the roles are discussed, as well as how to best work with each.

SIX
Identifying Buyer Roles

There are many excellent formal sales methodologies available. For example: *Challenger Sale, Conceptual Selling, SPIN Selling, SNAP Selling,* and *Solution Selling.* Each adds valuable structure to your sales processes—if they are followed. I have successfully deployed the Miller Heiman Strategic Selling methodology many times and prefer their terminology to define the roles of the buyers in the sales process.[25] I will use their terms "Economic Buyer," "User Buyer," "Technical Buyer," and "Coach."[26]

Prior to 2015, sellers typically met with a small group of individuals who did the bulk of the evaluation and the selection at the prospective company. There were often two or more people from the business or end-user area, and one or more from the information technology (IT) organization. Business area people normally ran the buying process, but sometimes this responsibility was ceded to IT because they had more expertise in choosing technological solutions. The team leader

25 Copyright © 2021 Korn Ferry. ALL RIGHTS RESERVED
26 Robert B. Miller, Stephen E. Heiman, and Tad Tuleja, *The New Strategic Selling: The Unique Sales System Proven Successful by the World's Best Companies* (New York, NY: Grand Central Publishing, 2005), 85-102.

then made a recommendation to an executive sponsor and if it was compatible with the budget and the IT infrastructure, and not inconsistent with the corporate strategy, it was routinely approved. For many corporate purchases, this normally occurred within a three-to-six-month timeframe.

However, as I've said before, enterprise sales is no longer a simple linear process. It now bounces around like the ball randomly going from flipper to flipper in a pinball game, mostly guided by which person or group has the greatest urgency.

Buyers Are More Educated Now

Buyers are much more knowledgeable now than in the past. They can do extensive research before contacting the sellers. Enterprise sales cycles are far more complex than they were just a few years ago. Instead of that small group we discussed earlier, now there will likely be six to twelve members of a cross-functional evaluation project team who must reach a consensus about purchases. Previously, the sales process was linear and followed defined steps, but now it has become much more multi-directional with concurrent paths. There are often sub-teams focused on specific areas. The team recommendation is then passed on for final approval. The Economic Buyer or final decision maker may or may not be involved in the evaluation process. The complexity of the process is often driven by the greater sophistication of the evaluation team, the more elaborate definition of requirements, the increased role of procurement, and a desire to have a more rigorous selection process. Some buyers are familiar with the process, and some are not, causing more awkward sales cycles, with stops and starts, and sometimes misinformation. You can help the buyer by explaining best practices to them. You can also guide them through some of the more difficult stages, such as building agendas for the presentations and demonstrations, as well as contract negotiation.

Buyers Now Have Limited Interaction with Sellers

In addition to the challenges listed above, we can add the increased inaccessibility of buyer's staff, which Gartner, Inc. has cited is as low as 17 percent of the buying time for ALL seller teams combined (meaning that if there are three sellers, the mount allocated to each can be as low as 5 or 6 percent).[27] This points to the necessity of maximizing, and not wasting, any interactions you have with the prospect, whether in person, on the telephone, or via videoconference.

The 17 percent estimate was pre-2020, so with the onset of the coronavirus pandemic this contact time has most likely been reduced to an even lower amount, thus making the selling process more difficult by decreased face time with the buyer. As a result, you must maximize the interactions that you do have with the buyers.

In the past, buyers often relied on sales pros to provide them with the information they needed to make an educated decision. Since more people are now involved in the process from the buyer's side, it has become much more difficult to determine who the person or persons are who are making the buying decision. Sometimes it is volatile and changes throughout the sales cycle.

Even though buyers have greater access to information they often have become less able to determine which offer is the

---

27 Brent Adamson, "Traditional B2B Sales and Marketing Are Becoming Obsolete," *Harvard Business Review*, February 1, 2022, https://hbr.org/2022/02/traditional-b2b-sales-and-marketing-are-becoming-obsolete.

best fit for their needs and, as a result, along with the increased role of the procurement or legal departments in the selection process, have sometimes defaulted to making decisions based on price and not on best fit or value. This is somewhat of a contradiction in that they seem more intelligent in the research phase, but less qualified in the evaluation phase, thus changing the landscape in which sales pros now operate. Many buyers do not understand the normal steps in the buying process or what the best practices are that will enable them to make a decision that will result in the best outcome for their organization. Sales pros are now challenged to shift this trend of purchasing the least expensive option without consideration for the value that each alternative solution can bring to their company. This has intensified the tension between the buyer and seller, and resolving it is key to the dual success: the sales pro wins the decision, and the buyer finds a solution that best meets their needs.

Unless you are the luckiest sales pros in the world, or are unconsciously competent, you will not be successful without understanding each of the buying roles and identifying the appropriate people in each role during the sales process.

A frequent mistake I see sales pros make is that they fail to realize when people's roles change during the dynamic sales process. This is because sales pros often gravitate to the people who seem to be most receptive to their calls or solutions and avoid others who they perceive as oppositional. Since most enterprise decisions today are collaborative, each buying influence needs to receive the proper amount of attention and their needs must be addressed and covered.

The Economic Buyer

The Economic Buyer has the power to "give final approval to buy. There is always only one person or set of people (the Economic Buyer may be used plurally), playing this role for a given sales objective."[28] They have both influence and authority and "can say yes where everybody else has said no. They can also veto everybody else's yes."[29] They may not attend many meetings with potential but will normally attend the meeting where there is a recommendation or proposal. During the past few years there has been a trend toward an ad-hoc small group (typically three people from different functional areas) playing the role of Economic Buyer and decisions being reached by consensus, especially in enterprise sales. This has slowed down and lengthened the evaluation processes. Decision making has become similar to juries reaching a verdict.

Takeaway 8: The Economic Buyer Gives Final Approval to Purchase

Identifying the Correct Economic Buyer Is Crucial

The Economic Buyer or decision maker must always be identified and contacted several times, not avoided, during the sales cycle. Identifying the economic buying influence may be difficult and getting to this person can be even more challenging. This person normally does not identify themselves as such when you speak or meet with them. The easy answer is to ask

---

28 Robert B. Miller, Stephen E. Heiman, and Tad Tuleja, *The New Strategic Selling: The Unique Sales System Proven Successful by the World's Best Companies* (New York, NY: Grand Central Publishing, 2005), 68.
29 Ibid, p. 85.

the person who has been identified as the Economic Buyer by your contact, or others, if they will approve the expenditure and sign the contract or purchase order. If yes, then you have found the right person. If no, then you need to find who is.

Sometimes the Economic Buyer is misidentified to the sales pro by the other buying influences, intentionally or unintentionally. When asked who the final decision maker is they tend to identify an executive in their area, or the person most active in desiring a new solution, or their direct manager. But that person may not be the final decision maker. Also, there are situations in which the Economic Buyer role changes during the process due to such events as a reorganization or an acquisition of the buyer's company. A lack of recognition of the Economic Buyer change could cost you a sale, so it is important to re-validate this throughout the entire sales process, with various contacts—and the Economic Buyer themselves.

It is best to establish access to the Economic Buyer as early in the sales process as possible. It is easier at this point because you have not yet established relationships with a few contacts, so it is less threatening. Access can be via email, telephone, or preferably in person. Some sales pros are reluctant to directly contact the Economic Buyer, perhaps because they are intimidated by the person's executive position in the organization, or because they are afraid of offending their contact by going over their head. This is a serious strategic mistake as your competitor is probably meeting or speaking with them. Furthermore, you have a right to meet with them if you are going to invest the time required to provide a proposal. Also, a refusal to grant you a meeting may be a message that your solution is no longer being considered by the organization. That is not a death sentence, but it does call for a step-up in your efforts or a recognition that it is time to go on to the next opportunity.

If you did not already establish contract with the Economic Buyer when you initially contacted the company, the best way to handle this is to request access through your User, Technical or Coach contact. The danger is that sometimes they will decline. When this happens, I explain to the contact that I am just doing my job, and I will keep them informed as to what I am doing. If that doesn't work, I recommend working with the executive assistant. You need access to help determine if the opportunity is real and if it is important to the Economic Buyer. Did this person authorize the project, and how much is invested in its success? Once you have access to the Economic Buyer, do not stop speaking with the User and Technical Buyers, or even decrease the amount of time spent contacting them. Having access to the Economic Buyer will also result in a smoother sales process, as the person has met you or your manager and can contact you if any important issues arise.

It is important to gain an understanding of the Economic Buyer's priorities. Typically, this person has a large area of responsibility and strategic goals. It is a good idea to ask what their current operational focus is, other than the project, and carefully listen to her explain their goals for the organization and any business issues that are on their mind. They normally are interested in the return on investment or in increasing operational efficiency as a result of the purchase. For example, if goals are to increase customer loyalty, you could ask how they plan on accomplishing it. This will give you a much better idea of priorities and how you can assist in other areas as well. Be sure to have a carefully thought-out agenda for your meeting with the Economic Buyer and do not waste their time. The Economic Buyer will be keenly interested in how other relevant organizations in the same industry or geography, or the competitors, have solved similar problems using your proposed solution.

Be ready to provide the Economic Buyer with information that attests to your value proposition: Why will their company be better off if they purchase from your company now? Economic Buyers are usually very strategic and anything you can do to help them will raise your status as a solutions provider to the company.

Other areas that would normally interest them are current trends or best practices, such as recent topics in the Harvard Business Review, Gartner, Inc., or The Forrester Group, or hot topics like increasing customer stickiness, understanding if blockchain or bitcoin is worthwhile for the organization, or transitioning to a "green" operation. When researching the company and meeting with the Economic Buyer's subordinates, always ask what the company's current strategic priorities are, such as an international expansion or closing an unprofitable operation. You can then try to link your proposal to achieving any of those goals. This will greatly increase your chances of closing the sale.

Sometimes sales pros focus only on the Economic Buyer and neglect the User and Technical Buyers. These are the people that will make the recommendation to the Economic Buyer, so ignoring them, especially when they oppose your solution, is a terrible strategy.

Takeaway 9: User Buyers Cannot Approve the Purchase

The User Buyer

The User Buyers' role is "to make judgments about the potential impact of your product or service on their job performance."[30] These are the people that have the greatest understanding of the current gap or problem they are trying to solve. They also will be greatly concerned with changing from the status quo and the impact of a change on their day-to-day tasks. So it is important to deal with their fears of disruption or training on new processes. Will it make more work or less for them? It is important to address their concerns. And the User Buyers are usually the most accessible.

I have established strong, positive relationships with User Buyers, and some are still personal friends of mine after twenty-five or thirty years. But remember that the User Buyer cannot pull the trigger on a purchase. They can only recommend it. Sometimes their recommendation is approved by their manager, and then another manager, and then another manager and eventually it may be seen by the Economic Buyer.

It is a good idea to ask the User Buyer what you can do to make their job easier, make them look better to their manager, or help them achieve a high-performance review rating for the year. Sometimes it might be as simple as an email complimenting them on the success of the project at its conclusion, with a copy to their manager. They often respond positively to this since they now understand that you are not out to negatively disturb their place in the company. And, since these people may move to another company at a later date, they will be favorable to you at their new employer. I have sold to the same person at three different companies.

---

30 Ibid. p. 68.

The Technical Buyer

While both User Buyers and Technical Buyers are often charged with the responsibility to research possible solutions, the Technical Buyers "make recommendations based on how well it (your product or service) meets a variety of objective specifications."[31] Though they may speak with authority, it is likely they do not have any. The Technical Buyers have the important role of assuring that the solution being considered is properly vetted, compatible with current operations, and does not violate any corporate standards. They are tasked to help determine how well the features and functions of your product or service, and perhaps even your contract terms, will fit the buyer's organization. They can be technical, engineering, legal, or financial, or any other role (not necessarily technical, as in the IT field) that are often asked to be advisers to the project team during the sales process.

Technical Buyers may want to test your product or service before buying, or assess the risks, as they will be called upon to give their "stamp of approval." They are sometimes called by the derogatory term "Seemores" by sales trainers. The reason is that they always want to *see more* and have an interminable quantity of questions. Most of these questions need to be answered, but be aware that, at some point, these questions may take a lot of time away from your other sales activities. It is often difficult to know when and how to disengage from a *seemore*.

Takeaway 10: Don't Challenge a Technical Buyer

Technical buyers should never be challenged during a group meeting. Allow them to be the know-it-alls. They should

---

31 Ibid.

also not be asked "what further information can I provide?" as they will always ask for more, even if it is not important. If you promise to provide information to a "seemore" and the committee, it is essential to follow through. It is preferred to have a separate meeting with the "seemores" so that they do not derail the meetings with the larger groups. Also, make sure that you understand what they are asking. Often there are differences in terminology. If you find the questions to be completely outside the areas being discussed, it is permissible to ask them why they are asking for this information, in a non-threatening manner. These individuals will often operate from a checklist or a due diligence document. Assist them in properly completing it. They will do this for many purchases, so this is routine for them. The Technical Buyer should be treated with courtesy, respect, and the understanding that they are only trying to do their job. They are not trying to introduce an objection that will kill the sale. Technical buyers will often tell you that they are the real decision-makers. They are not.

You cannot win an argument with a Technical Buyer, or any of the others, by arguing. Dale Carnegie, the famous writer said:

"Nine times out of ten, an argument ends with each of the contestants more firmly convinced than ever that he is absolutely right."[32]

Arguing with the Technical Buyer is foolish and should be avoided. Suppose you shoot his argument full of holes and prove that he is incorrect. Then what? You will feel fine. But what about him? You have made him feel inferior. You have hurt his pride. He will resent your triumph. And you have

---

32 Dale Carnegie, *How to Win Friends and Influence People,* Revised (New York, NY: Simon & Schuster, 1981).

made an enemy who will work harder to block the purchase of your solution.

> *"A man convinced against his will*
> *Is of the same opinion still."*[33]

Takeaway 11: Technical Buyers Cannot Approve a Purchase, But Can Impair It

The Coach

Takeaway 12: The Coach Is the Key to Closing Your Sale

The Coach is the true key to closing the sale. If they work for the company, they probably have a management-level or senior position, knows the company politics, the people involved, the company priorities, how decisions and purchases are made—and who has the real power to make them. I have often asked a Coach for help. The Coach should be approached carefully to make sure that they are willing to help you. This can only happen once trust has been established. I explain to them what I am trying to accomplish and ask them what the best way is to accomplish it. It needs to be in their interest to help you, so make sure they understand how your solution will help them. Once you have confirmed that they will assist you, it is important to maintain their trust—and never do anything that would reveal that they are providing you with insider information.

---

33 Chris Hallquist, "According to Dale Carnegie, You Can't Win an Argument—and He Has a Point," LessWrong, November 29, 2013, https://www.lesswrong.com/posts/HxWdXMqoQtjDhhNGA/according-to-dale-carnegie-you-can-t-win-an-argument-and-he.

Much of my success in selling has been the result of the relationships I have developed with internal (and sometimes external) Coaches. These individuals have provided me with guidance on how to identify and work with each of the buying influences in the organization. The Coach who is working with you wants the organization to acquire your solution. It is important to have credibility with the Coach, and this takes time. I have always respected the information that was given to me by the Coach and kept it confidential.

Observe the Roles

When you are in meetings or on teleconferences, or even one-on-one with a person on the project team, it is important that you listen closely to their responses to questions and even how they communicate with one another. If, for example, people mention that they need to go to Mary for approval several times, or if you observe people looking over to Mary during meetings to see what her reactions are to proposals, value propositions, and prices, it is likely that Mary is the real Economic Buyer, regardless of what you have been told. Or you may have noticed that when Mary came into the room the others became more formal and attentive.

"White Horse" Charger

The internal champion, or the person we often called the "white horse charger" (based on the television show "The Lone Ranger") is the person or persons who are most enthusiastic about your solution and are willing to assist you in selling it to their organization. The champion can be any of the above four roles but is most often one of the User Buyers. The champion could also be your Coach. It is possible to close a sale without a champion, but it is certainly much easier to do so with one. Nourish the internal champions and do whatever is necessary to assist their career success. One way is to compliment them, when appropriate, and copy their manager on your email. Another is to highlight the improvements that have been made due to their choice of your company as a supplier. The goal is to give them recognition within their own company. If appropriate, you could also ask them if they would like to participate in a case study that you will place on your website. Once they have been recognized or promoted in their company, they will be your friend for life.

It is unrealistic to assume that there never will be any team members that are unfavorable to your proposal. A mistake that I see sales pros make is to disregard, avoid, or ignore people that are negative toward them or their product. It is important to be respectful to these people and try to provide information to them that may help change their minds. Avoiding them often leads to a crisis later when they oppose your solution when providing input on the decision. They may object for a variety of reasons, but you can address them. Some that you may encounter could be:

1. They may have built the solution that you are proposing to replace.

2. They truly like another solution better due to functionality, features, or the manner they were presented.

3. The other solution may cost less.

4. The competitors' solution may be less disruptive to their department or area.

5. You did not contact them before the meeting to research their needs and the competitor did.

6. They had a prior negative experience with you or your company.

This chapter introduced the reader to Miller Heiman's four Strategic Selling buyer roles: The Economic Buyer, The User Buyer, The Technical Buyer, and the Coach, and their functions. Each role provides a different contribution to the buying process, and they should be treated uniquely. An understanding of how each person feels about your opportunity, and their needs and priorities, is essential. It will help you prepare better sales strategies and better navigate the sales cycle for each opportunity. These are usually influenced by their role. **The Economic Buyer** is the person or group that can approve the sale. They may or may not have been an active participant in the evaluation team. **The User Buyer** is most concerned with how the new purchase will affect their day-to-day work activities and environment. **The Technical Buyer** is concerned about fit and meeting corporate standards, and they can derail the sale if they deem it does not. **The Coach** can provide guidance and help steer you in the right direction, so the importance of finding such a person cannot be undervalued.

In the next chapter we will review the buying process, and then in the succeeding chapter discuss the real reasons why people make purchases. A greater understanding of the buying process, not just the steps of the sales cycle, will help you become more skillful in your efforts to successfully close more sales.

SEVEN
Understanding the Buying Process

"The sales process must be aligned around the way your customer buys, rather than the way you want to sell."[34]

—Girish Ramachandran
Tata Consultancy Services

Sales pros are trained to employ a sales process that follows the lifecycle of a lead to a sale. But most sales pros are unfamiliar with the new corporate purchasing process or buying journey, which has become more complex in the 2000s. Perhaps the increase in complexity was driven by the large quantity of failed projects, where goals were not met, as well as by increasing pressures to reduce the spending rate. This has resulted in situations where many sales pros are uninformed about the need to be more buyer-centric, the new purchasing processes, and the often-disruptive procurement role in their sales cycles.

Takeaway 13: The Corporate Purchasing Process Is Not Linear

---

34 Sean Callahan, "22 Sales Quotes to Inspire You to Make 2022 Your Best Year Yet," LinkedIn, January 3, 2022, https://www.linkedin.com/business/sales/blog/modern-selling/sales-quotes-to-inspire-you-2022.

The corporate buying process is not simply the obverse of the sales process. It is not like looking from the other end of a telescope. The buying process is more complicated, with paths that sometimes resemble a corn maze. There are a lot of moving parts that may be coordinated or not. Or they may desire them to be coordinated, but they are not. And they usually are not as linear as the sales process. Decisions are not as simple as sellers would like them to be. Most of the activities of buyers are not visible to the sales pro. There is an often quoted, perhaps rogue, statistic that "buyers have, on average, progressed 57 percent through their buying process before they engage a salesperson."[35]

The process of corporations buying products or solutions has evolved significantly in the past few years. And it has continued to evolve with more innovations based on automation and artificial intelligence applications, as well as the emergence of procurement as a value-added component of the buying process. To be successful, you must adapt your sales approaches to recognize these new buying practices—rather than the buyer adapting to your company's sales methodology. The best way to determine how to do so is to ask your contacts to explain their buying processes to you, up front and in detail, and for you to follow them as best you can. Many sales organizations say they have made the necessary changes, but they haven't. Mary Shea, the Global Innovation Evangelist at Outreach.io has commented:

> *"I hear companies talk about having a buyer-first mentality, and then it's funny—when you dig a little deeper, you see they have a linear sales process.*

---

35   Donal Daly, "Why Understanding the '57%' Buying Process Will Help You Sell Better," Business 2 Community, July 5, 2014, https://www.business2community.com/sales-management/understanding-57-buying-process-will-help-sell-better-0935491.

They have sales-stage milestones designed to facilitate pipeline reviews and management reporting—versus reflective of how the buyer would engage with you if they were interested in your product or service. When you dig in, you see the process is not buyer first at all. There is still a big gap between how buyers want to buy and selling organizations' ability to deliver those experiences.[36]

The effect of you not changing to adapt to the buyer's process not only increases the likelihood of a lost sale, but it will also result in a more disruptive and complex sales cycle. The Gartner, Inc. research firm, in a recent study of 750 business-to-business buyers, found that 77 percent stated that their latest purchase was complex or difficult.[37] You can stand out as an exceptional sales pro if you try to bring this percentage down by simplifying your interactions with buyers to make their decisions easier. Approach your prospects and customers with the attitude that you are there to provide them with the industry's best practices, insights into what other leading companies have done to solve problems, case studies of other companies that have utilized your solutions that brought significant improvements to processes, and latest innovations and technological breakthroughs, while not constantly pressing them for a sale. By doing this, you are bringing value to them, while at the same time enhancing your credibility as a thought leader. The buyer will then remember that you are a subject-matter expert that is willing to bring value to them and will consider you as a potential solution provider.

---

36 Sean Callahan, "22 Sales Quotes to Inspire You to Make 2022 Your Best Year Yet," LinkedIn, January 3, 2022, https://www.linkedin.com/business/sales/blog/modern-selling/sales-quotes-to-inspire-you-2022.
37 "The New B2B Buying Process," Gartner, accessed April 18, 2022, https://www.gartner.com/en/sales/insights/b2b-buying-journey.

Certain people in the buyer's organization may be more receptive to your marketing efforts or have a greater interest in your product. These could be in any functional or horizontal area, but they typically align with your product and value proposition. It is your responsibility to identify these people and orient your efforts in their direction. For example, if you were selling marketing research to consumer-packaged goods manufacturers you will want to seek out the marketing research director. You would also want to understand what the marketing research director's typical concerns are and how their performance is measured.

What Are Buyer's Personas?

Buyer Personas are fictional, generalized representations of your ideal customers. They help you understand your customers better and make it easier for you to tailor content to the specific needs, behaviors, and concerns of different groups.[38]

I have found it useful to prepare an internal worksheet that lists the goals and objectives of each persona (the CFO, VP of IT, VP of Engineering, etc.) involved in the decision and customize my message accordingly. The worksheet will also help you prepare questions and personalize your dialogue. Here is an example:

---

38 Protocol 80, "The Ultimate Buyer Persona Guide (for Beginners)," HubSpot, accessed April 24, 2022, https://cdn2.hubspot.net/hubfs/1547213/ContentOfferFiles/Ultimate_Buyer_Persona_Guide_For_Beginners_by_protocol_80.pdf?t=1459517429021.

Persona of Donna, The Market Research Director at Golden Eagle Corp.		
Job Title	Market Research Director	5 years, previously at P&G
Responsibilities	Assist in selection of data, provide analysis to product managers, manage team of 6	Will lead in negotiating new contract
Personal Driver	Get promoted to VP of Marketing	Rival is Pat who is on the project team
Business Driver	Have new research contract in place by Year End, increase market share	In her KPI for this year
Known Issues or Pain	Current provider, DEF, has had many errors	Credibility of market research department has decreased due to errors
Other Important Information	Price is important, has tight budget	Donna reports to Margaret Shakespeare, Exec. VP
Demographic Information	Married, advanced degree	Has more than 500 connections on LinkedIn.com

The persona identifies the person's job title, job level, responsibilities, personal drivers and challenges, buying criteria, business drivers, personal aspirations, short-term and long-term goals, the typical requirements for this persona, role in the decision process, who they report to, risk appetite, and what their typical day is like. What are their typical personality traits, needs, issues, objections, and place in the corporate hierarchy? For example, if you were calling on the Chief Financial Officer (CFO), what should you expect their role to be in the company and the purchase decision? You know that typically they would be at a management or executive position level in the organization and usually report to the Chief Executive Officer. Normally CFOs are accountants and are detailed oriented. They also like to see the return on investment (ROI) or the total cost of ownership calculations. In addition, what are their compensation goals and measurements (increase market share, successful introduction of new products in x market), the company, its industry, its size, and the current provider? What is important to them in choosing a vendor? Why would they consider an alternative now? What are the known issues or pain points? What does a "win" look like for them? Do they have personal hot button issues? You can also list personality traits, and demographic and biographical information, such as age, gender, education level and schools attended, social media platforms utilized, and location.

The persona information is very useful in helping you build your sales strategy and to personalize your messages to the prospect. In many cases, the personas of people in similar roles will be comparable.

The Goals of Corporate Procurement

Starting in the 2000s, corporate procurement, sometimes called "strategic sourcing," began having greater power in the buying process. In the past, they would not have even been a participant. This requires an adjustment on the part of sales organizations that must understand how to better work with this function.

Corporate procurement's primary goals are to act on the corporation's behalf to reduce sourcing risk and maximize value. This includes reducing the spending level and negotiating lower prices, mostly in the supply chain, but also in other areas for the corporation. Sales pros have tended to view procurement as a roadblock that obstructs the sales process, often at the end of the sales cycle once the supplier has been chosen as the preferred solution, in other words—the enemy. Now, many procurement professionals may be involved at the beginning of the project and remain part of the evaluation and selection team as corporations seek more control over purchasing practices.

A recent study of 750 business-to-business buyers by the Gartner, Inc. research firm found that 77 percent stated that their latest purchase was complex or difficult.[39] You can stand out as an exceptional sales pro if you try to bring this percentage down by simplifying your interactions with buyers to make their decision easier. Approach your prospects and customers with the attitude that you are there to provide them with the industry's best practices, insights into what other leading companies have done to solve problems, case studies of other companies that have utilized your solutions that brought significant positive improvements to processes, and information about latest innovations and technological breakthroughs, while not constantly pressing them for a sale. By doing this you are bringing value to them, while at the same time enhancing your credibility as a thought leader and as a potential solution provider in the future.

---

39 "The New B2B Buying Process," Gartner, accessed April 18, 2022, https://www.gartner.com/en/sales/insights/b2b-buying-journey.

Takeaway 14: Educate or Be Educated

Either try to educate your prospects or be educated by them. This requires you to stay on top of the latest developments in your industry by reading journals, postings, and browsing the internet.

Sales pros need to be aware that, even as corporations have made their purchasing processes more rigorous and the availability of information on the internet is unprecedented, businesspeople will still need the assistance of sales pros to provide them with additional insights that will help them make the best, most informed decisions. There are situations where the buyer freezes the purchase process because they did not know what to do next and were afraid to make a mistake. It is to your benefit to familiarize them with the best practices that other corporations have used. If you do not take action, it will result in a slower or a stalled sale.

For example, you can provide the buyer with a list of steps that most corporations take and advise them on what activities normally happen in each step. You can also provide them with sample evaluation criteria (that would normally favor your solution) which may help them build their own. If you do not help the buyers, the evaluation or procurement process spins out of control and goes off the rails. And, if the decision is made primarily based on the price, the sales pro owns part of the responsibility for this failure.

Start-up organizations are typically led by entrepreneurs that are subject matter experts in their fields but may not have had a lot of experience with corporate purchasing decisions and the buying process. This is also typically true of their employees, who joined the company because of the founder's vision and usually have specific skills, such as in technology, marketing, or finance. It is an excellent opportunity for you to familiarize them with the typical buying process and how to select a solution that best meets their current and future needs.

Many corporations have asked their procurement function to be more concerned about company social responsibility (CSR) and what could be termed "ethical sourcing:" i.e., whether their suppliers embrace diversity, create initiatives to reduce their carbon footprint, decrease greenhouse emissions, manufacture more sustainable products, enhance the environment, raise animals in a humane manner, or employ favored labor practices. If your company excels in this area, it could be a significant advantage to you.

A positive takeaway for sales pros is that corporations are no longer as loyal as they once were with existing suppliers and are now more willing to look at alternative suppliers rather than retain long-term relationships. Where they might have had single-source suppliers in the past, corporations now are more interested in reducing their risks and reliance on one supplier. This creates more opportunities for sales pros who can take advantage of the opening and be creative with their approach. On the other hand, it could be the "double-edged sword" where you need to deploy strategies to keep your existing customers happy—or you could lose them—while creating new strategies with new companies.

Although some sales pros feel threatened by procurement's increased involvement in the sales process, you should be excited by the possibilities you will have to replace a company's current suppliers, thus allowing you to sell into more corporations as a result. You can't be afraid to involve yourself in new ways because that is exactly how you will make the most sales.

Takeaway 15: Sales Pros Need to Be Proactive

The best practice for sales pros is to be on top of or ideally be ahead of, any possible sales opportunities before or exactly when they are needed by maintaining communication with each of their accounts. Don't wait for prospects to come to you. You should be constantly monitoring your top prospects' business needs, problems, and identifying solutions for them—sometimes before they even know they need it themselves! High-performing sales pros are *proactive*, not reactive. You should either be in contact with various (not just one) people at the company shortly after the kernel of an idea arises or be planting the seed that turns into the kernel. In this way, you may end up being the single-source supplier because of your expertise. If other suppliers are considered, you will have the advantage since you have been working with the buyers for a longer time and have a greater understanding of their needs. This could also result in the buyer not even bothering to issue a Request for Proposal document because they have already decided to work with you. However, be careful here. This does not obviate the requirement to qualify every opportunity early and often.

EIGHT
The Real "Why?"

"Qualifying the buyer" refers to the essential activity of determining whether or not the buyer is actively interested in your product or service, whether they are willing and able to purchase quickly, or if they are a "tire-kicker"—somebody that is just looking but is not going to buy, has already decided on a competitor, and is just using your company to provide a comparison to move forward, or will maybe buy in a year or two. It is the next step after sourcing or receiving a lead. As a sales professional, you should contact the company and try to reach the appropriate person to ask the typical qualifying questions (you've probably learned these in traditional sales trainings):

» Is this project or purchase in your budget for this year?
» What is the timing of your project?
» Is there an executive sponsor? If so, who is the executive sponsor?
» What are the problems or issues ('pain points') with your current solution that you hope to fix?

» What is working or not working with your current solution? What other solutions or competitors are you considering? (Or are they just curious and surfing the web?)

As noted in Chapter 5, the determination of whether this lead is qualified is quite important. You don't want to be working on an unqualified prospect who will just waste a lot of your time. It is the costliest mistake that many novices and even highly experienced sales pros make. Your time is important, and you need to value it as much as, if not more than, money. Sometimes important qualifying information is not revealed by the prospect until late in the sales cycle, which makes it even more important to qualify the prospect as early as possible. The prospect is normally not going to voluntarily reveal this information. It is your job to ask the tough questions as part of your qualifying process. If the prospect is evasive and refuses to answer questions or does not allow you access to the proper people, then perhaps this is not the prospect that you want to devote a lot of time to now. Be wary of spending a lot of time on a prospect who is unwilling to provide you with enough information so that you can do your job. One of the hardest things for a sales pro to do is to know when to walk away from a lead or suspect that may be a waste of time.

Some sales pros fail to understand what can be termed "The why?" of the buyer. It is a deeper dive into what caused the company to trigger a buying cycle. This information is more important than the routine qualifying questions above and is not normally revealed when running through your qualifying checklist. This info is often hidden, very rarely offered, and difficult to discover, but it may be some of the most important reasons why a company would decide to change. It should always be asked, to as many people as possible, as often as is permissible, and if they do not know the answer, help them discover it! This just might be the most important explanation of "the why."

What are the reasons that are driving this decision—right now? Do they have a sense of urgency? What is their motivation to make a change? Which people are motivated, and is there a personal incentive? Have they had a recent negative experience that is driving this now, such as a large fine or regulatory sanction? Are there any known risks driving the decision? And most importantly—what are the consequences to the company if they do not make a change? These are often not adequately explored—by the company or sales pros.

I have attended account reviews in which the sales pro could not tell their sales manager why the company was buying right now or what was driving the decision for their client. You should not proceed without knowing this information. To determine the real "why" you need to establish a trusting relationship with your contacts and ask the proper open-ended questions to drill down to determine "the why" as best you can. Once you know this information it will help you plan the appropriate sales strategy.

Discover the Why

Takeaway 16: Discover the Real "Why" That Drives the Purchase Decision

Understanding the buyer's "why" is as important as the qualifying questions and is often neglected by under-achieving sales pros. The "why" may be to achieve the company's strategic goals while others may be personal, such as career advancement, transitioning to a new industry or profession, or meeting the performance goals for this quarter. Some people want to take on additional responsibilities to prove greater value to the company. Others are motivated by fear, such as not meeting their manager's expectations or worrying about being fired from their job.

Perhaps a good analogy for this is the decision to buy a new car. As a customer, you may have decided that you like two or three of the new car models and have begun comparing them. That is your decision process—which car do you choose? But the real reason why you are doing this is that the maintenance costs on your current vehicle that has over 125,000 miles on it have become excessive, and you no longer want to continue to invest in it. For a sales pro, this information would be very helpful, so that they can stress the reliability of their model and their low-cost maintenance program. Without that information, you are just comparing features and price versus the other options you are considering.

If an evaluation began due to performance issues, or to obtain a lower price, staying with the status quo delays them from addressing the problem. Continue to stress the benefits that the company will derive due to a change in suppliers. Sometimes companies are talked out of making a change by an appeal for a second chance from the current supplier and a promise to do better in the future. Sadly, their tactic to buy more time rarely works out for the customer, and they will resume a search for alternatives at another point in the future. Your commitment to providing a better solution to the customer will win out if they trust you and believe your value proposition.

As much as we want to take credit for inspiring the buyer

to purchase through our presentation or persuasion skills, the reality is that "People buy for their reasons, not yours."[40] Some theorize that buyers are either motivated by emotions that result in feeling good or from avoidance of a problem. I do not think it is that simple.

As in the car purchase example above, when you know the real why that is driving the decision to purchase, you can prepare an optimal strategy that takes advantage of this knowledge. You can customize your messaging, marketing collateral, value proposition, and proposal to best position your solution to resolve their problem or need. For example, if you discovered that the real motive for the purchase is that the CEO has decided that there is an urgency to fix a supply chain issue to enter a new market, it provides you with helpful information to explain how your solution will help the buyer gain better control of the sourcing and delivery of the necessary components that are needed to build the product for the new market, reducing company risks.

Some decisions have serious consequences and subsequently are the reason the evaluation is taking place. For example, when my team met with the market research director of Coca-Cola, he reminded us that the sales data we provided to them had to be accurate because people's jobs could depend on it. If their regional manager in Houston was losing market share to their competition, it was likely that they would be replaced. So the choice of reliable market share data was imperative.

The real "why" also includes the notion that buyers purchase what the product does for them, the outcomes, not the tool or process that provides it. For example, Harvard Business School Professor Theodore Levitt said, "People don't want to

---

40 Jeb Blount, *Sales EQ: How Ultra High Performers Leverage Sales-Specific Emotional Intelligence to Close the Complex Deal* (Hoboken, NJ: Wiley, 2017), 238.

buy a quarter-inch drill, they want a quarter-inch hole."[41] The drill is the means to the end. So if you are selling the tool, provide and emphasize a vision of the results, not your product or service.

Contrary to what many product marketing experts advise, features rarely drive corporate purchases. I suggest that the "why" is rarely the "bells and whistles," or features and functions of your solution. I closed a sale where the customer had recently received a multi-million dollar fine and unfavorable publicity for having an inadequate program for detecting money laundering. That fine certainly resulted in an incentive to move away from their current in-house system.

Some customers, the "early adopters" are attracted to purchase items when a new technology is released. In that case, the psychological impact of buying the latest technology is stronger than other considerations.

Product features are normally "nice-to-haves," which are extraneous to the real "why." They are the byproduct of the whys, not *the why*. People are more motivated to buy must-haves, not nice-to-haves. The features may be more important to your company than to the buyer. The buyer is not buying the artificial intelligence (A.I.) functionality that you have touted in your marketing solution. They are probably looking for a solution to an existing problem that they likely first recognized and brought to the attention of the executives. Your A.I. solution is a means to address the real why—which is perhaps the realization that the customer's information data is deficient for marketing purposes. It is what the customer has in their mind when they started researching to search for a solution or the vision of the finished solution. Or it is what the CEO or

---

41 "No One Wants a Drill. What They Want Is the Hole," Quote Investigator, March 23, 2019, https://quoteinvestigator.com/2019/03/23/drill/.

executive sponsor determined should be a priority for this fiscal year and is perhaps an objective that the project leader will be measured on in their annual performance review. Or it may be the result of a significant customer issue or regulatory fine that re-ordered most of the planned projects.

Want vs Need

Takeaway 17: Know the Difference Between Want and Need

It is important to understand the difference between *want* and *need*, and how emotions affect your why and your inclination to make purchases. For a business, a *need* may be something critical for its operations, whereas a want is a desirable thing, but optional; we can survive without them. They are a choice. But they could still be important, especially for individuals involved in the sales process. We all need most of the same things, but we each want different things. Wants are emotional and needs are practical. It is your job to understand which emotion or logic is driving the buying decision and to frame your offer accordingly to satisfy one or both.

We do not just purchase the items we need; we also purchase the ones we want. Often, we make emotional buying decisions and then try to justify them logically afterward. This is especially true with impulsive purchases. We convince ourselves that we needed the purchase when we know we did not. I do this all the time with sports memorabilia and golf clubs. And the buying instinct that makes us buy something that we do not need is very powerful. It also elevates the urgency of the purchase.

Other motivations for buying might be the "fear of missing out," (FOMO) or potentially, it could be due to office politics. For the former, the buyer has anxiety because he perceives others are getting the benefit of buying something and he is not, even if he does not need it. This is also called the "fear of regret." For the latter, office politics frequently influence purchases. One person has certain interests to promote and views the purchase as a path toward that goal. Or they are trying to curry favor with the person in power. Sometimes the motivation for a purpose is not disclosed because it is embarrassing to the company (such as a fine) or due to circumstances that they do not want to make public. In such instances, the budget is often unlimited. There can be many levels contained within the "*why*."

My exercise coach, Kevin Coleman, has a sign in his studio that says: "When your WHY is stronger than your resistance to change you will succeed!" It is on us, the sales pros, to gain an understanding of "the why" behind every purchase decision. It's our job to help our customers succeed. To do otherwise is the same as flying an airplane in the dark, without instruments. Yes, you might arrive at the destination, but it is far easier, more certain, and far safer if you have the right information.

NINE
Who is the "Real" Competitor?

When I ask sales pros who their number one competitor is, the response is usually the name of another company they often face in the marketplace. But *they are wrong!*

Takeaway 18: The Real Competitor Is Not Who You Think It Is

The real competitor in most B2B sales situations today, the one you must worry about and the toughest to beat (because it is often invisible or not mentioned during the sales process)—is the status quo: *doing nothing,* no change, or keeping what they have. It is a black hole—the lack of inertia to make a change. Buyers are naturally biased in favor of the status quo, ("We have always done it this way"). They know it, have lived with it and are often comfortable with it. It is often the easiest and least risky choice. Anything else will result in an adjustment, and most people do not like change. The default position is to stay with the current solution, even if it is recognized to be suboptimum—unless there is a compelling reason to make the change. Why does this happen? Here are seven possible reasons:

1. Reduced staff (and those who remain are stretched thin, especially in IT. That limits bandwidth and limits the willingness to take on new projects.)

2. Lack of satisfaction with the solutions offered.

3. Estimated costs exceeding budget and concerns over ROI.

4. The business and/or technical risks are too high.

5. They did not consider the costs of not making a change.

6. Lack of an executive sponsor.

7. Sales pros are selling features and functions, not value.

The Cost of Doing Nothing

The cost of doing nothing is a paradox that is often overlooked. But if this is not properly addressed, it will often result in a stalled sales opportunity. To avoid this outcome, I suggest utilizing a three-step process:

1. First, look for an executive sponsor during the qualification phase—an executive who is willing to stake his reputation on the line to facilitate a change. This is not necessarily the Economic Buyer, but it could be. If you cannot find one, it is a red flag. Then you must decide whether to continue pursuit of the opportunity. If there is one, you must arrange to meet with the sponsor and determine if this project has enough high-level interest, has a budget, or has a sense of urgency to spend now, assuming a proven value proposition.

2. Second, ask questions during the qualifying process (in addition to the other questions) that focus on the real "why" (from the preceding chapter) and their willingness to make a change. Is there a sense of urgency? If not, what are you or they doing that will prevent a "do nothing" decision?

3. Third, you must build a compelling business case for making the change. What are the benefits of your proposed solution? The best value propositions result in an increase in profitability or greater efficiencies, an expansion into a new market, or an alignment with a key company strategy. It needs to be measurable and quantifiable. Be sure to include both "hard" and "soft" dollars. Absent these three reasons, the result is likely to stay with the status quo. The cost of doing nothing needs to be quantified and included in their ROI calculation. For example, the proposed solution may result in an annual cost savings of $500,000, which is then measured against alternatives. But what if nothing is done? Will that result in an additional cost of $100,000 to replace a machine? The same is true for the expansion of product lines or increases in marketing budgets. Has there been a compliance issue that needs to be addressed? What about the likelihood of fines, bad publicity, or the possibility of injury to workers? Most prospects are more concerned about avoiding losses, receiving negative publicity, or attracting their manager's ire, than making an investment. To achieve a sale over the status quo, the decision-makers need to conclude that the proposed solution results in greater benefits to the company than that of doing nothing and the costs of the investment. It is on you, the sales pro, to help provide the proof.

4. Absent these three actions, the result is likely to be a no-decision or to stay with the status quo.

Gartner, Inc. conducts a survey into enterprise buying dynamics in the technology area every eighteen months. In 2016, they published the results of the survey and noted that 94 percent of enterprise buying teams abandoned a buying effort with no decision in the past two years.[42] Gartner Vice President Hank Barnes noted:

> *"Let me be clear, this is not saying that 94 percent of the projects that B2B buying teams consider end without a purchase. If a respondent was involved in ten projects and one of them ended in no decision in the last two years, then they are part of this 94 percent number."*

This study is saying that 94 percent of our respondents have started down a buying path and then decided to do nothing. The message: it is far from uncommon for significant buying efforts (where the organization was seriously contemplating change) to end with no action at all.[43]

In doing further research Gartner's Barnes found that many companies had multiple instances of staying with the status quo. Forty percent of those having "high-quality deals"

---

42 Hank Barnes, "94% = Enterprise Buying Teams That Have Abandoned a Buying Effort with No Decision (in the Past 2 Years)," Gartner, September 20, 2016, https://blogs.gartner.com/hank-barnes/2016/09/20/94-enterprise-buying-teams-that-have-abandoned-a-buying-effort-with-no-decision-in-the-past-2-years/.
43 Ibid.

had zero-project cancellations, 23 percent had one to four cancellations and 17 percent had five or more cancellations. A "high-quality deal" or HQD, is "defined as a situation where the customer feels pretty strongly that the purchase is meeting expectations *and* they either did not settle for something less than they had hoped *or* they purchased a premium solution from a tech vendor. High-quality deals can be thought of as good for everyone involved."[44]

The respondents cited more than one reason for abandoning their project, as those shown in this chart add up to greater than 100 percent. If you look at the top four reasons, you can see that many determined that either the solution provider could not address their needs, either they or the supplier could not prove an acceptable return on investment (ROI), or that the projected costs exceeded the perceived benefits. These reasons can be easily summarized: the value proposition failed to make a compelling reason to move forward. The status quo ended up being better than the "solutions." However, I wonder if that was the case, or if the sales pro would have had better success if they followed my steps above.

44 Hank Barnes, "The Cost of No Decisions May Be Greater Than We Think," Gartner, July 30, 2019, https://blogs.gartner.com/hank-barnes/2019/07/30/cost-no-decisions-may-greater-think/.

Remember, you are asking the customer to make a change that will involve a disruption of some sort, either in staffing, resources, or training. There is always an incremental cost involved in such a decision, both direct and indirect. Sometimes you are also reminding them of a poor decision that they made in the past, which may have cost the company a lot of money or a significant opportunity cost. Some people do not want to own up to their mistakes, especially those that are identified to upper management. When that happens, sales pros help them spin it a different way, so they are not embarrassed or personally affected by an additional expenditure.

All of these reasons in the Gartner, Inc. study resulted in a "no decision," or to stay with the status quo. When this happens, everyone loses; the buyer does not acquire a new solution to a problem, and the supplier not only does not acquire a new client but has wasted a lot of time and resources throughout the sales cycle. This chart should be posted on the wall of every sales pro to remind them that their task is to address these issues—early and often.

Could this be due to the company culture? Has this happened a lot before? If so, it is on you, the sales pro to recognize it. It should be included in your questioning.

Some companies penalize their employees for taking risks. If the project did not work out, the people that led the purchase decision were publicly humiliated or terminated. Thus, when faced with difficult decisions employees are usually stalemated which is their safest career choice. While I understand their reasons, that is not a good model for success.

Preventing No-Buys

One area that is often neglected in sales training programs is how to prevent a no-buying decision or how to handle it when it happens. The subject should be given equal importance to a session on how to deal with common objections, which is *always* discussed in formal sales training and at sales meetings. Dealing with it when it happens is normally something that cannot be fixed, but it is worth trying to determine the cause and then addressing it.

Another "do nothing" or status quo decision is the objection "I want to think it over." This is normally a stall tactic but could be due to a legitimate scheduling conflict or a desire to do further research. This does not always lead to a status quo stall, but as time goes by the sense of urgency decreases and the prospect will normally lose their interest. When confronted with this objection the sales pro should respond by asking the prospect how much time they need and then informing them that you will call at that time.

Some sales pros focus on what they need to do to out-maneuver opponents X, Y and Z, when they did not recognize that "none of the above," or "do nothing" may be the option chosen by the buyer.

And sometimes the project team gets over-ambitious and grows the scope of the project beyond the perceived value or ROI. I called on a major international financial institution that needed a better, easier solution in their electronic international wires area. They wanted to make it easier for their retail customers to go into a branch and send a wire to another country, perhaps to their relatives. We worked with them to design a simple solution that would meet their needs. However, the project team decided to fix other areas and build a much more elegant solution than what was needed. They thought they could convince executive management that they could build and buy a solution that would solve many problems, not just the primary need they had and were tasked with solving. They requested $20 million for their project and were turned down. They could have put an excellent solution in for $5 million, which would have been easy to justify, and it would likely have been approved since they had an executive sponsor who recognized the need. They added their "wants" to their "needs." As a result, this financial institution wasted a lot of their time, and our time, and then continued to use an antiquated solution that was inferior to their competitors, and probably lost business as a result. The lesson here is to encourage your buyer to focus on solving the problem they are tasked with, within the allotted or perceived budget and time, and it will have a greater likelihood of being approved.

As companies continue to desire to be more "inclusive" they increase the size of their project teams to comprise many functional areas of the organization. This increases the probability of greater "buy-in" throughout various functional areas of the organization and perhaps the success of the project. But there is a greater likelihood that the project team will not reach a consensus due to the larger size and diverse interests of the group. When few people are involved, the decision tends to move quicker. As you add people it becomes more difficult to schedule meetings and the project gets extended. And, of course, each person may have a personal agenda.

Sometimes, after a long period, the urgency to make a change decreases or executives feel more comfortable staying with the current situation. They may also have frustration with the inability of the project team to reach a consensus and cancel the project. It's easy to understand why. Just look at our justice system. In most criminal cases, our jury system requires twelve people to reach a unanimous or majority decision, which is intentionally difficult and favors the defendant. There must be a greater degree of certainty for twelve people to reach the same decision. I am sure that a lesser amount of five or six, or even eight people might have been able to reach a decision, but adding more people introduces more opinions, which could cause a stalemate. The same goes for business meetings and decisions. Furthermore, the addition of people who only attend your meetings occasionally, not regularly, will negatively affect the dynamics of the decision-making process. Yet this has become common, so be prepared for it.

Now that we have covered this topic, let's look at a real-world example where you can see the three steps applied.

Let's assume that while calling on a company, Access Manufacturing, you learned that the Vice President of Human Resources, Ms. Martin, the project sponsor, is willing to meet with you and has the budget to make a decision in the next few weeks. She has asked her team to gather information about the leading applicant tracking offerings in the marketplaces and you are one of more than five companies that the company will be considering. Now what?

I suggest that you begin your conversation with Ms. Martin by asking questions to gain an understanding of the current situation and the reasons why they are considering a change. This should be an in-depth conversation of at least thirty minutes. Focus on how strongly the executive sponsor feels about using time and budgeting money to replace the existing process or product. Are they having issues now with their applicants? Have they increased the volume of their hiring? Also, is this being done because of an expected increase in ROI, decrease in costs, or to increase operational efficiency?

What is the cost to them of not making a change? Will staying with the current environment drastically improve the situation or is this a "nice-to-have?"

We should ask them which other suppliers they are considering, and if not forthcoming with this information, the question should not be pursued. Do not make negative comments about any of the competitors they name, but rather, say something positive, such as "they are a good company with good products" or "we see them a lot in the marketplace." Any denigration or "trash-talking" about competitors is unprofessional and is also a comment on your buyers' abilities to determine which companies to look at. Besides, if they are looking at a company that you consider an inferior competitor, it is in your best interests for them to remain in the field they are considering. Knowing which competitors they are considering will assist you in building a strategy for winning this opportunity.

Takeaway 19: Know Your Products Before Worrying About Your Competitors' Weaknesses

Let's assume that you are familiar with the competitors that Access Manufacturing is looking at. One is a low-cost provider; another is primarily located in Europe; the third is a small company with limited funding. You can now customize your value proposition, for example, to not only emphasize how you can improve their current applicant tracking process but also to emphasize that you have fair pricing that is based on the value you are bringing to them, you are located in the U.S. in case of support issues, and you have the resources to be around for a long time to support them today and in the future.

Since all prospects have access to unlimited information on the internet "It's important to remember your competitor is only one mouse click away."[45] If you do not know your competitors, begin by researching them: look at their websites, LinkedIn.com, and contact your team and other sales pros to find out if anybody has encountered them in the marketplace. Do not assume that an opponent that you have never heard of cannot win a competitive sale. There is a reason why the buyer is looking at them. Find out why. What is it about them that attracted the attention? Often this is because either they received positive publicity in a recent article on the web or perhaps because they know somebody else that chose them. This is important information.

If you have a good relationship with your contacts, you can also offer to assist them in their evaluation of competitors' offerings. A way to do this is to provide them with a sample generic requirements list that will help them review the competitors and compare them to yours. It can be positioned as a "starter kit" for their evaluation. This list will, of course, include your product's strongest features and functions and some of the competitors' known weaknesses. Do not provide them with the information on each alternative. If you did that, they would check it anyway, so let them do the legwork and arrive at their own conclusions. It is essential to be perceived as a credible subject-matter expert in your field. They will also respect you more if you can add value to helping them fix their problem, even if they do not choose your solution. People want to work with others that they believe are smarter than they are or have more knowledge about a specific area because they know their

45 Jim Belosic, "21 Insightful Quotes About the Power of Good Customer Service," Inc.com (Inc., June 26, 2015), https://www.inc.com/jim-belosic/21-insightful-quotes-that-link-customer-service-to-profit.html.

knowledge is limited to what their company has dealt with and the possible solutions they have tried or deployed.

In summary, always assume that each opportunity will be competitive (including a "no" decision), especially when calling on a new customer. There may be opportunities where an existing customer is extremely loyal and only considers your company, but this is not common. Consider these to be bonuses—like getting a front-row seat at a concert. Always remember that many corporations are experiencing cost pressures and are interested in reducing costs, especially with existing suppliers. Always assume that each existing contract is always at risk, regardless of how satisfied they tell you they are. That may be true today, but not necessarily tomorrow.

TEN
Why Didn't it Close?

You may have worked with a prospect over many months. Your contacts have given you positive feedback about your proposal. You have had access to the Economic Buyer or decision-maker and received favorable comments. You believe your offering is a good fit for their needs. You have mutually determined a favorable ROI which indicates that the solution will bring value to them. There has been no resistance voiced to your sales price. The sales opportunity has been on your sales forecast for many months, but it has not closed. It is like you are fighting a ghost army that you cannot see or hear. But they are there. Perhaps they have gone "radio silent," or are "ghosting" you, and have not returned your telephone calls and emails. Why?

Has your deal gone to the "opportunity graveyard?" If so, what should be on the tombstone?

> **Takeaway 20: Deals Stall for Many Reasons, Mostly Because They Were Not Qualified or Lacked Executive Sponsorship**

In Chapter 8 on the "Real Why" I listed several qualifying questions, which would also apply to a deal that stalls. However, stalled deals can occur for other reasons as well. Here are some additional factors to consider why this happens:

» Sometimes the sales opportunity is like a Hollywood set—there is an exterior that appears to be real, but there is nothing behind it. And what you thought was a real opportunity vanishes. Simply put, if it is not a qualified opportunity it will not close. It is a "false positive."

» Was there a recognized need or was just one person shopping or putting his "toe in the water?" Some sales pros spend many hours meeting with prospects only to find out later, sometimes after months, that the person who initiated a search to find a solution to a problem did not have executive sponsorship.

» Sometimes a prospect will be interested in a product when approached by the sales pro, but again, an approved project does not exist. This does not automatically mean that you must disengage from the prospect, as I have been able to close non-budgeted projects when there is a recognized need or a very positive ROI.

» How much information did they share with you about their company or issues during the discovery process? If they shared none, or very little, it is a sign that it may not have been a qualified prospect, or that you are losing the sale.

» Did they request a formal proposal (RFP)? That normally indicates a valid project.

» Did you ask for buying affirmations, solicit feedback, and gain commitments throughout the sales cycle? Did you test your contact with trial closing questions from time to time, such as "Is our solution still a viable option for you?" "What are your team's (and your) thoughts about our proposal?" "What do you see the advantages we have over our competitors," and "If you had to make a decision today, would our solution be one you would choose?" It is unacceptable to fail to ask for the order and just wait for it to come on its own. A suggestion is to ask your primary contact a question such as: "My manager is working on our sales forecast for this month. Should your company be included in the forecast?"

» There is a natural point in the sales cycle for you to ask a closing question such as "Are you ready to go ahead with our proposal?" A hint that you are at that point is that the buyers begin asking post-purchase type questions, such as about training, delivery, and implementation. They may have asked for a sample contract. It is at this point that you have earned the right to close. If you are not sure where the opportunity is, it is best to triangulate and ask several different people to find out the truth.

» Alternatively, did you try to close too soon? A premature close before the buyer is ready can result in a stalemate. Throughout the sales process, ask the buyer what the timing is of their decision and where you stand. The trainers that tell you to close at every opportunity are mistaken. That will, at best, annoy the prospect, and at worst, result in them shutting down communication.

» Did the prospect decide to remain with the current supplier? This is often due to the buyer's reluctance to change to an unknown supplier, and it presents a different challenge. It is rational to be risk-averse when considering a change. One recommended strategy is to offer a less strategic or costly product or even to provide several deliveries of the product being considered, at no cost, for them to compare quality, pricing, delivery, and after-sale service. You can also refer the buyer to some of your other customers to allay their concerns.

» Some prospects do not consider issues other than price when they view the alternatives. They see alternative A costs more than B, or it costs more than they have in their budget for the year. And they have no experience with alternative C. Does that mean they should buy B? Or stay with the current solution? To address this, you need to know the impact of their current solution in terms of any of the following costs:

> Financial risks
> Additional resources (excessive staffing, overtime, potential reductions in waste)
> Elimination of pollution or improving air quality
> Avoidance of machine breakdowns, missing deadlines
> Employee absences, replacing dissatisfied employees, or morale issues
> Customer issues or delivery problems

> › Inventory shortages, additional costs for rushed shipment
> › Lost customers due to quality problems
> › Additional health care costs
> › Potential fines from state, local or federal government for non-compliance issues

» You received a verbal commitment, but they have not issued a purchase order or signed a contract. There could be many reasons for this happening. Frequently contracts get backed up in the legal department. Also, company priorities are dynamic, and what was important one month ago may not be important today. I had a proposal with a telecommunications company that determined it had a 2000 percent return (due to decreases in fraud and billing issues) stall because there were other projects with greater returns and not enough IT resources available to handle them all.

» Did you miss a hidden objection or an unaddressed concern? Review your notes to assure that something did not slip through the cracks. Sometimes these are not vocalized by the buyer, so you must ask questions to seek them out. For example, "Did I address all of your concerns in the meeting today, or are there any others that I can follow up on later?"

» Perceived risks often freeze decisions. Think of what you can do to reduce the buyer's risks. For example, discuss a money-back guarantee, an extended warranty, or relaxed payment terms. That may help put the project back on track.

» They may have already chosen another supplier—but

have not informed you. Most people do not like to deliver bad news, especially to somebody that they have been working with for several months. Many people are respectful and do not want to hurt your feelings. And buyers do lie, by that I mean that they will tell you that you are doing well when you are not, or that they prefer your solution and they do not. Lying to you is easier than telling the truth—that they do not like your solution, or maybe do not like or trust you. Your contact is procrastinating and is not informing you that they have decided, and your solution was not selected. In this case, I would ask the buyer directly "Have you chosen anybody else?" I would also follow this with a request for a de-brief call or meeting to find out why you lost. This information can be valuable and should not be ignored. You might find out information that will be helpful in the next competitive situation, such as a new feature or a lower price.

» Were you listening to the buyer, or did you have "happy ears" because you believed you were winning? Were they giving you verbal cues that this was not going to close, or that they favored another solution, and you ignored them? Some sales pros only hear want they want to hear. They filter out other information, such as unfavorable comments that are made about your proposed solution or that they are "too busy" now to move forward.

» Is the buyer burdened by "sunk costs?" The concept of sunk costs is that some costs have been incurred and cannot be recovered. They should not be considered in a decision about what to do now, but rather the buyer should focus on the economic benefits of moving forward. What is the opportunity cost of pursuing this project further, rather than using the same resources on an alternative project? The fact that the buyer may have invested a lot so far is irrelevant when deciding what you do now. This is often difficult for people to process, for both emotional and financial purposes. They either continue to "throw good money after bad," or they often become frozen and indecisive.

» Tests, or a "proof of concept" (PoC) can be very valuable to prove that your product or solution will perform to the buyer's expectations. Perhaps your product does not have a lengthy track record of success, or the prospect is highly skeptical of your product's ability to handle their special circumstance. For example, large financial services enterprises, such as the major banks, brokerages, insurance companies, and money transfer businesses, may be extremely concerned about your ability to handle their high transaction volumes.

» Before a test is performed, it is important to define the objective, establish proper test criteria as to what determines success, agree on a fee and a project timetable. Resources need to be committed by both the buyer and seller. The prospect should pay for the test so they have "skin in the game" and it demonstrates that they are serious. You may offer to apply the fee to the total cost should they decide to buy. (Sometimes a prospect may want to build a working prototype of the desired result. I would normally not agree to this unless it was defined as a non-refundable fee project.)

Case in Point

Early in my sales career I called on a large manufacturer in Ohio. Their accountant, Nancy, was interested in automating the depreciation computations using a fixed assets accounting system, but Nancy was worried that transitioning to a new system could result in a radically different calculation, which could affect profitability. Nancy asked if we would perform a test on one of their units and we eagerly agreed. I collected the information and worked with others over a weekend to manually enter the data in our system and run the reports. I could not wait to go back to see Nancy and show her the depreciation calculation printouts. Incredibly, our depreciation calculations agreed with Nancy's to the penny! Both Nancy and I were quite happy, and I asked when they would license our system. Nancy said that she would request approval to do so. From that day until the day I left the company twelve years later, Nancy's company never licensed our fixed asset system—or any others. I learned many lessons because of this stalled sale.

Even though we knew the purpose of the test was to compare our depreciation calculation with the prospect's, we did not agree on what actions would be taken from a successful or unsuccessful test. We also did not agree on what would constitute a success. There should be a written agreement on the purposes and consequences of the test, as well as a non-disclosure agreement to protect both parties.

The prospect did not pay us for the test, or for my expenses and those of my colleagues who worked on this over a weekend, so there was no financial commitment or investment on their part. The company manager was also not interested in Nancy solving his problem and he had not done sufficient internal selling. It was not a strategic priority. Let poor Nancy work overtime doing the work manually. It was also apparent that she did not have any power or authority to move forward. This then resulted in a stalemate. And it was mostly my fault for not better qualifying the opportunity. I was overconfident and too eager to prove to Nancy and the company that our solution could meet their needs.

Re-energizing a stalled opportunity is certainly very challenging. Once an opportunity ceases progressing to a close, or is "put on a shelf," it quickly loses its momentum and you lose the buyer's interest, sometimes irreversibly. (This is discussed further in Chapters 10 and 21.) I have not found a guaranteed method to rescue such opportunities. Some sales trainers advise trying different closes (see those listed in Chapter 4), but I have usually found that to be counterproductive. It can make the prospect suspicious of your motives. If you have built trusting relationships, asking your coach or contact for guidance is a good place to start. If they cannot assist you, then you need to go to others to seek more information.

One idea is a questioning method that I have termed the "Columbo method." Lt. Columbo was a popular television detective in the 1980s that was effective at getting people to let their guard down by asking innocuous questions, often appearing to be baffled. One technique he used was to seem to be concluding a conversation, but then he would turn around and ask another question on his way out. For example: "Just one more thing, throughout the sales process you mentioned to me that on-time delivery and customer service were important to you in determining your supplier. Is that still important to you when you make your selection? If so, it was my impression that you agreed that our company excelled in this area." Then wait for the response. It may be more informative than the original message. It is possible that on-time delivery was not as important as you thought it was, or that the competitor convinced them that they could deliver better than you could.

Deals stall for many reasons, but I have found that most are due to the lack of executive sponsorship. Perhaps the opportunity just gets caught in a logjam in the legal or procurement departments. Sometimes other projects erupt with higher priorities and must be handled before your proposal. That is not a "death sentence" to your opportunity, but it likely will be stalled for a while: I had a large opportunity with a major insurance company that was ceased twice over two years and then started for the third time in the third year when I closed it. During that time the decision-maker and evaluation teams changed as well.

A difficult decision that you will need to make is whether to continue to invest selling resources to a stalled deal or to pursue another opportunity. Often, it is wiser to do the latter. In the next chapter, we will look at value propositions and how they help you overcome stalled sales and close sales.

SECTION 3

There are some specific actions you should be taking throughout the year to increase or replenish your pipeline and close more sales. First, in Chapter 11 we will discuss value propositions and how they can help you sell your product or service. Sales pros often emphasize product features and functions as they have been traditionally trained to do. But selling features and functions to a prospect who does not understand the need, or is not interested in those features, can be a distraction. Instead, we will focus on how you can research their needs and explain the value or ROI that your product or service will provide to your prospect and how they can assess your calculation.

Next, in Chapter 12 we will go over the concept of "value-based pricing," in which the price the buyer pays for your product is determined as a function of the value they derive from using it, not by a standard pricelist. This can be awkward, but when done properly will result in happier customers and will also often increase your revenue.

By this point in your career, you likely understand the model of the funnel pipeline, in which one starts with a larger set of prospects that is reduced to smaller quantities over time by working the sales cycle. However, I have found that many sales pros do not understand the mathematics involved in this funnel, or how to maximize sales by managing their activities. In Chapter 13 we will discuss the mathematics of the sales funnel, and how you can focus on all or any of these factors throughout the sales process. Chapter 14 then introduces you to the "Sweet Spot" to prospect. By understanding this concept, sales pros can increase their pipelines (and sales) by calling on higher probability prospects—those where their needs, your value proposition, and competitive strengths intersect.

In Chapter 15, we discuss an area of controversy amongst sales trainers and managers: Whom do you call at a company when prospecting—high-level executives, middle-managers, or lower-level user contacts? Many experts say that sales pros should only call high-level executives to be successful. However, most sales pros like to call lower-level people because they are more accessible and often friendlier. In this chapter, I explain why the best strategy is to call at *several* levels at each opportunity and why this can be such an effective strategy.

One of the unique benefits of this book is the inclusion of a step-by-step guide to using the popular LinkedIn.com social media website for business development. Most people are familiar with LinkedIn.com as a tool for job searches, but I have found it to be invaluable for networking and reaching targeted prospects. I have also found that it is under-utilized because many sales pros have either not tried it or do not see its potential. Chapter 16 includes simple, easy to use, step-by-step

instructions on how to use LinkedIn.com for business development that can be utilized immediately.

Finally, in Chapter 17, we address how to master phone
conversation techniques and the best questions to ask. Some
sales pros will freeze when they reach a prospect on a call and
are at a loss for words. Others read from a script which gives
the call an inauthentic tone. Instead, we are going to cover
more than one hundred sample questions you can use in a wide
variety of situations. By the end of this section, you will be prepared to deliver a well-researched pitch and proposal to your
prospective client.

ELEVEN
Value Propositions and How They Help Sales

What is a value proposition? This is a term that has been used a lot, especially by marketing departments, and means something different to different people depending on industry and profession. A simple definition is that a value proposition is the unique, positive, business, or monetary value that your product brings to the customer and represents your competitive advantage. It provides the potential buyer with valid, measurable, and quantifiable reasons to do business with you instead of another competitor. It tells them explicitly "what's in it for them."

Takeaway 21: Your Value Proposition Must be Strong and Quantifiable.

Your value proposition needs to differentiate your offering from the competition. If your prospects cannot differentiate between offerings, then price—not value—becomes the differentiator by default. Your value proposition needs to be strong enough that it is consequential. If not, it becomes meaningless to the buyer. What problems will your product or solution solve for the customer? What are the benefits they can expect from you? It should be compelling, and if possible, link to the prospective company's strategies and/or mission. It could be the reason the company exists, as with my last employer—helping to prevent the bad guys from laundering or transferring money through the world's financial network. It might be as simple as "We provide the fast-food restaurant market in Cincinnati with the freshest produce each morning by 7:00 a.m.," or "Our solutions provide the easiest customer experience when sending money across international borders to university children studying abroad."

The value proposition can also be the result of "mutually agreed outcomes" between a seller and a buyer.[46] An example would be that the value proposition of a new machine will be a reduction in production defects of 10 percent.

Many sales pros struggle with discovering and succinctly articulating their product or service's value proposition. They may understand the features and functions of the product and the customer's needs, which can be value statements, but are unable to articulate a simple value proposition or even a short, thirty-second "elevator pitch." This challenge must clearly state the financial benefits as well as customer satisfaction and other measurable outcomes associated with your product. You can then link the successes that others have had to the success you can bring to this buyer if they choose you.

Takeaway 22: The Validity of the Value Proposition Is Determined By the Buyer, Not the Seller.

---

46 Frank V. Cespedes, *Sales Management That Works: How to Sell in a World That Never Stops Changing* (Boston, MA: Harvard Business Review Press, 2021), 116.

Instead of regurgitating the pitch given to you by your product marketing department, say it aloud and think "If someone approached me with this, would I react to it positively or negatively?" I have found that when I practiced this simple test many value propositions failed. I often think of the 1984 Wendy's TV commercial with octogenarian, Clara Peller, where she had that innocent look and kept asking about competitors' hamburgers, "Where's the beef?"[47]

Sometimes sales pros are advised by product designers and marketing people that the product's value proposition is a "cool" feature or something in its design. For example, design people will gloat over something like a very user-friendly interface. But the value proposition is the benefit that your solution, service, or product provides to the customer, *from their unique viewpoint—not yours.* It is "what it does for a customer—functionally, emotionally, or in terms of perceived social impact or risk reduction."[48]

Value Propositions — Weak versus Strong

An effective value proposition should draw interest from the buyer. They should want to learn more about what you can offer them. Amongst all factors that can win or lose a sale, the value proposition is the most important. A weak sales pro can win with a great value proposition, but even an outstanding sales pro will have difficulty winning with a weak value proposition. A strong value proposition can also help overcome out-of-date or ineffective marketing collateral, a sub-optimal formal presentation or proposal, and poor questioning. An effective value

---

47 "'Where's The Beef?'" w/ Clara Peller - 1984 Wendy's Commercial #1," YouTube, accessed April 19, 2022, https://www.youtube.com/watch?v=eANcbFSPHyA.
48 Frank V. Cespedes, *Sales Management That Works: How to Sell in a World That Never Stops Changing* (Boston, MA: Harvard Business Review Press, 2021), 198.

proposition with metrics, combined with a business driver and an executive sponsorship, will result in a sale.

I attended a sales presentation where the presenter, borrowing from the company- produced marketing material, kept emphasizing that our company offered over ninety anti-money-laundering sanction lists. The customer was supposed to be impressed, as ninety is a large number. But what if a competitor had 125 lists, would that mean they have a better solution? What if you only had twenty-five? What difference does the *quantity* of lists mean to the customer? Probably not much. The value proposition to the customer should have been "If you license or purchase our solution, we can ensure that you do not make any payments to any sanctioned entities, anywhere in the globe, which will result in fines or negative publicity. We currently do this for all the major financial institutions in the world today." That explains the positive outcome the buyer will acquire by purchasing that solution.

Apple's value proposition is the experience that one undergoes with their products, whether the iPhone, the MacBook, or the Apple Watch. The iPhone doesn't emphasize its features and functions, many of which are available with their competitors. They focus on how the iPhone affects your life, including its apps and advanced security. The Apple Watch proposition emphasizes its health benefits.[49] Apple's competitors' products all cost less, yet their customers are notoriously loyal.

If your marketing department or sales enablement functions do not provide strong value propositions to you, and in many cases they don't, it is on you to develop your own. It is not as difficult as it may seem, and you may go through several iterations before arriving at something that seems to make

---

49 "Apple Watch Series 6," Apple.com, accessed April 18, 2022, https://www.apple.com/apple-watch-series-6/.

sense. First, test it on yourself. "If I were the buyer, how would I respond to it?" If it does not motivate you to learn more about the offer, then keep working on it. It should be explicit—not implicit or hidden. "If you buy from me, this is the positive result that you can expect to happen."

A weak value proposition will often leave you on the outside looking in, while other more marketing-oriented competitors, perhaps with inferior features and functions are inside with a less valuable value proposition. Today most business executives are extraordinarily busy. If you cannot present something that grabs their attention and provides an answer to the question "What's in it for me" you will lose their interest. All of your interactions with the buyer, marketing sizzle, and thoughtful work on PowerPoint slides will have been for naught.

Your value proposition should address critical issues, such as:

» Does your product or service *increase revenues, double profitability,* or *increase market share*? Does it accelerate the go-to-market of a new product or enter a new market? Does it speed up the availability of a resource, provide a competitive advantage, or remove one of your competitor's advantages?

» Does it *decrease costs or inventory?* Does it *increase operational efficiency* or aid in automating an existing process? How does it help improve quality, or increase customer or employee satisfaction? Will it withdraw the company from unprofitable markets or implement new customer-oriented systems?

» Does it help accomplish *a key corporate strategic goal?* Does it gain a competitive or first-to-market advantage, or become recognized as the market leader in a chosen industry?

It is important to take emotion into account when considering the effectiveness of value propositions. Emotions can be powerful and often overrule an analytic or empirical data. As entrepreneur Elon Musk said: "When something is important enough, you do it even if the odds are not in your favour."[50]

Have you ever analyzed a situation, made an informed decision, but then purchased something else? I have, especially with automobiles. Author and sales trainer David Sandler notes that "people make decisions intellectually, but they buy *emotionally*."[51] A few years ago I went to a car dealership to consider buying a new car. I intended to purchase a sports utility vehicle (SUV) but saw a slightly used cherry red Mercedes 230 SLK hardtop convertible with a red and black interior (the colors of the Chicago Bulls and Blackhawks, two of my favorite sports teams) in the showroom. It was a two-seater and impractical for my use. We left the dealership and were having lunch at a restaurant when we saw somebody else test-driving the car. When I saw the car drive by, I decided I *had* to have it and we went back to the dealership and purchased it. It was an impulsive, emotional decision.

People will often decide on their choice and then work on self-justifying their decision, especially when they purchase a luxury item. Buying that $1,000 (or $10,000) watch cannot be justified when considering only utility. A $50 Timex wristwatch will tell you the same time and has a history of reliability.

---

50 Elon Musk, "Elon Musk Quotes," Goodreads (Goodreads), accessed April 18, 2022, https://www.goodreads.com/author/quotes/7221234.Elon_Musk.
51 David H. Sandler and John Hayes, *You Can't Teach a Kid to Ride a Bike at a Seminar: The Sandler Sales Institute's 7-Step System for Successful Selling* (Pegasus Media World, 1996).

However, your emotions and perhaps a desire for the luxury item overrules the rational choice. The value proposition that has been agreed upon with the buyer could be the justification that they are looking for, but you must be able to connect emotion to value when the mathematical value is not enough.

Do not overwhelm prospects by presenting too many value propositions, even if you believe there are many for your product or solution. Ten value propositions would be far too many. I would advise you to choose the best one to three that apply to *this* customer, not what the marketing department lists on the website for all prospects. The value proposition should be customized for each target audience and relate to the buyer's specific needs or where you think they would add the most value. If you are calling on a bank, the value propositions should be specific to banking and financial services, not manufacturing, distributions, non-profits, health care, insurance, transportation, or utilities.

The time that you invest in developing and testing a compelling value proposition will always be worthwhile. I encourage you to think "outside the box" and not blindly accept the one that is provided by your marketing staff, unless they also meet with prospects and customers to find out how the product or service is being used and where they derive the greatest value.

The consequence of a poor value proposition could be elimination from further consideration for this opportunity by the prospect, regardless of how well your product meets the customer's needs. There are a lot of excellent products on the marketplace that have not been properly positioned to buyers and because of that, they sometimes fail. You cannot assume that the buyer will link their needs with your product without your help articulating how it will fulfill, or better yet, exceed their needs and expectations. A strong value proposition can be the instrument that helps propel your opportunity to the top of the executive's pile of urgent documents to be signed.

TWELVE
Value-Based Pricing

"If there is no price to be paid, it is not of value."

—Albert Einstein[52]

The concept of Value-Based Pricing (VBP), also known as Return on Investment (ROI), is that the price the buyer pays for your product or solution is based on the value that your solution or product provides to them. In other words, the price is a function or percentage relationship of the quantifiable benefits received by the buyer. It is directly related to the prospect's expected benefits, which establishes a mutually beneficial relationship between the two parties. This is contrasted with cost-plus or list price, pricing, where the seller adds a margin to its cost to cover its overhead and provide a profit.

Takeaway 23: There Is No Standard Price List With Value-Based Selling

Let's look at an example: A medical practice is looking for a new records system. The adoption of an electronic medical

---

52 "Memorable Albert Einstein Quotes," ASL Associates, accessed April 18, 2022, http://www.asl-associates.com/einsteinquotes.htm.

records system would have a different (lesser) value for an office of five doctors than the same solution would have for a 1,000-bed hospital. The hospital would derive a much greater financial benefit, perhaps millions of dollars of savings, compared to the smaller doctor's practice. They would also derive other benefits such as easier accessibility of test results, usage across multiple facilities, reductions in mistakes due to inability to read physicians' handwriting, or automated assessments for potentially dangerous drug interactions.

The VBP should include both "hard dollar" and "soft dollar" costs. Hard dollars, such as reductions in headcount or increases in quality are easier to quantify. But soft dollars, such as savings from increases in customer satisfaction, reductions in training, or decreases in medical errors need to be included in the ROI computation.

Here is another example: The pricing for the same product (perhaps a software application), would be different for a small local retail organization with five stores than for Kroger, the fifth largest retailer in the world. If the product saved $7,500 annually per store, Kroger would receive over $20 million annually in benefits, while the small chain might save $37,500.

Many sales pros who have not worked with VBP may have a lot of trouble adapting to this concept. It is much easier to use a price list. But using a price list does not consider that some companies may derive greater financial benefits from using the solution than others—and there is likely a difference in scale.

VBP recognizes this relationship and results in variable pricing. If the price to the small retailer, as in the example above, is a license fee of $9,375 (25 percent of the benefit), then the price to Kroger should be about $5 million. It is relative to the overall benefits realized by implementing the solution.

In either case, try not to provide a price to the prospect until the value they will derive is mutually quantified. This is often uncomfortable for the sales pro when the buyer is interested in your offering, maybe has even engaged in solutioning, and is now asking for a price. Traditionally, sales pros work a deal until the point when a buyer asks for a price, then gladly provides it. In VBP, you must change this process so you are not prematurely providing a price that has no relationship to the value or savings your customer will derive.

You have been gathering most of the information necessary to provide a price throughout the discovery process. However, you may only have 60 to 80 percent of the information you need, so continue to ask questions to quantify the value you will be providing. Determining the value is an exercise that should be shared with your contact or coach so that your premises are validated. Providing a price before determining a value should be discouraged at (almost) all costs. I have rarely seen it work out positively when you don't. Price lists are *only* for selling commodities when *the difference in value between offerings is insignificant.*

A buyer may resist the VBP model by insisting that they pay the same price as any other company. It is then your job to explain to the buyer that your company does not sell using a standardized price list, that the pricing model is based on the buyer's company receiving benefits that are proportionate to the value that the company will receive. Presumably, that means that if there are no benefits to be derived there should be no cost. If there are no benefits, then the buyer should not be purchasing the solution, and you should not be selling it to them. Many procurement professionals do not like VBP as their performance is often measured by the savings they accrue by reducing costs.

Once VBP becomes standard in your company, the need to offer discounts or selling on price becomes rare. Besides—and I consider this an even greater benefit—the usage of VBP should result in a shortening of the sales cycle and an improvement in your close ratio, as the decision-maker has a proof statement of the economic or other benefits to the organization.

Motivation and emotion are important components of value. If the security officer needs to fix a vulnerability that resulted in a data breach, do you think their motivation to do so in the next few hours is more important than price? The same would be true if there was a possibility of a fine from the Environmental Protection Agency (EPA) due to a leak of harmful substances into the air. If a CEO is committed to reducing their company's carbon footprint, do you think a minor increase in costs will hinder their decision? If somebody has a built-in bonus/salary increase in their formal performance goals that is dependent on completing a replacement of an inefficient process, do you think they will be sufficiently motivated to move forward this year? Absolutely!

The company where I was most recently employed made the switch from using a standard price list to VBP at the direction of the CEO, Hugh Jones. It was not an easy change because of the prior reliance on price lists and prospects requesting prices early in the sales cycle. It took more than a year before it was completely implemented. It was also difficult to use VBP with a Customer Relationship Manager (CRM) system like Salesforce.com that tracks quotes and approvals. Yet, this change, plus investments in products, resulted in a more than 15 percent compounded annual increase in revenue. More importantly, we now demonstrated our value to our customers, which ensured greater customer satisfaction and continued business.

Value-based pricing is best deployed with mid to high-value products and services. Lower-priced products and services, which are often considered commodities, are best kept with the traditional price-list model. The primary obstacles to deploying VBP are determining the value of the product or service and communicating it properly to the customer. The benefit is that the pricing is aligned with the value the customer receives and therefore reduces friction between the buyer and seller, which should make purchase justification easier. If you aren't using the VBP method, I encourage your sales team to make the switch. And be patient because it may take a while before all have adopted it. Every sales pro on the team will benefit! And the customer, your company's shareholders, Board of Directors, CEO and CFO will be delighted with the financial results.

THIRTEEN
The Mathematics of The Sales Funnel

Understanding the mathematics of the sales funnel, and how to increase sales, is essential for sales success. For years we have been taught that closing sales is a function of a "numbers game." In other words, greater activity creates more sales. But this is too simplistic, and it certainly is not valid. Let me explain.

The term "funnel" has been chosen to represent a model that begins with gathering a set of sales prospects, usually through a company or sales pro-initiated marketing campaign, and then winnowing them down to a smaller group that you will invest time and efforts into to close a sale. Some may turn out to be legitimate, qualified leads and many will not and will be discarded. Once they are qualified, you spend more and more time with each, until such time that you decide to either invest more time or cut your losses. Your goal is to waste as little time as possible on unqualified prospects. The top sales pros spend more time on qualifying leads than the average and below-average sales pros, and they have acquired the knowledge to identify the best opportunities (as explained in the next chapter) and not invest a lot of time on mediocre or lower probability leads.

As you aggressively work with the leads in your funnel, the quantity of prospects will naturally decrease over time due to your qualifying activities and attrition. Those who show interest in your product or service, and meet other criteria, are considered "opportunities."

Your investment in *each opportunity* increases—inverse to the shape of the funnel, as prospects proceed through the stages of the sales funnel. There is no standard quantity of stages in a funnel, but my advice is to keep them between five and ten.

I prefer to utilize the Miller Heiman funnel categories that has five stages: Universe, Above (the Funnel), In (the Funnel), Best Few, and Order. [53]

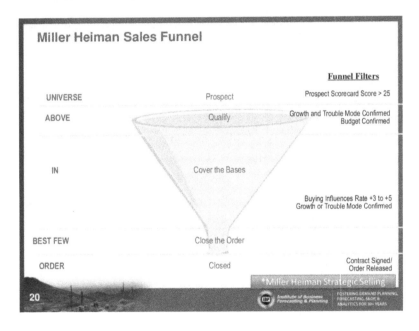

---

53 Copyright © 2021 Korn Ferry. All rights reserved. Used with permission.

The Stages of a Sale

Below are some of the activities that occur in each stage:

- » Universe
  - › Marketing or sales program definition
  - › Any company can be considered as a prospect
- » Above the Funnel
  - › Selection of targeted companies
  - › Contact the prospect/personal introduction
- » In the Funnel
  - › Qualifying the lead—make a go/no go decision
  - › Survey/Discovery
  - › Build the sales plan
  - › In-person meeting with a prospect
  - › Solutioning
  - › Building trust
  - › Determining value
  - › Presentation meeting/demonstration
  - › Answer questions
- » Best Few
  - › Financial proposal
  - › Follow up/objections
  - › Best few options
  - › Ask for commitment
- » Closed/Won
  - › Consensus and affirmation
  - › Confirmation of decision
  - › Contract negotiation and finalization
  - › Delivery, fulfillment, customer service
  - › Post-sales assurance

Moving Through the Funnel

The movement of a sales opportunity through the stages of the funnel is not affected by the passage of time, or even by certain actions, such as holding a meeting. An opportunity moves from one stage to the next when the buyer commits to specific actions. These actions must be measurable and quantifiable, tied to a timeline, appropriate, and necessary for that stage. For example, buyers commit to determining an ROI, or total cost of ownership, to go ahead with the purchase, or the consequences and cost of not purchasing now. Sellers' actions should not move an opportunity without a corresponding buyer commitment.

Listed below are examples of the types of actions by the buyer or sales pro that will result in the sales opportunity moving from one stage to the next stage.

To move from the Universe to Above the Funnel:

- » There are conversations or receipt of an inquiry from the buyer that indicates some interest in your product or solution.
- » There is an agreement by the buyer to an initial call or meeting with you.
- » Open conversations are held between the seller and buyer to discuss issues of concern to them, such as possible growth or trouble with a business situation.

To move from Above the Funnel to In the Funnel:

- » The buyer gives you, or allows, access to other members of the buying team that have a voice in the decision process, including the Executive Sponsor.
- » The buyer's team agrees there is a "need to do something."

» The buyers get involved in "discovery" or "solutioning" meetings to identify the problems and how to solve them.

» They provide documentation (spec. sheets, workflows, etc.) that is needed by the sales pro to help understand the problems.

» They have all the right people attend presentations and/or demos—but only after participating in all the discovery work that has been done.

» They review and make constructive comments on a "draft" of the solution.

To move from In the Funnel to Best Few:

» They accept your proposal as one of the best—show positive "buying signals."

» They might want to have discussions about the price or ask for price concessions.

» They discuss the decision-making process and guide you through that process.

» They get the right people involved in the final approval process.[54]

If there are too many prospects in the funnel that have not been either properly qualified or discarded, you may have a "constipated" funnel, according to sales consultant Bill Hoffman.[11] They are stuck, and action needs to be taken to clean them out. A "whistle" funnel is one in which sales pros try to work a small number of leads from the top to the bottom. Instead of a wide funnel, this one is narrow from top to bottom. A "martini" funnel has many leads that have been worked but are at the top of the funnel and are not being moved to the next

54 Weinberg, Steve. B. Hoffman Personal Conversation. Personal, January 4, 2021.

stage or closed. The sales pro may be meeting and entertaining the prospect, but not enough sales activity is taking place. Thus, the shape is like a martini glass, very wide at the top and thin from that point on. A true funnel shape shows that the sales pro is properly working the leads and opportunities.

Funnel stages are sequential and are not concurrent. Do not proceed to the next stage without satisfactorily completing the prior. And each will take whatever time is necessary, not a prescribed amount. For example, do not qualify a prospect while doing discovery, or while concurrently presenting a solution on the same opportunity. And do not try to close a prospect after qualifying and then, if it does not work, go back to solutioning.

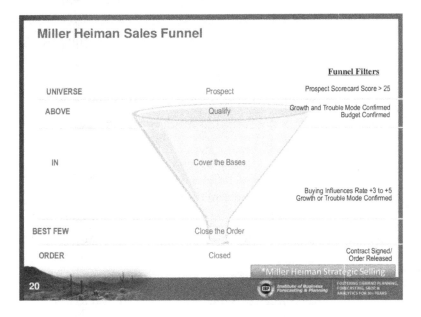

Now, let's analyze this equation. Putting some numbers into this concept looks like this example:

- » Above the Funnel
  - › Direct mail campaign to 5,000 targeted companies
  - › One hundred people show interest (respond to the direct mail piece or visit the link to your website)
- » In the Funnel
  - › Twenty qualified leads—call or meet and discuss needs
  - › Twelve people/companies interested in a solution and follow up
- » Best Few
  - › Ten make decisions, two do not
  - › Five wins (50 percent win rate)

In this example, you started with 5,000 unqualified companies, and after proceeding through the winnowing down of the sales cycle you have closed five sales, a 0.1 percent, conversion rate.

The funnel value is "monetized" by applying your price quote, or average sales price, and the sum of all opportunities is termed "the pipeline." The purpose of a pipeline is to perform sales forecasting. Normally the opportunities are arrayed by those closing this month, next month, this quarter, next quarter, and so on.

Takeaway 24: Sum of Your Pipeline Goal = At Least Three Times Your Annual Target

The optimum pipeline should equate to three to five times your annual goal due to attrition. Many opportunities will not close this year, and that is just the nature of the business. Some sales pros try to mislead their managers by leaving unqualified or dead opportunities in their pipeline to show a greater pipeline value. This is foolish and hurts the sales pro as much as their manager. It can give you a false sense of accomplishment instead of working on a remedy.

Takeaway 25: Five Ways to Increase Sales Revenue:

1. Develop More Leads,
2. Increase the Average Sales Price,
3. Change the Quality of Leads;
4. Improve the Win Percent;
5. Hire More Sales Pros.

6. Develop More Leads: You could increase your number of contacts by deploying lead-generating activities. This requires an investment in finding new prospects, which may mean you must increase cold-call prospecting. More inputs of leads or suspects at the top of the funnel will increase the quantity that makes it to the bottom—a "waterfall" effect. In this example, if you increased the universe from 5,000 to 10,000 companies, using the same mathematics it should yield ten wins—double the amount. More leads will increase the size of your pipeline, but it does not automatically lead to more sales. The key is to add higher quality leads. ("Garbage in/garbage out" applies with leads as well.)

7. Increase the Average Sales Price: Or you can increase the average sales price, which is usually either a function of the market, your price book, or your value proposition. This can be very difficult.

8. Change the Quality of Leads: Changing the quality of leads results from more precise targeting of leads. That will occur if the pool of prospects consists of companies in the targeted "Sweet Spot" of prospects, which is where your value proposition, the prospect's needs, and your competitive advantage are aligned. (More on this in the next chapter.) Again, this can be difficult.

9. Improve the Win Percent: Or you increase your win rate from 50 to 65 – 70 percent, for example, which will then yield seven wins instead of five in my example. Increasing the win rate is the most difficult change because it requires more efficiency in all phases of the sales cycle. That requires changes in the sales pro's behavior which includes selling style, positioning, and more effective explanations of the value proposition.

10. Hire More Sales Pros: Hiring more sales pros is normally frowned upon by the company because it increases costs and by sales pros because it results in reducing sales territories. But if each sales pro is expected to close a certain amount of sales, adding more sales pros will increase total revenue.

Dedicate Time for Prospecting Every Day

Consistent prospecting needs to be done to put more "unqualified" leads into the top of your funnel. Author, salesman, and motivational speaker Zig Ziglar called the unwillingness of some sales pros to prospect "the sin of the desert, which for sales pros is not prospecting every day that often results in periods of no sales."[55] It's true most sales professionals don't like this aspect of the job, and yet it is one of the most important.

If the company's marketing programs, website, and direct mail campaigns do not yield enough qualified prospects, and many do not, then you must make more initial calls to fill your funnel. I advise sales pros to dedicate *at least* one hour per day to business development. A goal is to make at least twenty call attempts per hour that result in at least five conversations with one ending up a qualified prospect. We also know that leads will become stale or lost if they are not promptly followed up with an email or phone call. Far too many leads are wasted by sales pros who were too lazy or too unmotivated to pick up the telephone.

Personally, I am not a fan of over-stressing funnel velocity to the point where the sales pro tries to prematurely close sales. That will backfire and result in increased losses or stalled sales. However, adding sales incentives can be effective. This can be done by leadership, but you can also determine your own incentives. For instance, if you meet a certain goal, maybe you buy yourself a trip somewhere, or even something as small a as a nice dinner. Do whatever works to motivate yourself to do this least-favorite part of the job.

Most sales pros do not spend more than 10 to 15 percent of their working time on prime selling activities. Your daily work priorities and your time investments should not be in the sequence of the funnel, but rather:

---

55   Zig Zigler, *Zigler on Selling* (Nashville, TN: Thomas Nelson, 1991), 46.

1. Close sales (last stage)

2. Input more prospects in the Funnel

3. Qualify the prospects

4. In the Funnel activities: solutioning and covering the bases

Don't Be a "Quota Sloth!"

Sales pros often make the mistake of prospecting just long enough to gain some leads and then cease the activity until they run out of opportunities. Others concentrate on working only the best few because they require steady attention, and they see the possibility of closing some of them soon. But when they close those few sales, they have a dry pipeline and can go months without a sale. Some sales pros try to find large deals ("whales") and concentrate solely on seeing those through to completion. This strategy is like going to bat in baseball and trying to only hit home runs. Very few of those baseball players succeed. These people are all various versions of "quota sloths."

Prospecting for more leads must be a continual process that you do throughout the year. I advise working with prospects at various stages in the pipeline every day so that there are prospects at each stage. Do not try to add new prospects to the pipeline from accounts chosen from the universe—instead try qualifying those that have already been contacted and those that are Above the Funnel to determine which are more promising prospects and then dedicate sufficient time to those to close. As a bonus, not only will you see increased success using this method, working each level increases variety and makes your day more interesting.

Calling on opportunities at the various stages in the funnel, not just those at the bottom, will also result in better coverage of your opportunities. In my own experience, I've found that the ideal quantity of opportunities I can manage effectively at any one time is about twelve. Any more than that results in decreasing attention to each opportunity, which leads to losing those opportunities.

Sales managers use the funnel, or pipeline, to manage the behaviors of sales pros. They will be looking at things like time allocation, prioritization of selling tasks and prospects, qualifications, closing percentages, and whether the sales pros are following up on all issues and open items. These are valuable analytics that can be derived from the funnel; however, I caution sales managers against using them to manage sales pros. Being successful in sales cannot be reduced to a formula. If you track these analytics, make sure they are not the only thing you are assessing.

In summary, understanding the mathematics of the funnel will help you determine how you can best increase your sales. There are (only) five ways to increase sales revenue and the easiest of these is to do more generation of your own leads. Prospecting companies in your Sweet Spot, which will be discussed in the next chapter, must therefore be an essential part of your daily activity, not done occasionally or just when necessary. Targeting the most likely buyers will also improve your chances of success. The lesson is that there needs to be a funnel that contains enough prospects at *every level* to be successful each month, each quarter, and each year.

FOURTEEN
The Sweet Spot to Prospect

"How can I find prime prospects so that I do not waste my time on companies that are not going to buy from me this year?" This is one of the most common questions I've received throughout my career. I have found that as many as 50 percent of a sales pro's pipeline consists of prospects that are not well-qualified—they are not the companies most likely to need or use the seller's product or service. The result is that sales pros waste a lot of time on companies that do not buy, take an excessive amount of selling resources to convince, or that become unhappy customers.

There is a strategy that you can use to increase your chances of finding the best prospects, and it is not as difficult as it may seem. The clue is to decrease the universe of all prospects to just those that genuinely need your product or service, and this means researching the companies. An analogy could perhaps be made to fishing in the ocean: Use generic bait and you're just hoping to land a fish sometime in the next week, versus fishing in a specific pond or stream where the desired species of fish are known to be and using bait that you know is reliable for that specific fish. In the latter case, your chances of catching the type of fish you desire are much greater. Fishing for just anything that comes your way can work on occasion, but it is not a model for continued success. This applies to sales: creating a sub-set of likely prospects works the same way.

To find the best prospects you need to know:

» Your value proposition
» Your competitive strengths
» Which prospects are likely to have needs that you can fulfill

Your value proposition is the unique positive business value that your solution, product, or service brings to the marketplace. Your competitive strengths are the advantages you have over the other suppliers, which can include their weaknesses. There can be overlaps (see the diagram below) with the value proposition. The prospect's needs are sometimes disclosed, but often need to be found during the sales pro's discovery process.

Let us review the Venn diagram below that consists of three intersecting circles for each of these questions.

» The white circle represents your competitive strengths.
» The black circle represents your prospect's needs.
» The gray circle represents your value proposition.

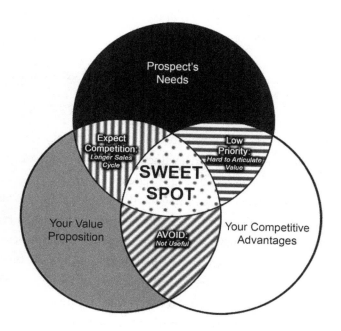

The diagonal shaded area includes prospects that do not have needs that match your value proposition and strengths. They are a waste of time and should be avoided.

The horizontal shaded area includes prospects that have needs that are in your competitive strengths but do not match your value proposition. That can happen if the prospect requires a low price, for example, which may be one of your competitive advantages, but they may not see as much value from your solutions. These prospects should receive a low priority unless your strategy is to be the low-cost provider in the marketplace.

The vertical shaded area includes prospects that have needs that match your proposition value but are outside your competitive strength. These prospects should be targeted, with the realization that the deals will be extremely competitive and that you will need to work harder to establish greater trust with the buyer to be chosen.

Takeaway 26: The Sweet Spot is the Best Place to Prospect

The polka dot area in the middle is your "Sweet Spot." This is where the prospect's needs, value proposition, and competitive strengths are aligned. These are the prospects that you want to seek. You will have an advantage and your probability of closing the sale is much greater. The "Sweet Spot" is more desirable than the "ideal customer profile." The latter only describes the type of prospect, from amongst the universe, that is the best fit for your product or service based on functionality or vertical market characteristics. (Vertical markets are a group of companies in a specific industry or market segment: i.e., automotive manufacturing, health care, pharmaceuticals, financial services, etc.) A company could be "ideal" if it looks like it meets the criteria; however, that does not mean it is a prospect that has needs you can meet.

Finding prospects in the Sweet Spot requires you to master your value proposition and competitive strengths and then identify those companies that would likely need a solution that your company offers. Next, make a list of all the job titles that would normally purchase from you and then use LinkedIn.com, Hoovers, or another source to find the primary contacts' names, telephone numbers, and email addresses. You can approach the individuals through cold calling, direct mail, or LinkedIn.com, or all the above.

Let us consider some examples and determine which, if any, are in the Sweet Spot. We will assume that your company's value proposition is that your solution will lower overall energy costs by 20 percent per year. Your company also markets this product globally through offices in most major countries. You are intentionally *not* the low-cost provider in the market.

There are four hypothetical prospects for your energy-saving device:

» Fortune Manufacturing is a medium-sized boutique company. The procurement manager is charged with the task of reducing energy costs and has identified the primary deciding factor to be the lowest price. They do not have any urgency to change suppliers.

» Besides International is a large, growing global organization. The VP of Operations has a stated goal of reducing their energy spend by at least 15 percent this year. The CEO wants a recommendation next month.

» Meredith Company is an international petroleum processor. Their Plant Superintendent's primary need is to replace old, rusting infrastructure, but recognizes the need to reduce energy costs and has included it in their long-range plans.

» Divot Plastics is a specialty domestic manufacturer. The plant foreman contacted you for information on your product. He seemed interested and was eager to have us and other suppliers visit them. However, they do not need to reduce their already low energy costs.

COMPANY	NEEDS	VALUE COMPETITIVE ADV	COMPANY
Fortune	√		
Besides	√	√	√
Meredith	√		√
Divot			

Fortune Manufacturing has the need, but the decision is being managed by the procurement manager who is most interested in price. They do not align with our value proposition or competitive strengths. To sell to them you would need to get the prospect's businesspeople to take control of the decision. They would fall into the vertical shaded area of our diagram.

Meredith Company would benefit from our global network, which is a competitive advantage, and they have long-term needs, but this is not a priority for the plant superintendent who is mostly concerned with upgrading the infrastructure. This person may not see the value in purchasing from us. They would fall into the horizontal shaded or lower-priority area.

Divot is a domestic company that does not need to reduce costs, so our product is of less value to them. They are not international, so would not benefit from our global capability. Even though they seem eager to engage us they are in the diagonal shaded area.

Besides International has the immediate need for our product and they have a sense of urgency. The VP of Operations will understand our value proposition and being a global company will benefit from our international support network. They are in the polka dot Sweet Spot.

To be highly successful in sales you must find more companies like Besides, and to a lesser extent, like Meredith. Work on finding enough prospects that you do not need to call on those like Fortune and completely avoid companies like Divot. They are a waste of your time.

How Do I Find Sweet Spot Prospects?

In this example, first try to find information on which companies consume a lot of energy that would be a good fit for your product. They have the financial strength to afford it and the infrastructure to be able to install it without a lot of modification. If you cannot find this information through web searches, choose twenty to fifty international, publicly traded companies, and look at the profit and loss (P&L) statement in their annual reports. These are normally available online, but always available by request. Their energy costs should be shown in the P&L report.

Review your existing customer list and identify which are receiving the greatest benefit from and are the most satisfied with your product. What do these customers have in common? Are they in the same or a few vertical markets within the industry? If so, that is another clue as to where to find more prospects that are in the Sweet Spot.

Once you have a working list of companies, expand it to at least a hundred by including similar companies in the vertical market or geography. For example, if one or more of the companies was a manufacturing company, add similar manufacturers to the list.

Secondly, consider your competitive strengths. For instance, your product is globally available and supported. Your primary competitors have regional solutions. There are major competitors in Europe and in the Asia Pacific region, but none of these products are similar in international opportunity and that presents several issues. Your marketing messages should emphasize that support for the purchase is available in all the major markets and the advantages of working with a single source globally, rather than with several regional suppliers.

Next, find the appropriate contacts at each of these companies as well. Follow the same steps you did the first time. What are the titles of the people who would most likely utilize your product? Perhaps it is the Plant Manager or Operations Vice President. Who do these people normally report to? List the titles. Now search on LinkedIn.com for those titles at your target list of companies. You can try to connect to these people through your existing connections as I describe in the next two chapters. Or you can try to obtain their contact information from Dun & Bradstreet or other list providers. The result will be a list of companies, with the primary contact targets and their contact information.

Your next step is to contact these prospects and qualify them to determine if you want to pursue them. This will include determining if they are interested in reducing their energy costs and what their sense of urgency is as a possible buyer. We've covered that in earlier chapters, so once again just employ those techniques. As a result of your conversations with several contacts at each company, you will determine each target's category or color.

If you do not have enough prospects in the polka dot, vertical shaded, and horizontal shaded areas, it is advised that you review your product's value and strengths to then identify the companies that would benefit the most. Restart and try again. By following this process and concentrating solely on these prospects you will be fishing in the "Sweet Spot" pond.

FIFTEEN

Effective Lead Generation

Sales pros often need to conduct personal marketing campaigns to generate leads for themselves, but unfortunately, not all are skilled at generating the leads necessary to build their pipelines. If your goal is to exceed your sales target and your company does not provide you with enough leads, you must own your sales success and start prospecting now. When a sales pro is evaluated, it is mostly based on closed or booked sales versus quota or target. So if the leads generated by the company are insufficient (and I have never worked in an environment where they are sufficient) you must generate the leads on your own.

I still have not met a sales pro who enjoys prospecting, especially cold calling people. Eight reasons most often cited are:

1. It is a waste of time.

2. The list of prospects is out-of-date and worthless.

3. It is difficult to reach people by telephone.

4. They do not return calls from voice messages.

5. They dislike rejection.

6. They don't know what to say when they reach somebody.

7. They don't like being told what to do.

8. They are too busy and are more productive doing something else.

Many sales pros are uncomfortable doing lead generation because they have never been trained on how to do it. During the course of this chapter we will discuss tips that will assist you—but just like riding a bicycle, or learning to swim, you must practice to improve as a sales pro.

Here are twenty-one essential elements to a successful sales pro-initiated marketing campaign:

1. What is the goal of the campaign? Is it to generate qualified leads? Is it to introduce a new product? Is it to educate the prospect? Are there sub-goals or objectives? Is it to upsell existing customers or to find new buyers? Is it to build a 2x, 3x, or 5x pipeline (x is your quota or target)?

2. The campaign goal should be SMART: Specific, Measurable, Achievable, Realistic, and Time bound.

3. Do not confine your efforts to one method, but rather use email, cold calling, LinkedIn and social media.

4. Include asking for referrals from your existing customers in your campaign. I have found them to be invaluable.

5. Establish a campaign budget. What is this going to cost? Will you be provided any funding, or will this be handled within the existing budget?

6. What is the campaign timeline and what tasks will be completed by each date? What has worked in the past? What has not worked? Why?

7. How much time is the sales pro going to dedicate to the campaign each day? The minimum should be one hour per day, or the results will be minimal.

8. Your message should be brief which will increase the possibility it will be read or heard. Another reason: it may be read on a smartphone.

9. What is your compelling message, or call to action, for both phone calls and emails for cold calling? The call to action should tell the prospect what you want them to do after they hear or read the message. What is the subject line of the email? It will determine whether the email is opened, deleted, or assigned to junk mail. It should be a compelling phrase that increases the curiosity of the recipient, but not trite, such as "What keeps you awake at night?" The email content should refer to your value proposition. What is in it for them—what do they gain?

10. Your calling scripts should incorporate a compelling message. These scripts should be in writing and should incorporate positive and negative responses—this is what to say if the targeted person says "no" or "yes." The scripts need to be as brief as possible. The scripts should also be varied based on the targeted person's function or title. For example, the message to the Chief Financial Officer would be different than one to the Inventory Control Manager. There should also be scripts for voice mail messages, should you decide to leave one. They should give the targeted person a *brief* business reason to speak with you when you call them back, or for them to call you.

11. Select a subset of companies from the universe that are in your "Sweet Spot," or perhaps in a targeted vertical market, geographic area, interest group, gender, or age group. Are they current or existing customers or non-customers? If so, the strategies and messages will likely be different.

12. Where or at what level are you targeting to contact the prospect? Your message should be relevant to those people. Are you going to try to work from the top down or the bottom up, or pursue specific functional areas? It is always easier to go downstream than upstream.

13. Do you have any existing marketing collateral that can be used? If not, you must create marketing material that supports *this* campaign, not something broad or general. Do you have any case studies or white papers that are specific to this campaign? If not, get to work and produce a few.

14. Prepare a list of current customers that are similar to your targeted prospects where you have had measurable successes. You can provide the references when requested. Can you point to any trade journal or web articles where customer successes were cited?

15. Obtain email addresses through a third-party firm, from your customer relationship management (CRM) system, or via visits to websites. There should be

several email addresses from each company. Assume that at least 10 (perhaps even 20) percent of them will be inaccurate. This is mostly due to employee turnover, as lists are often only updated annually.

16. Will you be using social media: Facebook, Twitter, LinkedIn, Instagram? Google, pay-per-click advertising? If so, how? Are you going to encourage the respondents to visit your website? If so, is there enough relevant information available for them to research? Are you going to utilize search engine optimization (SEO)?

17. A CRM system or spreadsheet should be used to track the calls. All leads, qualified and unqualified, must be followed up. An intelligent email system, such as Constant Contact or Mailchimp, are excellent for automated follow-ups, sometimes termed "drip messaging."

18. Do you have a plan about what to do with lead conversions—the prospects who show interest. Is it another telephone call, a demonstration, a free trial, a proposal, a "white paper" or case study, a return on investment (ROI) test, or a proof of concept (POC)? What is your pricing strategy?

19. How will you make in-course changes? If something is not working, how will you allow for changes? What is Plan B? If the campaign is successful, what will you do to improve it to make it more so? How can you expand the number of targeted companies?

20. How do you measure success? What will you consider to be a success for this campaign? What do

you want to achieve? There should be a measurable objective and metrics established before the campaign is undertaken. What are the key performance indicators (KPIs)? For example, is it fifty or a hundred qualified leads? Is it increasing sales by 10 percent in the next quarter? What are the financial projections for the campaign?

21. You should conduct a post-campaign evaluation to record what have you learned so that you can use it to do a better job in future campaigns. Another benefit of doing your own lead generation is that many of the opportunities that you develop will be non-competitive because you were the person that generated the interest, not the prospect. It is also likelier that you will avoid the issuance of a Request for Proposal (RFP) if you get in earlier.

Many sales pros want to be opportunistic and sell to whatever companies show an interest in their products or solutions. They want to go after the "low-hanging fruit" in the universe first, regardless of who they are, and then look for others that may show interest, without a target market in mind. I call this "pinball selling," after the game in which the ball bounces around and can land anywhere. It may work for some, or for a short-time with the "long-hanging fruit," but it is not a good long-term strategy. Since sales pros are usually measured on total sales versus a quota or target, some believe it does not make any difference whether a pet food manufacturer purchases your products versus a hospital if both see value in it. It is certainly true that all dollars are equal, but when considering which companies to target, the sales efforts involved in each, and your likelihood of closing the sale, it is more efficient and less difficult to market to companies that are similar.

Selecting an appropriate list of target companies that are derived from matching the initial targeted set to your "Sweet Spot" is your key to success.

Starter Set of Prospects

I recommend a prospect list starter set of 100 – 500 companies. Then score the companies against your Sweet Spot, using weights of one to ten, with ten being the highest. I would then call the tens first, then the nines, and so on down to the fives. Discard those that are scored less than five, as those companies are likely to be more difficult to sell to and may waste a lot of your time. Once you have your target list you then should choose the titles, personas, or positions of the people you want to target. Which titles are the most likely buyers of your product, service, or solution? For example, is it the Chief Financial Officer, Controller, Chief Technology Officer, Manager of Accounting, Treasurer, Director of Human Resources, Manager of Supply Chain, or Procurement Manager? There should be five to ten titles at each company.

There are times where you may opportunistically pursue sales prospects outside of the Sweet Spot. However, this should be infrequent and there should be a sales-related reason for it—a lead that resulted from a meeting at a trade show, an introduction from a mutual friend or customer, or an incoming lead where somebody has shown interest in learning more about your solution. But remember, the likelihood of a sale to a company outside the Sweet Spot is normally statistically small.

Sometimes people with good selling skills do not achieve their quotas because they spent time chasing companies far outside their Sweet Spot.

Other clues can help us target companies that are more likely to make purchases in this fiscal period are:

» The company is growing and doing well financially. Companies that are growing are more willing to invest and consider alternative solutions. Their needs include where to find additional qualified staff, office space, equipment, additional distribution channels, native language speakers, cash flow, spreading the company culture, and developing new strategies.

» Companies that have recently had negative publicity or have incurred regulatory fines are ripe for solutions that address those situations, although normally the company has begun remediating those before the public finds out about them. If your company has a product that eliminates environmental waste, then it makes sense to look for companies that have had significant waste or EPA issues. At Accuity, we wanted to assist companies in their anti-money laundering efforts, and we looked for companies and banks that incurred fines for not being careful enough.

» Companies that have had a significant change in management, especially at the Chief Executive Officer level will often be in the market for solutions that will help them address known—and unknown— issues. New CEOs typically will be change agents when they join the company.

» Technology and start-up companies are often good prospects because they make quicker decisions and are not married to past processes and solutions. Many have been in business for less than ten years and have no anachronistic procedures. They are more open to creativity, and you do not hear "we have always done it this way." They are more agile, much less bureaucratic, and typically will act quicker when presented with an opportunity to expand markets, increase revenues, or reduce costs. In many cases, they will empower middle managers to act without requiring executive approval. On the other hand, they will demand more innovative solutions.

» Companies that are expanding globally, especially into emerging markets, are often good candidates for products and solutions that will facilitate their strategic goals, and they tend to make quicker decisions. It is a plus if your company has offices and/ or experience in international markets.

» Government agencies, such as the Departments of Defense, Homeland Security, Labor, Housing and Urban Development, and the Food and Drug Administration do a lot of spending, especially during times of economic prosperity or national emergencies, such as wars and devastating storms. You can look on their websites for requests for proposals. Often your company must be pre-approved on the federal Government Services Administration (GSA) list.

» Look for women and minority-owned firms, as the federal and state governments, as well as socially conscious corporations, are increasing their spending with these companies. That benefits you as the sales pro because these companies may now be looking to expand or may need additional services as a result of these contracts.

» Look at companies that are currently being merged or acquired or have been recently merged or acquired by another company. In such cases, most large, non-essential purchases are normally frozen until the new organization and new priorities have been established.

» Contact companies where previous contacts now work. According to the US Bureau of Labor Statistics, the average annual turnover rate for corporate employees is about 12 to 15 percent or roughly one in eight people.[56] This is even greater in Silicon Valley, where turnover is even higher. These people are resources for you to contact at their new companies. Since you already have worked with them, it is easier than a cold call.

» Do not limit your prospecting to the traditional jobs that have previously purchased your products as there may be ancillary areas that might be new markets in addition to the supply chain and procurement areas.

» Consider company partners or potential partners who may be interested in co-marketing with you. Be sure to explore these opportunities.

Once you have a list of target companies the next step is to research them using Hoovers, LexisNexis.com, or a similar resource before you make any calls. If your company does

---

56 "Job Openings and Labor Turnover," Bureau of Labor Statistics (US Department of Labor, March 29, 2022), https://www.bls.gov/news.release/pdf/jolts.pdf.

not subscribe to Hoovers, your local public library likely does. You will want to look at the financials (if available), recent press releases, management, products, markets, the stock price (if public), and their trend—whether they are expanding or contracting.

Takeaway 27: The Prospect's Annual Report Contains Strategic Information

Annual reports of public companies are full of important information, including the CEO's annual message (be sure to read it!), their financial results, their products, and a listing of their officers. They are usually available at the company's website. CEOs often explain their strategic goals in a message to shareholders and employees. For example, the CEO might write that "our goal this year is to reduce fixed costs by 10 percent," "we have begun an initiative to expand into new markets," or "the company's goal this year is to replace our current inventory system with one that will be much more efficient and yield cost savings." These are the marching orders that the CEO has given to the first-line managers. Suppose you had a solution that enabled the company to accomplish any of those goals, or one that is ancillary. You would want to contact the person(s) responsible for executing the CEO's vision. My experience is that very few sales pros research prospects by reviewing their annual reports.

At this point you should have determined the prospects in your "Sweet Spot"—their need, your competitive advantage, and value propositions should all be in alignment. You should have also researched the company to understand their strategic goals, recent information, their markets, and any issues affecting their industry. If you are targeting more than one company in a specific industry there might be some common issues affecting all companies—for example, the need for greater e-commerce capabilities for retailers.

The next step in the process is to use the information gained from your research to prepare succinct and compelling messages that link what you found to each company's value propositions. For example, perhaps you found that the company is expanding into more international markets, and you are selling a foreign currency solution. You can then prepare a brief message to explain how your solution can assist them to achieve their global expansion. If they are concerned with inventories or transportation, you might explain how your (logistics) product will help them take advantage of solving the supply chain problems that many firms are currently dealing with.

Takeaway 28: Your Prospecting Objective Is to Get the NEXT Call, Not a Sale!

By this point, you should now have a message that resonates with your prospect and a script that has a "hook" that stimulates your prospect's interest. Studies have shown that you have only a short time, as few as eight seconds, when you reach the intended target to grab their attention with a concise (twenty-second) message before they lose interest in speaking with you.[57]

Scripts Can Be Useful Tools

Written scripts are always helpful, but only so long as you don't sound like you are reading from one. Using a script will ensure

---

57 Kevin McSpadden, "Science: You Now Have a Shorter Attention Span Than a Goldfish," *Time*, May 14, 2015, https://time.com/3858309/attention-spans-goldfish.

that you are following a pattern that optimizes what is said at each point. I prefer to use my own wording rather than one that is written by someone else as it will also sound more authentic and natural. Here is an example:

> Prospect: "Peter Jones here."
>
> Me: "Hi, Peter. My name is Steve Weinberg. Have I called you at a good time?"
>
> If no:
>
> Me: "When shall I call you back? Is Tuesday at 3:00 p.m. good for you?"
>
> If yes:
>
> Me: "Peter, we have worked with many companies in your industry to help them increase revenues by improving their grocery displays. I would like to set up a call to discuss this further with you, and any other people you might want to invite. Does Tuesday at 3:00 p.m. work for you?"
>
> If no:
>
> Me: "When is a better time? I'll send a calendar invite. Thank you for your time."

Here is another example that is a little longer:

> Prospect: "This is Mary Smith."
>
> Me: "Mary, thank you for taking my call. Are you in charge of payroll operations?"
>
> If no:
>
> Me: "Can you please direct me to the person that handles payroll operations?"

If yes:

Me: "Do you process payroll in-house or is it being handled by somebody else?"

If in-house:

Me: "Have you considered outsourcing it? Are you the person in charge of the decision of whether to outsource? If not, can you please tell me who is responsible?"

If already outsourced:

Me: "May I ask which payroll vendor you are using now? Can we discuss how we can provide greater service and better reporting to you than you are currently receiving? Can we set up an appointment for next week to discuss this in further detail? When is a good time? Is Thursday at 10:00 a.m. good for you?"

I always hoped that the targeted person was willing to speak with me when I called. However, later in my career, when I re-entered direct sales, I preferred that the person tell me that they were too busy to speak with me now, but they would speak with me at a later date. I would then schedule the call with them at a more convenient time, and I would follow that up with a calendar invitation. That would put the call on their calendar, and I would usually have a scheduled, undisturbed, twenty minutes to converse with them. These scheduled conversations seem to be more relaxed and productive.

Who to Call When Prospecting?

There is a controversy among sales trainers and authors as to whether to contact higher-level executives, such as the

Economic Buyer or other decision-maker, or to contact mid- or lower-level employees, such as first-line managers or analysts. Some sales experts recommend the former as they hold the "purse strings," or budget, and the decision-making power. They believe it is a waste of time to call on lower-level staff.

This approach results in working on a smaller pool of more qualified prospects. That is not always a negative, as sales pros are normally measured on closed sales, not on the number of prospects they call on. But decision-makers are busy and are often hard to reach. They often have built-in protection from cold calls and non-scheduled interruptions, usually in the form of an executive assistant screening calls. It is important to be prepared and have something ready to say that is relevant and interesting. A "Hello, how are you?" or "How is the weather in San Jose today?" is not what they want to hear from you. Get to the point quickly and do not waste their time. If you can quickly capture their interest, the likely outcome is that they will refer you to their subordinate who is charged with the responsibilities for that area or project. When you then call on that person, you can inform them that the CEO has advised you to call. It is much easier to go down the organization hierarchy from executives to lower-level individuals than working one's way up.

One caution: you may only have one opportunity to call the Economic Buyer. If that does not go well, or if they do not take your call, you may not have another opportunity later. Do you want to use your one shot on a cold call, which may not be successful, or do you want to use it later, after the sales cycle has been established, and you want to have a high-level conversation? This could be about information needed to satisfy questions about your solution and whether or not it will meet their needs, or whether the value proposition that has been discussed is realistic. I usually prefer to use it during the sales cycle, yet when I initiated the largest sale in our company's history I contacted the Economic Buyer, a Senior Vice President, through LinkedIn, who referred me to the employee he had just hired to handle the problem. It can work; just be aware of the risks.

On the other side of the issue, some sales pros prefer calling lower-level contacts because the people at these levels are usually available and often are the people doing most of the legwork on the project. They are the worker bees of the colony. They are also normally the end-users, the subject-matter experts, and they deal with the everyday issues. However, the lower-level workers may not be in contact with the executive sponsor, or have budget or project authority, nor the awareness of the organization's goals. Many product-knowledgeable sales pros like to engage in conversations with this group because they can show off their knowledge of the industry and the appropriate jargon. Some sales pros stay at this level throughout the entire sales process because they are comfortable there and do not want to deal with people whose titles may intimidate them or who might ask them difficult questions. But this is a serious mistake and indicates that the sales pro does not have confidence. These sales pros are not meeting the senior managers and executive sponsors who are making the decisions, but it is likely that their competition is. Don't be that type of sales professional.

Once you have established contact with the lower-level person, there is a risk in calling above them later. Some contacts will take offense to that. They do not understand why working with them is not sufficient for you, especially if all has gone well up to that point. They may be embarrassed by it. Worse, they may be called on it by their manager or another high-level person in the organization. They could be accused of not having control of the suppliers. The consequence is that you could change your contact from being a positive buying influence into a negative, which could cost you the sale.

In such a situation, my advice is to never call over your primary contact's head without their knowledge, but not necessarily with their consent. You will need to explain why you are doing it; perhaps blaming it on your manager. Tell them your manager insists that you contact the person that will ultimately approve the project to introduce yourself. A good manager will back you on this. Copy or blind copy your contact on your emails to that person so that they feel included in the process.

This risk can be worth it, especially if the sales cycle has not been going well and your contact has been giving you indications that they are going in another direction. If you decide to take this path, be sure not to disparage your contact. One explanation you can give is that you would like another in-person meeting to do a better job in making your case. Take ownership for them leaning in another direction. It is your fault. That way you are not attacking the integrity of your contact or their selection process.

A good guideline is to contact prospects at three vertical levels in a given company (perhaps your contact, their boss, and their subordinate) as well as three wide (your prospects' peers across other functional areas.) This will ensure that you obtain the best possible information, as well as determining who is agreement with your proposal and who is not.

Takeaway 29: There Is a Reverse Relationship Between Authority and Accessibility

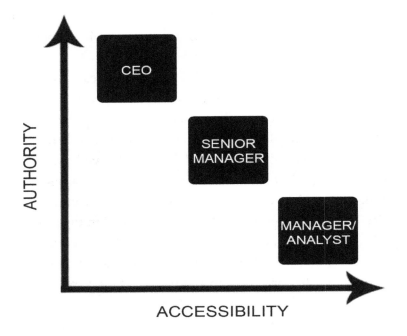

As you can see in the chart above, there is typically a reverse relationship between the *authority* level and *accessibility* in most corporations. The CEO is often more difficult to reach but has more authority. The manager or analyst is easier to reach but has much less authority.

The third alternative strategy for first contact with a company, and the one I prefer, is to first attempt a high-level contact at the targeted company. If that does not work then target people in the prospective organization, at multiple levels, according to function (for example, Chief Financial Officer, Treasurer, Accounting Manager), and try to contact people at multiple levels in the organization—executives, mid-level or senior managers, as well as first-line managers and analysts. This could be termed a "shotgun approach."

You then work with whomever responds positively to your call, email, or marketing campaign. Once initial contact is established, continue to work with this person, but also begin contacting others as you learn more about the organization and decision-making progress. I call this strategy "land and expand." Once you have met with several members of the team during the initial qualification or solutioning meetings or at a formal presentation, you should follow up with each one after those meetings. I prefer to do so with telephone calls and individually addressed emails. Another reason to take the shotgun approach is that when you first contact the prospect, and sometimes for a while afterward, you may still be unaware of who the real decision-maker is. This approach covers your bases.

In some organizations the Economic Buyer or a business line executive will have the ultimate decision on whether to purchase a solution. In others, it could be the mid-level managers. In some, (especially in Silicon Valley and Toronto) it may be the result of the consensus of the team. Since you do not know this information upfront it makes sense to contact as many people as possible, at multiple levels, in the organization to find out.

Your conversations should also be different depending on with whom you are speaking. The CEO should receive a different pitch than with lower-level people. CEOs think more long-term, are more strategic, are risk-averse, and are usually not interested in product features and functions. They are also less encumbered by budgets and company politics. Since they are usually very busy it is important to not waste their time.

One negative to the shotgun approach is that you may

receive conflicting information from different people at various levels or functions within the organization. This is quite normal. Sometimes the differences are the result of timing. It was true yesterday, but it changed today. People also have different interests, biases, political agendas, or they sometimes hear or interpret information differently. When this happens, I note what each tells me and then try to sort through the information to determine which version makes the most sense. Another negative is that you could become distracted by a person who is unimportant to the decision process.

In summary, the argument of whether to call high or low in your prospect's organization is one that should not be settled by a simple rule. Those that tell you to only call high may have valid reasons, but it may result in less opportunities and fewer subsequent sales. It is always easier to move from higher to lower when calling in to a company than it is to do the reverse. Call each of the people on the evaluation team. Find out who the Economic Buyer or decision-maker is and call them early in the cycle—do not wait until the end or it may be too late. You should make the effort to build a relationship with a person who will act as your (internal or external) coach on this opportunity. Once the procurement function has gained more control over purchases, I advise calling them as well. If you receive resistance from your contact about calling above them, you will need to explain that you are not trying to embarrass them but are simply following the sales practices of your company. By calling all the people that may be involved in the purchase decision you will have all the necessary information that you need to win and close the sale.

Should You Leave a Message If You Receive a Voice Mail?

I have gone back and forth on whether to leave a voice mail when the person you are calling does not answer the telephone. Many purposely never answer their telephone and use voice-mail to screen their calls. My conclusion is that the benefits of possibly receiving a call back outweigh the negative of leaving one that is not returned.

My advice is to leave a *brief* voice message regarding why you are calling, such as "Peggy, this is Steve Weinberg of Acme Chemicals. I am calling on Monday, January 11th at 10:35 a.m. to discuss how we can help you reduce the amount of your inventory while not negatively impacting your manufacturing operations. Please call me at 312-XXX-XXXX to discuss this further." I have told Peggy who I am, when I called, why I called, and how she can reach me. It is unlikely that Peggy will return the call, but it could happen. I will often wait about one week to ten days. If she doesn't return the call, I will call again at that point. I will try at least five more times, with intervals of five to seven days between each call so I am considered a "pest" before I relegate Peggy to the bottom of my pile to call after I have called all the uncalled leads.

In many cases, will reach a person and you will be told that they do not have anything to do with the area that you are inquiring about. That is fine. Then ask that person to refer you to the proper person who does handle that area. You then call that person and tell her that you were referred to her by the person you just spoke with. They are more likely to speak with you when you mention their co-worker's name.

When speaking with the prospect that you worked so hard to reach, I recommend that you stand rather than sit at your desk. I find that when I do so I am more alert and can react quicker. You can also refer to and take notes when standing. If you are using Zoom, or another videoconferencing tool, be sure to be properly dressed and groomed with a plain or uncluttered background.

Remember—it is all right to fail while cold calling; most people do. You might think it is not worthwhile, but it is. For every hundred calls you make, you may only reach a few people. If you consistently prospect every day, you will eventually build a workable pipeline—and you will become better at cold-calling. But you must make the effort!

SIXTEEN
How to Use LinkedIn for Business Development

My very successful sales career can be divided into two distinct phases:

1. The period before I began using LinkedIn.com (LI) as a business development tool.

2. After I began using LI in 2004 (I was an early adopter). LI is to sales as detergent is to washing machines. It makes the job much easier. It is also part of what I consider "the Edge."

Most people are familiar with LinkedIn from job searching and networking, rather than business development, as it is used extensively by recruiters and professional job seekers today. As of March, 2022, there are approximately 756 million members who have a profile on LI, and about 310 million active users in over 200 countries, many of whom work for corporations.[58] LI has 61 million users that are senior-level influencers

---

58   Salman Aslam, "81 LinkedIn Statistics You Need to Know in 2022," Omnicore, April 15, 2022, https://www.omnicoreagency.com/linkedin-statistics/.

and 65 million are in decision-making positions. It is estimated that "Four out of five people on LI drive business decisions."[59]

Approximately 40 percent of LI users visit the website daily.[60] Of this total 146 million are in the US or about one of every three Americans.[61] Executives from each of the Fortune 500 companies are members. LI is the ubiquitous business networking tool, and your usage of it should be a no-brainer.

Takeaway 30: LinkedIn.com is the "Secret Sauce" That Will Help You Develop Leads

This chapter is focused on how to begin utilizing LI for business development, specifically to develop quality leads, which should lead to increases in sales. It should be thought of as another tool in your sales toolbox, used to identify and contact possible buyers at target companies. I recommend that LI be included in every company's business development process. (*Note: This chapter was written based on successful usage of LI and has not been endorsed by LinkedIn.com*).

Six Degrees of Kevin Bacon

It is easy to understand how LI can be used for business development if you think of the popular parlor game of "The Six Degrees of Kevin Bacon." The idea of this game is that you can find movie actors connected to Bacon through no more than six acquaintance links, or degrees of separation. For example, Bacon can be linked to Kate Winslet in three degrees because Bacon was in the movie *A Few Good Men* (first degree) with

59 "37 LinkedIn Statistics You Need to Know In 2021," Social Media Marketing & Management Dashboard, accessed April 18, 2022, https://blog.hootsuite.com/linkedin-statistics-business/.
60 "55+ LinkedIn Statistics," 99firms, May 27, 2021, https://99firms.com/blog/linkedin-statistics/.
61 Ibid.

Jack Nicholson. Nicholson was in *The Departed* with Leonardo DiCaprio (second degree). DiCaprio was in *Titanic* with Kate Winslet (third degree.)

So if you wanted to reach a targeted person you could contact a person who knew that person or knew a person that knew that person and ask them to introduce you to their connection. Or you could request to be connected directly to that person!

Here are seven easy steps that you can use to begin using LI effectively for business development:

1. Build your personal profile. Go to www.LinkedIn. com and click on the "Join Now" option. You will then be guided through the sign-up process. Your profile includes biographical information, such as your academic degree, and the employment information that you decide to share. Do not post your entire resume as a profile, but rather include the key accomplishments that you want to highlight to other people when they review your profile for networking (or possible employment).

   › I suggest you upload a professional "headshot" photograph. This is not Facebook and photos with your friends drinking at a bar, on your last vacation, or with your dog are not appropriate on LI. (in fact, they may be harmful.)

   › It does take a substantial time investment to optimally set up your profile and establish hundreds or thousands of connections, but it is well worth the effort. LI provides an excellent primer for setting up your profile.[62]

---

62 "55+ Linkedin Statistics," 99firms, May 27, 2021, https://99firms.com/blog/linkedin-statistics/.

› Consider the headline you choose to use. It is one of the first things that the reader will notice because it is directly below your name and is used by the LI search algorithm. This is especially important when you are searching for a new position and the headline informs the reader of who you are and how you can help them.

› LI offers a useful tool to measure the effectiveness of your completed profile. It is called a "Profile Strength Meter."[63] I recommend that you utilize it.

› LI has added the capability to include a thirty-second video profile, available only by mobile.

2. Invite people you know to connect with you. You can import your Outlook, Google, or iPhone contacts, or individually invite your friends, former co-workers, and acquaintances one at a time. Personalize the invitation and tell the person why you want to contact them. And do not write that you want to connect to sell to them or their company. For example, "Sally, we are both members of the SAP Users Group. I would like to connect with you so that we can network with each other." An email will be sent to them asking them to "accept" or "ignore" the invitation.

I encourage you to be liberal in whom you decide to invite. However, be careful when inviting people you do not know to connect, or who are more than one connection away from you, without explaining to them why you want to connect. Your LI privileges

---

63 "Viewing Your Profile Level Meter," Viewing Your Profile Level Meter | LinkedIn Help (LinkedIn), accessed April 18, 2022, https://www.linkedin.com/help/linkedin/answer/391/viewing-your-profile-strength-meter?lang=en.

may be temporarily suspended if your invitations
are ignored, left pending, or marked as spam by the
recipients. When I receive an invitation to connect, I
read the reason they want to connect with me (if they
give one) and then conduct due diligence by reviewing
their profile, and sometimes even use Google to see
what their background is and if we have any common
areas before accepting.

> › LI business networking usage intends that you
> will only invite people that you know, or one of
> your contacts knows, to connect with you. Most
> people follow this practice, but some users are
> super-networkers, called "open" networkers, and
> they welcome invitations from almost anybody.
> I suggest that you cast a wide net, meaning that
> you invite good friends and relatives, college
> classmates, current and former colleagues,
> neighbors, and people that you have met through
> business and social activities. It is also acceptable
> to invite people who are members of the same LI
> Group as you. A good start is a minimum of 250
> personal contacts.

> › Attend in-person networking events, local,
> regional, and national, to meet more people and
> enlarge your group of personal contacts. You can
> speak with the people and find out what they do,
> how you can assist each other, and collect their
> business cards. Afterward, write down on the
> back of the business card where you met them
> and what you learned about them. Later you can

refer to this when you invite them to connect with you or when you want to contact them about a common interest.

> Remember, using the "six degrees of separation" concept, the more people you know the greater likelihood you will be able to utilize your network to reach people that you might want to connect with at some point in time.

Takeaway 31: Join and Participate in LinkedIn.com Groups

3. Join thirty to fifty LI Groups. (The current limit is one hundred.) There are many types of groups: For example, industries, occupations, college alumni, special interests, team sports, military veterans, pet-lovers, and geographical for local networking. Members of groups post news items or articles of interest every day. The benefits of joining groups are networking, education, current news, job searches, and obtaining sales leads. People will often look to see which groups you are a member of when deciding to accept or reject an invitation. Besides, there is a greater probability that you will get a connection acceptance, or even an appointment, with somebody that is in the same group as you.

> There are two ways that you can find groups to join. You can search for groups by name or keyword, or you can browse groups recommended for you by LI.

> › You also can create a new group for an interest that may not already be in existence. For example, I could form a group for "Sales Book Authors Sharing Best Practices." Then I could invite friends, connections, or others that may be interested in joining it. I would encourage them to invite others and begin posting articles or blogs to share information and ideas.

> › After you join a group, all communications, postings, and comments must be professional and respectful. It is fine to disagree with a posting or a position that someone shares, but there should be no negative personal comments directed at the person. There should be minimal self-promotion of yourself or your products or services and no spam.

4. Prepare a list of targeted companies. Search the company's name for people who have titles indicating they are normally buyers or users of your product or service. You will then see a list of people that currently or previously worked for it. Next to the individual's name will be a numerical designation, such as *2nd*, which indicates that the person is two connections away from you. To reach the person, you will need to contact one of the people listed under their name to request an introduction to the person listed. LI does not show anybody beyond a 3rd level. You can also search the "Company Pages" for information about the targeted company, including the latest company-provided updates.

5. Contact the listed person directly by sending an invitation to connect with a message explaining why you want to connect with them, such as that you are both members of the same group. It is important to understand the goal of making contact is to obtain a conversation, not to make a sale during the contact process. It is also important not to be perceived as a pest or stalker, as it can turn off the contact or potential buyer.

6. You have the option to upgrade to LI Premium to take advantage of being able to send a certain number of InMails to anybody on LI. These InMail's allow you to send direct messages to people to whom you are not connected.

7. Finally, assuming that you have been introduced to the targeted person or that they accepted your invitation to connect, you can request to set up a telephone or video conversation with them. That is the beginning of your sales cycle.

This is simple, but special attention needs to be given to building a quality professional profile, inviting people to connect, determining which companies and people to target, crafting messages, and then attempting to connect with targeted individuals. Your efforts will be worthwhile and help you achieve your sales goals.

Once you are established on LI, it is a good practice to post, re-post, or share articles or links to articles that are interesting to you and may be to others, especially those that apply to your group, industry, or your customers. In my case, this has often been financial services, technology, money laundering, and financial crimes and electronic payment routing. This enhances your credibility within the LI community and your groups, and also signals to your connections—and would-be connections—that you have subject matter expertise in a chosen area. When you post an article there is a chance it could reach an audience of hundreds of millions, including many potential buyers and influencers.[64] That reach is mind-blowing. It is a great opportunity for you to become known as a subject matter expert by potentially millions of people, at no cost other than your time.

By posting and sharing articles, especially those you author, your targeted connections will be willing to connect with you and will be able to see that you have common interests. An example would be an article on the latest in banking technology or virtual currency if you were in the financial services business. The article can be from newspapers, magazines, websites, or bloggers.

My advice is to never post anything political, religious, or controversial on LI. To do so could result in somebody refusing to connect with you due to different political philosophies or if they are offended by a posting. LI is a professional networking site. Non-professional posts belong on Facebook or Twitter, but I would caution people who are using LI for both business development or for seeking employment, that potential employers will often review your LI, Facebook, and Twitter postings. I have recently discussed this with several recruiters, and they told me they look at the social media websites and will subjectively eliminate from consideration anybody that looks like they could cause problems, or exhibits immaturity, poor judgment, or even bad grammar. Remember, in most cases, the

---

64 "55+ Linkedin Statistics," 99firms, May 27, 2021, https://99firms.com/blog/linkedin-statistics/.

recruiter will have received hundreds of resumes or web applications for a posted position, so they are looking for ways to reduce the pool of candidates.

It will be time well spent to build a professional profile, invite people to connect, determine which companies to target, craft messages, and then attempt to connect with targeted individuals. I assure you that using LI will be worthwhile and help you achieve your sales goals.

LinkedIn Best Practices

The best way to explain how LI may be utilized for business development is to use a hypothetical example:

Let's say I want to sell a new type of logistics software application to Acme Manufacturing (a fictional company) in Chicago, IL. To do so, I need to contact several people at Acme to find somebody who might have an interest in learning more about how I can bring value to their company. How do I find out whom to call or email? Before the internet, many companies purchased lists of corporate executives from list providers such as Hoovers or INFOusa and then sent out direct mail pieces, hoping for a one or two percent response rate. I have found that as many as twenty percent of the people on purchased lists have moved to another company since it was compiled. With the arrival of the internet in the early '90s and search engines such as Google, I can search for the company to gather facts on it and browse the targeted companies' websites. I look for the About Us section of the company's website, or the Financial Reports section and look for Officers' and Directors' names on the company's public website. However, the executives listed are generally not the people who would respond to cold calls or direct mail pieces.

If you have any connections or second-degree connections to people who currently work or have worked at Acme, they will be listed, as I described above. I will discuss what to do if you do not have any first or second-level connections later.

Takeaway 32: Do Not Make Sales Pitches on LinkedIn.com

Your objective when contacting a specific person is to obtain a meeting or conversation, preferably in person, or via telephone or videoconference, where you can learn more about their operations, needs, requirements, priorities, and pain-points. This is not telesales or telemarketing—the goal is never to attempt to make a sale during the contact process. A sales pitch is not appropriate. This will often result in a rejection from the person you contacted, and they might ignore all future attempted contacts from you. The goal is to form a connection and then build a professional relationship on trust and credibility. I always regret accepting an invitation to connect from somebody who then immediately follows up with a sales pitch. I will ignore the sales pitch and expect that others do the same.

If there is already a direct connection between the targeted person and you, I suggest sending a message such as "Mary, can we set up a time so that I can learn how your company currently handles shipping logistics and what you envision your future needs are." If it is a second-level connection, I would send a message to the first-level connection like this "Derek, can you please pass this message on to your contact Mary Smith in the logistics department" and then include the previous message. A response rate above 20 percent is excellent. The positive response rate is influenced by:

» Whether this person is a first or second-level connection. My experience is that first-level response rates should be greater than 50 percent and the second level approximately 25 percent.

» Whether or not the person uses LI regularly. This can often be inferred by the number of contacts shown in their profile or how often they post articles. An indication of "More than 500 contacts," posted articles, recommendations, and endorsements in their profile is a positive indicator that the person actively uses LI and is more than likely to accept an invitation to connect with you.

» Whether you and this person belong to the same group. If so, you could say "Mary, we are both members of the Logistics and Suppliers Group. Can we set up a time to discuss the latest developments in increasing logistics efficiencies?" If you want to be bolder, you could say "I wish to discuss your company's needs in the area of increasing the efficiency of your supplier onboarding process."

» Your personalized message is extremely important. A simple, non-personalized "Steve wants to connect with you" is often ignored.

» Subjective factors, such as what kind of day the person is having, the gender or perceived age of the person sending or receiving the contact, or even sending a photograph also influence a connection's acceptance. Sometimes I receive invitations from people in geographies that I would never do any business with or are known havens for scammers, and I ignore those.

» The willingness of the recipient to network or to pass a message along is another influence.

» The relationship between the recipient and the target will affect connections as well. Do they know each other? (There could be more than 20,000 employees at the company.) Do they like each other?

If you search the company and determine that you don't have any first or second-level connections listed, then treat this more like a cold call. It takes patience, persistence, and dedication to be successful in cold calling. One must commit to making a certain number of calls each day, even if there are no positive results that day or that week. You cannot take rejection or the lack of people returning calls personally. It is normal behavior for people to ignore unsolicited calls to save time and avoid scams during busy workdays. As I have said before, I also do not believe you can succeed in business development without developing better cold calling skills and consistently devote daily or weekly time to this activity.

So now you have identified and approached a few people at the targeted company, Acme Manufacturing, and one or two have accepted your invitation to connect. What next? This is where it becomes more difficult and more of an art. Several approaches may be used, perhaps many, to find one that is the most effective and comfortable to use. As previously noted, I discourage an immediate sales pitch message, such as "Tom, now that you have accepted my invitation to connect, can I contact you on Thursday to discuss our solution." If you are that aggressive, they will either disconnect you (yes, they can do that) or, more than likely, ignore your message.

I usually wait five or ten days after a new contact has accepted my invitation before approaching them with an email, a telephone call, or another LI message. I thank them for accepting my invitation. I will often send them a link to a current article that might be of interest to them. Then you can do any of the following (they are not mutually exclusive):

» Send a non-aggressive message through LI such as "Pat, can you please advise me who is the person responsible for making purchasing decisions on logistics or supply chain solutions. Thank you in advance. —Steve," or "Pat, can we set up a conversation so that I can learn more about XYZ Company."

» Send an email to them by looking for their email address in their profile, which is disclosed to you once you are connected.

» Call the company's switchboard and ask for them by name.

You may not be successful in reaching a targeted connection using LI for business networking. It does not always result in a qualified lead. Nor does any other tool or method, such as email or telephone calls. But I have found it to be a valuable tool and I believe it will increase your chances of success versus a telephone cold call or unsolicited email.

At some point in time continued attempts to contact the person can cross the line and be considered inappropriate or unprofessional. That can alienate the contact or potential buyer from a legitimate solution. I have found that if the person does not respond after three attempts it is best to move on to another person or company. If I am convinced the target company is in our "sweet spot." (identified in the qualification process), or if it is an assigned account that I must penetrate, I will seek another person at the company, either one in another area or one that is lower on the organizational chart. At that point, I will initiate a similar contact and try to work my way into the company for a meeting. The new person may point me back to the person who did not return my calls. When that happens, you can ask them to make a "warm" introduction of you to the target person. Alternatively, it may be worthwhile to ask the person to help familiarize you with the corporate culture, priorities, whether there is something exceptional happening now (perhaps a merger or acquisition), or other guidance on how you can gain a greater understanding of how to approach other people in the company.

Tips for InMail & Email

I am often asked which LI email template works best in reaching the buyer or in getting the buyer to respond. I have found there is no single, foolproof way to word an LI message or email that works all or most of the time. Use the style that you are most comfortable with and continue to refine the message, making sure to use excellent grammar and spelling. (One of my pet peeves is the usage of poor grammar or excessive bad spelling. If I receive such a message, I usually discard it, no matter how useful the item or solution may be to me or my company. I assume that it is a "phishing" scam, or from someone not educated enough to be involved in business operations.)

Most businesspeople receive an excessive quantity of emails every day. The goal is for your message not to be perceived as spam, but to be read and hopefully result in a response. Be judicious about the volume of emails you send out; Any more than one unsolicited email per two- to three-week period is too many. Also choose the best time and day of the week to send out your emails; One study showed it is best to send a message that will be read early in the workweek and early in the morning, by 9 a.m. and not after 11 a.m. to try to position the email so that it is at the top of the person's email box when they sign in.[65]

A few sales pros have told me that they have not been successful in reaching potential buyers by using LI. Like most anything else in life, some things work for some people and not for others. I do not know how hard they worked at it nor whether they gave up after a few tries. Also, what works once or twice may not be scalable to an entire group of people. My answer is to not give up, change the messaging, and make sure that the correct people are being targeted. Sending an invitation or a message to a person that hardly ever uses LI will have a low response rate. But that doesn't mean it will never work.

Let's look at an example from my own experience. I recently closed the largest sale in my employer's history by starting a conversation with an executive at one of my targeted companies using LI. Here is a synopsis of how it happened:

I had been calling on a target corporation in our "Sweet Spot" which I will call ABC Co., and after reviewing their company page, I selected an option to "Follow" them. I learned from a company press release that they hired a new Chief Compliance Officer, whom I will call Morris. I then sent an LI connection invitation to Morris asking him to please connect with me. I noted that I had been calling on ABC Co. for several years and had been in contact with members of the previous compliance staff. Morris accepted my invitation shortly thereafter. I waited a few days to send a message to Morris. That message said, "I would like to discuss your company's compliance needs

---

65   Sami Halabi, "Dear Salesperson: It's Not Me, It's You," Blogs.oracle.com, January 14, 2019, https://blogs.oracle.com/cx/post/dear-salesperson-its-not-me-its-you.

with you at your earliest convenience." A few days later Morris responded and told me to call him on Friday and provided his telephone number. I called Morris and we had a short conversation. He told me that he was familiar with my employer, and they were interested in learning more about our compliance solutions. He asked me to follow up with a person named Guy whom Morris had recently hired to handle the implementation of a better solution to screen their payment transactions. I set up a meeting for us in New York City that was also attended by two of my colleagues who were more familiar with the solution that Guy was interested in than I. Guy explained at that meeting what their objectives were and the hurdles we would have to overcome, which included a "build it here" bias at ABC Co., as well as a need to handle heavy transaction volumes at sub-second response times. I set up additional meetings in New York and at the company's headquarters in California. Eventually, after several lengthy problem-solving and technical meetings, ABC Co. decided to go with our solution, and we began contract negotiations. The elapsed sales cycle was approximately nine very intense months.

This may not have happened without my initial contact from LI to the newly hired ABC Co. executive.

Takeaway 33: LinkedIn.com Is a Terrific, Easily Utilized Networking Tool for Business Development.

As you can see, it takes time and persistence to derive the greatest benefits from LI. Invest the time to create an effective profile, join groups, post interesting articles, and invite connections to build a network of critical size. In my opinion, the sales pros who do not understand the new business development benefits from LI have not invested the time to learn how to properly use it. Some people have been reluctant to use LI because they feared there would be a financial commitment to do so, or because of privacy concerns. It has been nearly twenty years and those fears have not been realized. Others choose not to be LI networkers. That is fine for them, but none of them should be in B2B sales. Utilize the tools you have—all of them—to ensure you maximize your success in sales and meet or exceed your sales quotas.

SEVENTEEN
The Best Questions to Ask

Since every prospect is unique in their needs, budgets, priorities, senses of urgency and decision-making, you must approach each one in different ways. It is vitally important to obtain valuable and actionable information from your prospect that will enable you to develop winning sales strategies and tactics. To do this you need to skillfully question your contacts throughout the sales cycle. The difference between winning and closing the sale, or losing it, is often the result of utilizing the information that you were able to obtain through adept questioning. The questions you ask are far more important than anything you can say to the prospect. Best-selling author Daniel Pink states "In the new world of sales, being able to ask the right questions is more valuable than producing the right answers."[66] The answers to your questions should guide you to the best solution for the prospect, and to help you determine the best sales strategy. If you optimize your questions, the answers will better equip you to develop customized strategies and tactics. As eighteenth-century French writer and

---

66 Daniel H. Pink, *To Sell Is Human: The Surprising Truth About Moving Others* (New York, NY: Riverhead Books, 2012), 147.

philosopher Voltaire said: "Judge a man by his questions rather than his answers."[67]

Open-Ended Questions

I am often asked what the best questions are to ask a prospect when making a cold call, when doing discovery, during a sales presentation, during follow-ups or solutioning, when closing the sale, and during contract negotiation.

There is no simple answer to this; the best questions would vary according to the company you are calling on, where you are in the sales cycle, the solution you are selling, and the level of the person we are calling on, as different questions would be appropriate for each. Also, the prospect's willingness to answer or be forthcoming with information will often direct you to the next logical question. My advice is to ask more (but not exclusively) open-ended questions, sometimes called the "who, what, where, why, and how" questions, which should result in broad, descriptive answers. Closed-end questions are normally answered by short, simple answers, such as "yes," "no," or other single-word answers. You will not learn much from those answers. The objectives of the questions are primarily to begin a conversation with the prospect, secondarily to elicit discussions, and thirdly to solicit important information.

Examples of open-ended questions I frequently use:

» Can you please share with me your (or the executive sponsor's) objectives for this project?
» What do you consider to be the highest priority projects for this fiscal year and why?

---

67 "Voltaire Quotes," Goodreads, accessed April 18, 2022, https://www.goodreads.com/author/quotes/5754446.Voltaire.

» What prompted your company to look at solutions at this time?

» Can you please describe your current system and what you like and dislike?

» If you were designing a new system, what high priority features or functions would you include?

» What information would help you make your selection?

» Can you please describe your vendor selection process?

» How does your decision support your goal of reducing expenses this year?

» Why does the inventory control system need to be updated manually?

» How is the treasurer currently tracking payments to the lockbox?

» What challenges do you currently face in doing your accounting closing in three business days?

» What is your expected result for this project?

» How have you handled this problem or issue in the past?

» Please describe your current procedure for handling customer service issues.

» Who are the people responsible for this process and how do they feel about continuing to use it?

» Your CEO described their goal to enter new markets this year. How will your department support that effort?

» What other solutions are you considering to improve the management of your inventories? (Could be any of their processes.)

The response to each of these should be one or two sentences, not one word, during which time you will not lead or interrupt the prospect. Also, do not argue with their answers. Normally you would follow one open-ended question with another question on the same track, such as "Can you please help me understand why . . ." I advise keeping the series of questions relevant and not overbearing.

Closed-Ended Questions

On the contrary, sales consultant and author Thomas Freese prefers to start conversations with focused closed-ended questions and recommends preparing a list of diagnostic questions in advance that are customized for the products or services being sold. He believes that open-ended questions, especially when asked early in the sales process, do not help establish credibility and can sometimes be considered intrusive by the prospect. "Prospects are reluctant to answer questions until the sales pro has proven that he or she is indeed credible."[68] Freese also prefers to open presentations with closed-end questions. I have not done this, but I can see the benefits of this approach. They are far less threatening to prospects, and it is much easier to provide a one or two-word response, rather than elaborating your response. Freese believes that once the sales pro has been perceived as credible by the prospect, "then uncovering needs and presenting solutions is easy."[69]

Examples of closed-end questions are:

> » Would you be interested in hearing about an idea
>   that will increase your profits by 20 percent in
>   one year?

---

68 Thomas A. Freese, *Secrets of Question-Based Selling: How the Most Powerful Tool in Business Can Double Your Sales Results* (Naperville, IL: Sourcebooks, 2013), 118-119.
69 Ibid, p. 122.

» Have you heard about the new method that X company is using to increase inventory turnover?

» Would you prefer a lump-sum or hourly billing?

» Have you worked on a similar project like this before?

» How much have you budgeted for this expenditure?

» Who is the decision-maker for this purchase?

» When does your current contract expire?

» Would you rather have walnut or maple furniture?

» How many people are there in your quality control department?

» Do you prefer to buy or lease capital equipment?

» Do you have any plants in [Insert Country Name]?

» Have you decided to staff the open position you have for XYZ?

The quality of your questions, as evidenced by your preparation and relevance to the subject matter, will tell the buyer whether you know what you are talking about, whether you are wasting their time, and how interested you are in finding a solution for them. It will also affect your credibility with the buyer. Questions should not be capricious and are not to be asked without a purpose; this is similar to the adage that an attorney should never ask a witness a question that they do not already know the expected answer.

Questions should not be asked randomly and should follow a logical order. It is also important that questions are asked naturally and do not seem to be rehearsed or read off a list. Good sales pros will uncover as much information as possible from the prospect about the current environment, limitations, or barriers they face, any operational or regulatory risks, any employee or safety issues, office politics, budget issues, or other information that will assist them in determining which solution that may want to recommend at some future point.

The degree or intensity of the problem or pain needs to be uncovered as well, similar to an initial assessment by a physician. How much is this bothering the customer? Will they act on it now? Is there an executive involved in the solution? What is the cost or consequence of doing nothing, or remaining as is—the status quo? Questions that are asked properly also indicate that you want to learn more about the prospect, their position, their priorities, and their interest level in your company.

Listen with an Open Mind

Takeaway 34: When Asking Questions Be Sure to Listen to—and Understand—the Answers

Some sales pros cause prospects to become defensive because of the aggressive nature of their questioning. You should be prepared to ask the most important questions when given the opportunity and allow space for them to consider the question and answer, rather than engaging in a rapid-fire succession of questions. I like to frame open-ended questions with "Please tell me about . . ." or "How do you feel about that?" and then listen without interrupting. *Repeat—without interrupting.* The more they talk and the less you talk the more information you will receive. I have found asking the prospects to elaborate on any answers that are unclear or appear to lead to a secondary question that could yield more useful information to be an effective approach. Most people are more than willing to talk about their company and their roles.

Respect the position of the prospect you are calling. They are in that position at the company for a reason; in the majority of cases, they earned it. And they were either put in charge of the evaluation or are a key member of the team because somebody at an executive level believed they would do a good job in the selection process. Ask them to share some of their knowledge with you. They will usually be flattered that you asked. It is much more interesting to encourage your prospects to talk about their company and their issues than for you to tell them about your company, products, and solutions. They would also prefer to speak, rather than listen to you, unless you can provide some information of value to them. Do not introduce any sales solutions at this point—that will come naturally later—if you earn their trust.

Sample Sales Questions

Questions also allow the sales pro to provide a unique opportunity to provide their input on the path of the sales process. By asking certain questions you can initiate thoughts on areas that the buyer may not have considered, such as the cost of doing nothing, the computation of the return on investment, the hurdle rate to have projects approved, or even how you can approach the team with alternative suggestions.

Here are some example questions:

For initial prospecting (cold) calls:

» Is this a good time for you to speak with me for five minutes?
» If not, can I call you on Tuesday at X o'clock (I prefer this and will then send a calendar invitation).

- » Janet, have you heard of our previous business with XYZ (our company)?
- » Can you please familiarize me with how you do_____? (a process or area that you are probing).
- » Does your company currently have a solution for ____ _____? If so, what is it? Is it in-house developed or was it purchased or licensed?
- » Are you currently having a problem with _____(examples: inventory control, overtime, overstock, meeting shipping commitments, cash flow, receivables, regulatory issues, customer retention, distribution, foreign currency, filing payroll tax returns, employee turnover, financial reporting, etc.)
- » Can you please explain how (and when) the problem occurs and what is being done to remediate it now?
- » What do you think the solution to the problem is?
- » Are you interested in learning about how the latest technologies have been deployed to increase safety at manufacturing plants? Or decrease shrinkage at retail stores?

Do *not* ask them what is keeping them awake at night. That is trite. And silly. What if nothing is keeping them awake, or if it is a raccoon in the attic? Then what?

For discovery:

(These questions should be tailored to the level of the person you are speaking with and their functional area of expertise; the goal is to obtain more information, facts, and data. It is important

to demonstrate your mastery of the subject matter. The questions are not sequential.)

» Why have you invited me in today? (This is always a good opening question.) What is the urgency, if any?

» How long have you been with the company? In this position? What is your background? What did you do before you joined the company? (Possibly available in LinkedIn.com)

» Would you please tell me about your company? Its products?

» How is your company organized? Are there divisions, subsidiaries, centralized versus decentralized? Is each headed by a president or CEO? Which organization are you under?

» What are some of your company's key core strategies? (Ex. Green energy, entering new markets, diversity, lowering costs, acquisitions, etc.)

» What are some of the most important business issues your company is currently facing? (Competition, new markets, unprofitable divisions, merger, or divestiture).

» Do you see your company making any significant organizational changes soon?

» What is your company's target market? Which are your most profitable markets? Who are some of your most important customers?

» How much of your business is generated outside of the US? Will that change soon? Do you manufacture outside of the US?

» What are your company's plans for the next five years?

» What do you see are the challenges of entering new markets? (If applicable.)

» How would you describe your company culture?

» What are your current responsibilities, and what are those from the other people on the team?

» Whom do you report to? Whom do they report to?

» What is your fiscal year?

» How is the company doing financially this fiscal year (perhaps versus expectations)? Is your unit profitable? If not, why not? (Reason may be used in building a value proposition.)

» Why do people want to come to work here? (Why did you want to work here?)

» Who are your most difficult, or frequent, one or two competitors?

» What is your competitive edge versus these competitors (availability of inventory, services, low-cost, geography, response to calls, long-term relationships, innovation, or distribution network?)

» What are the greatest challenges in your position? (Internal and external.)

» When did you first decide to look at alternatives?

» Can you tell me how your company does _____? (Manufacturing, sales, inventory control, etc.)

» How many X do you currently have? (X is specific to your product or service.)

» Are you interested in upgrading to a new X?

» Is your company's IT architecture standard based on IBM, Microsoft, Google, or Oracle? Or another, such as LINUX? Or a combination of more than one?

» Will you vary from this standard?
» Please tell me about your current problem, process, opportunity, or need.
» What is your current process for_____?
  (The area you are probing.)
» How is the current process working?
» What problems does it cause?
» Who resolves these problems?
» What areas do you think need immediate improvement (in the next thirty to ninety days)?
» What alternatives are you currently considering?
» What do you see as the pros and cons of each alternative? (Or What do you like or dislike about each?)
» If they do not have any pros and cons, would they like assistance in evaluating the alternatives?
» Do you have any customer satisfaction issues that would be helpful for me to know about?
» If you made a change, what would be the first thing that you would do?
» Are you open to a change in processes if it can be proven to increase profit/reduce costs/increase inefficiencies? Is your manager or executive in charge of this area open to a change?
» What happened the last time your company made a major change? Was it successful or unsuccessful?
» When was the last time you upgraded the X system? How long did it take? What were the major obstacles?
» What do you do with the information that you currently obtain from process/software/data? What is the flow of the information?

» What are you trying to accomplish this year?

» What are your strategic goals for the next three to five years?

» What do you see as "roadblocks," "bottlenecks" or obstacles in the current process?

» What change(s) do you think would have the greatest positive impact?

» Who is the executive responsible for this area?

» Could you give me some background on your decision-making process?

» What is the consequence if you do not make a change now? This year?

» How would you feel if the company did not make a change? (You need to know where they stand on this.)

» Are you and your manager both aligned on this decision?

› If not, what are the differences?

» What software are you currently using for
_____?

» Is the software performing in a manner that meets your current and future needs?

» How long have you been using the software/hardware solution?

» What do you most like about your current solution?

› What do you least like about your current solution?

» What are the most recent significant changes in your industry?

» Do you sell your products globally? What is your sales or distribution channel (direct, distributors, Original Equipment Manufacturers (OEMs)?

» Who are your biggest competitors? (Theirs, not yours) Why?

» What are your primary advantages over your competitors? (Can be used later if price issue.)

» What are some of your most important MBOs or KPIs for this year? What are the metrics?

» What would happen if you changed the current outcome for ____ by 10 percent? 20 percent?

» What would happen if you do not fix the problem?

» Many of my other customers are having issues with __ _____. Is your company?

» Are you interested in benchmarking data, or industry studies, from others in your industry? (This is almost always a "yes." Don't ask this unless you have the data to share.)

» Can you explain your technical infrastructure to me? (To IT executives only.)

» Do you utilize cloud storage?

» Do you deploy Software as a Service (SaaS) applications? If so, which?

For after a sales presentation:

» How do you feel the presentation went? (Do *not* argue with their feedback. It is how they felt, not how you felt. Listen.)

» Did the presentation meet your expectations? If not, where did we fail?

  › How did our presentation compare to the others you have seen? If ours was better, why?

  › Did we adequately demonstrate or discuss how we can provide value to your company? If not, where did we fail?

> › What features or functions would seem to have the greatest positive on your operations?
> › What would have the least impact?
> › Did I or we cover all of the agenda items to your satisfaction?
> › If not, which did we miss?

» What would the best solution look like to you? How would it work? Where would the greatest impact be?

» If you were to make a change how would that affect your standing in the company? Does it help you achieve your MBOs, KPIs, objectives, or other performance metrics?

» When we last spoke, you were scheduled to see a presentation by our competitor(s). Was the presentation held? What was the group's reaction to their presentation? What was your reaction? What did you like? What didn't you like? Any special features that appealed to the group or you?

» Were there any competitor features that seem preferable to ours?

» How many alternatives are you now considering? When will you be reducing the list? When do you expect to make your final cuts?

» How would you rank the solutions that you have considered, as of now?

» Should you decide to purchase our solution, what would you see it accomplishing?

For follow-up calls or meetings:

» Have there been any changes in the project since our last meeting/call? If so, what?

» Where are you in your decision process?

» Have any new alternatives emerged? Which are they? Why?

» Have you decided that you will buy, not build?

» Is there an urgency to conclude this in the next thirty days? Sixty days? Ninety days?

» My managers keep asking me whether you are going to move forward with our solution. What shall I tell them? (I use this a lot.)

» Do you feel that our solution will provide you with greater value than your current state, or status quo?

» How does our solution compare to the others that you have considered?

» Have the target dates changed since our last conversation? If so, why?

» Do you feel that it is a good fit for your organization? If not, why not?

» How did the other attendees feel about the presentation?

» What is their reaction to the feasibility of our solution meeting your needs?

» How do you think we might be able to help you?

» Do you recognize a need for our solution? If not, why not?

» Do you feel that our solution is a good value? If not, why not?

» Would you like to speak to or visit any of our current customers?

» Would you like more clarifications on the IT infrastructure than was provided earlier?

For closing the sale:

» How do you think our proposed solution meets your needs?
  › If not, why not?
» Do you agree with the value proposition/ROI calculations that we arrived at?
  › If not, why not?
» Have the value propositions been presented to/ accepted by top management?
» Did we successfully resolve the objections that you previously raised in our meeting or our last conversation?
» What other information can I provide to help you make your decision?
» Have you identified the cost of not moving forward with a new solution?
» Have you decided which alternative solution to solve the X problem is best for your company?
» Is the business ours? Is there any reason why you could not do business with us? Are you ready to proceed to the contract stage?
» What is the next step in your process to conclude a contract?
» When will your recommendation committee make its decision?
» Which business executive needs to sign off on this purchase? Can you please introduce me?
» When would you like to schedule training and delivery?
» Should I keep the paperwork that I have prepared for your project or discard it?

» Are you ready to move forward and become business partners with us?

» If our management is able to offer an incentive, can we get the contract done this month?

For commencing contract negotiations:

» We need to formalize our agreement. Are you the person who handles this function at your company?

» What are the steps in your contract review process?

> How long does it normally take to go through the process? How much time should we allow to complete it?

> Do you have the authority to make contract changes? If not, who else needs to be involved? (We would prefer to negotiate with this person.)

> How have you handled similar negotiations in the past?

> Are the changes that you have proposed the entire list that we need to review? (We do not want to agree to them one at a time.)

» Who is the ultimate signer of the contract?

> Will this person be available immediately after the contract is negotiated? (This is especially relevant before the December holidays when executives tend to take time off.)

> Who will be the attorney that is assigned to finalize the contract? (Our attorney often wants to check out his or her background.) Is this person internal (an employee) or external counsel? (The latter costs more to the company, is often less flexible, and often does not understand what the client is purchasing or its value.

> › Of the contract redlines that you have provided to us, what are your priorities? Which are the most important to you?
> › Does your company require you to issue a purchase order before signing a contract? If so, what information can we provide so that you can proceed?

» When would you like to schedule training and delivery? This is the same as above, but ask it again when negotiating the contract?

> › Which of the proposed contract changes or redlines are the most important to you?

» Can we meet with your attorneys to discuss and resolve the open items?

» Can we schedule a contract signing celebration, lunch, or dinner?

> › Can we issue a press release that you have signed a contract with us? Whom shall we clear the language of the release with?

You have a unique opportunity to ask a lot of relevant questions, some of which you may already suspect you have the answers to when you assume ownership of an account. Even if the sales pro who previously managed the account has thoroughly briefed you about the company and the past, present, and future opportunities, I have found it to be extremely informative to play dumb and ask the key people at the buyer level to fill me in, in one or more meetings, on their experiences with your company. How do they see them? Did your company perform well? If not, what could you do better? Were there any personal interactions where your company did not meet their expectations? Are there any existing areas in which you could assist, perhaps some from your existing contracts? I call this a "Get Out of Jail" card that can only be used once with a client, but it can be invaluable, and most customers are glad to comply and provide this information. You must be judicious when using this opportunity, and it is a good idea to take thorough notes of the conversations. I guarantee that no matter the quantity or the quality of the information the prior sales pro has provided, you will learn a lot, and that is exactly how you will obtain the valuable and actionable information you need to develop winning sales strategies and tactics. It is the difference between closing the sale or losing it.

SECTION 4

Thus far, we have covered many valuable advanced sales concepts which will help you develop into a more effective sales pro. This includes advice on how to identify and pursue the best prospects in the marketplace to fill your sales pipeline and ask more effective, provocative questions that will save you from wasting time on opportunities that have a lower probability of closing. We have also discussed the importance of understanding buyer's roles and motivations for decisions. You have also been alerted that many of the sales training theories that you have received are obsolete and need to be discarded. In addition, you now understand and can better manage the enterprise sales process and your pipeline. Those of you that have been reluctant to use LinkedIn.com should now better understand its potential for business development and how to use it to your advantage to find prospects and close sales. By adopting my recommendations, some of which will take you out of your "comfort zone," you will become more proficient in how you approach your sales opportunities.

In Section 4 we will examine additional ways to optimize your sales performance to close more sales *now*. Included are many specific recommendations that will further enhance your sales skills.

In Chapter 18 you will learn techniques that will help you ace your sales presentation. These include how to build an interesting agenda, what to do when your prospect engages in solutioning during your meeting, how to test the content of your PowerPoint slides, and how much you should speak during the presentation. *Spoiler alert:* more is not better.

How to make your sales presentations more memorable is discussed in Chapter 19. Studies have shown that prospects forget much of your presentation, so it is on you to make it more memorable and to stand out against your competition. This chapter provides sixteen proven hints on how you can accomplish this.

I have a bias against competing in sales situations where the decision is based on which seller quotes the lowest price. Simply put, if the price is the major factor in a decision, why does the organization need a highly trained, professional sales-force? Price is usually the major factor in commodity purchases, such as when buying bulk paper, cardboard, crude oil, and agricultural items such as corn, oats, and soybeans, but it should not be used for other items, such as technology, automotive parts, solar panels, and financial services. In Chapter 20 we discuss how to avoid competing based on price.

Chapter 21 contains an original thesis on pinpointing the time of the prospect's greatest amount of interest in buying. My theory is that this occurs when the buyer makes the recommendation to management to go ahead with the purchase.

The purchase interest is lower every day before that point and quickly drops thereafter. The lesson is that you need to know when that happens and then close the sale as soon as possible before the interest level completely diminishes.

One of the greatest wastes of time, as well as one of the best sources of new business, is a Request for Proposals (RFP). There is a skill in deciding whether to respond to unsolicited RFPs. If you are correct, you have a chance to book a new sale. If you are wrong, you have squandered a lot of valuable resources in your company. Chapter 22 contains some ideas that may be helpful for you when making this important decision about whether you should respond to RFPs.

I have found time management to be a difficult skill to master—perhaps the most difficult. And the consequence of optimal versus poor time management can result in achieving your sales target or not. Often, I have kept busy doing something that seemed important at that moment, like emails, only to find out that I did not have enough time remaining to accomplish specific important goals. Chapter 23 provides ideas for you to prioritize your tasks and maximize your selling time.

I have hired and managed over a thousand sales pros over the past thirty-plus years across several companies. Many have become successful, and others have not. Some have become the top sales pro in their organization and others have been promoted to Vice President of Sales or even president positions. One earned a million-dollar commission check. When I hired them, I believed each would succeed, but sadly some did not. Why have some become successful, and others have not? In Chapter 24, which is intended to help hiring managers identify and hire top performers, I analyze the characteristics and attributes of high performers, based on my experience. This chapter will also allow sales pros to compare themselves to the best performers and build a self-improvement inventory.

I feel very strongly that the sales profession has a very bright future and that people entering it can be successful, both in terms of their personal accomplishments as well as their income goals. There have been many positive contributions in the past few years because of new technology, and leveraging those technologies is a key to your future success.

EIGHTEEN
Acing the Sales Presentation

The objective of a sales presentation meeting, or sales pitch, is *not* to make or close the sale at that meeting! Repeat— it is not to make the sale at that point! That is an unrealistic goal. And the purpose is not to convince the audience that you have the best solution for their problem, needs (which comes later), or to achieve their strategy, although this is a desirable outcome. The purpose of a presentation is to have a productive two-way discussion where:

1. you gain a greater understanding of the prospect's needs

2. they gain confidence in you as a potential supplier

3. the positive result is another scheduled meeting.

A successful presentation consists of a serious problem-solving conversation between the seller and the buyer, *NOT* a sales pro delivering a scripted monologue. It is not necessary to present a professionally prepared PowerPoint presentation or video to the audience, as long as the meeting achieves its goals.

For example, this could be a conversation at the conclusion of the presentation:

Sales pro: "In today's meeting my objective was to learn more about your company, to introduce you to my company, and convince you that we can be a viable partner in solving your short and long-term needs. Have I accomplished that today?"

Buyer: "Yes, you did. We are interested in learning more about how you can help us accomplish our goals."

Sales pro: "Excellent. When can we schedule our next meeting? How does one week from Tuesday look for you?"

Buyer: "That works. We will also ask Ted and Takesha, two department heads, to attend, as they would also be interested in your solution."

Sales pro: "I am looking forward to the next meeting."

Takeaway 35: The Objective of the Meeting Is Simply to Secure the Next Meeting.

The objective of the *second* meeting is then to gain a third meeting, and so on. Remember the American football analogy. You need to keep moving the first down markers down the field. At each meeting, your goal is to progress toward a conclusion where it is obvious to the buyer that your solution is the best fit for them. This will be achieved through understanding their needs and crafting a value proposition so compelling that they are eager to learn more about it at each successive meeting and by successfully navigating the sales process.

I consider presentation (especially face-to-face) meetings to be precious, usually crucial, and they can often be the difference between winning and losing the sale. According to recent Gartner, Inc. research, sales pros are being given less time to present their solution and each vendor is provided only approximately 5 percent of the total time expended in their buying process, so you must optimize the time you do have.[70] Bad things happen when a sales pro tries to "wing" a presentation. I will focus on some of the best practices for you to work on and some areas that should be avoided.

Best Practices

First of all, you need to invest a significant amount of time preparing for the presentation meeting. For me this involves calling or meeting with the other internal participants, discussing the objective and the agenda with as many prospect contacts as possible ahead of time, internal role-playing, and customizing the presentation material. If you are going to use the internet for an on-site demonstration, check with the company to find out if you can access the internet at the prospect's site. If it is going to be a virtual presentation, be sure that the prospect is familiar with accessing the specific website that you utilize. Prospects will often utilize a firewall, and you cannot assume you will be allowed access. Due to considerations like this, it is almost impossible to over-prepare.

Your mood, or emotional state of being, is also very important. Sometimes there will be situations when you are stressed or anxious. It may be caused by an issue with your manager, your children, car problems, traffic, the weather, or the internet connection, or other issues out of your control. Whether you realize it or not, it will affect your demeanor and performance. If something like this happens to you, it is best to take the time to regain your composure, as best as you can, before beginning the meeting, or plan to take a coffee break during the meeting.

It is important to build trust with the attendees as early as

---

70 Matt Dudek, "Gartner Research Webinar," *Gartner Research Webinar*, (November 13, 2019).

possible in your meeting. That will happen by being respectful and building rapport with all attendees. This means not just the executives, but also the administrative assistant who set up the meeting. Our paths to building trust include working with a pre-approved agenda, addressing their topics, sticking to the agreed-upon time constraints, offering your expertise, understanding their likely skepticism, showing empathy for their problems or issues, asking well-thought-out questions, actively listening to their concerns and objections, properly answering questions, honoring all of your commitments, apologizing for mistakes, showing personal integrity, not being argumentative, and refraining from jumping into the selling mode before it is appropriate (and that is rarely appropriate in the initial meeting). Building trust will be a differentiator that you will need later, especially if the buyer decides that any of the alternative solutions will work for them.

Takeaway 36: Never Pitch to a Prospect in Your First Meeting.

Formal presentations should never occur without these prior meetings, or, at the very least, telephone calls, with buyer representatives to discuss their needs, current and desired states, pain points, an understanding of the decision process, the names, and roles of each attendee, and learning whether the project is budgeted and has an executive sponsor. Failing to do so is comparable to a physician giving a patient a prescription before discussing the symptoms and current medications.

It is preferable to conduct a presentation in person in a conference room at the buyers' offices, versus on the internet, telephone, or your office. Ever since COVID-19, this may no longer be possible. Most sales presentations are now occurring via Zoom or Skype. Benefits to a meeting in person include greeting the people involved and seeing the body language and reactions to questions and discussion items during the meeting. In a virtual meeting, you miss the opportunity to meet the individuals in person, chat with them before and after the meeting, and observe the body language and hints that you may discern in person. Plus, it is easier to build a relationship when meeting in person. You will need to compensate by diligently following up with each attendee to gain their perspectives on the meeting.

In my experience, it is better if at least two people from your company attend the presentation meeting: the lead sales pro and a second person to take accurate and detailed notes. It is difficult, but not impossible, to present your content, answer questions, and concurrently take good notes. I also recommend meeting at their offices because there is a greater likelihood that there will be more attendees and it will give you a chance to learn more about the company. Meeting notes are important because you will often need to respond to questions, and it is important to know the context of those questions and who asked them. At a minimum, record any unanswered questions that need follow-up and who asked them.

The Keys to a Good Meeting

The first key to a good meeting is to make sure the proper people are attending from both the buyer and your company. Prepare a list of all the buyer's attendees, their titles or functions, their email addresses, and their telephone number before the meeting. And provide similar information from your company to the buyer. I always pass around a plain sheet of paper at the beginning of the meeting, and ask the attendees to list their name, email address, and telephone number. Even if you already have this information, there are often additional people who show up. This also enables you to follow up with each person. You will need it for follow-ups to specific questions and to record who was at the meeting.

Occasionally there will be representatives from the pro-curement department in the initial meeting, though they are usually brought in later. It is better to be more inclusive—have more representation from the buyer and enough from your company to answer at least 80 percent of the questions they will ask. It is rarely possible, or often not even desirable, to answer 100 percent of the questions. It is better to have a few items to follow up on after the meeting. The follow-up items, and who is responsible for each item, the prospect or the supplier, should be agreed upon at the conclusion of the meeting and noted in the follow-up email after the meeting.

A mistake that some sales pros make is to meet only with the person that they have been speaking with by telephone or email. They will often try to exclude anyone they know is in favor of other solutions. *Guess what?*—Exclusion does not work. If the buyer wants that employee to attend, they will probably be invited. They also may be key to the decision and take your lack of inviting them as an affront. Furthermore, the only way that you can resolve any negativity is through discussion. If the company cannot have all, or most, of the decision-makers and influencers at the meeting it is best to postpone and re-sched-ule, even if your contact urges you not to do so. You will likely only have a single opportunity to present to a group of people and the proper people must be in attendance. You do not want to have a meeting with just the contact and Technical Buyers.

If there is a key person who you have been expecting to

attend the meeting and who cannot be present, then discuss with your sales manager and the coach whether this meeting should be postponed. When that happens, state that you understand the unpredictability of these events and request to have the meeting rescheduled. An alternative is to meet and have a conversation with the available people but schedule the formal presentation for a later time when the right people can attend—and provide full-time attention. But remember, you may only be given a single opportunity to meet with them.

Takeaway 37: An Interesting Agenda Is Key to the Success of the Meeting.

The second key is to build an interesting agenda that captures the key areas the buyer wants to discuss, while also including items that you need to cover. The agenda needs to be discussed and agreed upon with your main contact *before* the meeting. It should be mutually owned by you both. Ask your contact, "What would you prefer to accomplish in this meeting," when it is scheduled and that should be the first item discussed during the meeting—after introductions, that is.

The agenda should include, at a minimum:

» an introduction of the meeting participants
» a review of their requirements and needs
» the solution you recommend
» time for questions and answers
» a meeting summary
» the defined next steps

The time allotted to each agenda item needs to be included as well as the total expected length of the meeting. The buyer needs to agree that there will be no interruptions, except for emergencies, and that you must be allowed to explain your proposed solution. One of the worst mistakes that occurs in a meeting is not allowing enough time for the entire agenda to be discussed and for the meeting to end without a summary, next steps and thank you for the opportunity. A premature ending, where people get up and leave the meeting because it is 4:00 p.m., for example, can be a disaster—and must be avoided. If the meeting appears to be headed to longer than the time allotted, the buyer should be asked, at least ten minutes before the scheduled end time, if the meeting can be extended, or if not, which items are most important to them to cover in the remaining time. The others can be postponed to a second meeting. The latter is not a bad result. Any additional time they spend discussing an item can be beneficial to the outcome.

Listen to what each person attending the presentation says during the meeting and take careful notes. This is another reason why having (at least) two people from your company at the meeting is beneficial. Often one person will hear, or observe, something that the other person missed, especially if you are conducting the meeting. You should also welcome, not dispute, objections during the meeting. Wouldn't you rather deal with these while the meeting is in progress than find out about them later when you may not have the opportunity to respond in front of the same audience?

Some sales pros have "happy ears." They only hear what they wanted to hear or what they deemed favorable. They missed the grimace from the vice president or the fact that she closed her laptop and left the room. Or they ignored the objections that were stated during the meeting and just moved on to the next topic. This is more common than you would expect and is a serious mistake. Two ways to prevent this are: first, focus more on your listening skills and not on preparing what to say when they finish speaking; and second, have at least one other sales team member take notes and focus on everything said by the buyer.

It is important to ask closing questions at the end of the meeting that can provide additional information to the sales effort. These could include, "How did we do?" "Did we cover the items you wanted us to cover?" "Do you think our solution is a good fit for your company?" "What do you see as problem areas?" "What do you like best/least about our proposed solution?" and even "Do other suppliers seem to have many advantages over ours?" This should not be done as people are exiting the room.

I was once in a sales situation where the buyer, a large New England insurance company, openly shared their vendor evaluation checklist with me before the meeting. It showed which requirements were most important to them and how each was going to be measured—for example, some had a maximum value of five and others a maximum value of ten, (it was not filled in yet.) When I met with our product subject matter experts and pre-sales pros the evening before to prepare for the meeting, they insisted on sticking to their prepared, company-approved PowerPoint presentation, rather than acknowledging the buyers' primary areas of interest. It was their opinion that if they performed the company's routine presentation the buyer would receive the information they need to make a favorable decision. They were wrong. *Very wrong.* We lost the sale.

So What?

A PowerPoint slide show should not be routinely used as

the primary sales vehicle for the meeting. When they are used, there should only be bullet points and very little, if any, other text. I like to keep it to a slide with the company overview, an agenda slide, and then move on to the main discussion from that point on.

Takeaway 38: Use the "So what?" Test When Evaluating PowerPoint Slides.

Whenever I review PowerPoint slides, my reaction is to say, "So what?" after each phrase. For example:

» "We are the most established business in the industry."
  › *So what?* What does it mean for the buyer?
» "We have been in business for 175 years."
  › *So what?* Millennials view this as a negative. The internet has been available their whole life and smartphones for most of it.
» "We have over five hundred customers using this solution."
  › *So what?* What does this mean to the buyer? Are any like them? When did they buy it? What were their requirements?
» "We have this feature that automates your inventory control."
  › *So what?* So you can do the wrong things quicker?
» "We have professional services people who have successfully deployed this solution at other companies."
  › *So what?* What can they do for the buyer?

And so on. It is not about your company, the product, or the service. It is about what your company can do for the buyer. The point is that each of the statements is meaningless unless they are tied to the value proposition being presented so that the buyer understands why it is to their benefit. These benefits should be articulated along with each statement so that the buyer understands what the value is to them. Using the above examples, you might add:

» "We have been in business for 175 years. We have been providing terrific solutions to companies for many years and will do so for you. So there is no financial risk of our company going out of business."

» "We have over five hundred customers using this solution. We are experienced in deploying the solution which will assure you a successful implementation."

» "We have this feature that automates your inventory control. This will result in less out-of-stocks and a 20 percent savings from your current run rate."

» "Our customers have experienced a return on investment of 150 percent in the first year of our solution deployment."

» "The total cost of ownership of our solution, including the realized benefits, will be less than your current spend rate."

» "We have professional services people who have successfully deployed this solution at other companies. These people will be utilized on your project, assuring you a successful, on-time, on-budget, completion."

Do not make the mistake of thinking that the sales presentation comprises the whole sales cycle, or even most of it. The key to winning a sale often occurs *before* the presentation. The presentation is important, but it may be more important to gather the necessary information, such as their key objectives, their pain points, their reason for making a change, who the decision-makers are, etc. before the presentation, and then to properly follow up afterward. The presentation will allow the sales pro to utilize much of the information that has been acquired in the fact-finding stage and will serve as a reinforcement that you understand the buyer's current situation and pain points. Some sales experts believe that sales can be made without a presentation, and perhaps in some cases, that is valid. But that is not my experience.

Here are some additional tips for different stages of the meeting process.

Before the Meeting:

» Decline participation in undesirable presentation arrangements, such as when the buyer schedules multiple presentations by different vendors on the same day, even if the buyer tells you that you will not be considered otherwise. Do the same if they do not allow you a sufficient amount of presentation time— for example: only fifteen to thirty minutes when you normally need more than one hour. There are two reasons: first, they will not remember what you said versus your competitors, so it is a waste of time (and your time is your most precious resource); and second, it will become a random decision unless it was already predetermined and you do not know it. In that case, it is likely to become a commodity decision based on price or be a "beauty contest" of who had the nicest graphics, for example. By withdrawing you are telling the buyer that you take this process very seriously and do not want to participate in something that does not result in the best opportunity for the buyer to learn about your company and its solutions.

Takeaway 39: Avoid Multiple Presentations by Different Vendors on the Same Day.

» Practice your presentations. It is essential to role-play and watch videos of your presentations. You will be surprised how often you say "ah" or "um." A terrific way to improve your presentations is to join your local Toastmasters International club (https://www. toastmasters.org/) where you will give speeches to your peers and receive feedback. You will also become more comfortable speaking in front of crowds or in challenging environments.

» Rehearse the intended presentation with your entire team before the meeting. All sales staff should understand their roles in the meeting and be on the same page. If there will be Buyer executives in attendance, your team should be briefed on who will be attending, their positions and responsibilities, and what you expect from team members. Discuss possible scenarios where you might encounter issues and be prepared to respond to them if they occur.

» Double-check the details of your presentation for

accuracy. If there is an error and it is caught by an audience member, who may or may not alert you to that fact, it will diminish your credibility. This also includes typographical, grammar, or spelling errors. Slow down, take your time, and get it correct. Steve Jobs, the co-founder of Apple, who was known to be a perfectionist and design minimalist who preferred simplicity said, "Details matter, it's worth waiting to get it right."[71]

» Check with your customer service people and the CRM system to assure that all outstanding issues have been cleared up *before* meeting with the customer. Sometimes a sales pro is "blindsided" both at the beginning and the end of a meeting when a customer brings up the fact that when they called in to your company's customer service their calls were not returned or there are outstanding issues or interactions that still have not been resolved. What do you think that person was thinking about during the meeting—what you came to discuss with them or the issue that hasn't been resolved? I suggest it is the latter and they are just waiting for the best time to bring it up during the meeting, so their full attention is not on you. This will also negate your statement or hurt your credibility when you say, "We have been the best customer service department in the industry."

» Find out if any of the buyer's attendees have any previous experience (other than customer service) with your company, or your competitors', and

71 "Steve Jobs Quotes," Goodreads (Goodreads), accessed April 18, 2022, https://www.goodreads.com/quotes/420161-details-matter-it-s-worth-waiting-to-get-it-right.

whether the experience was positive or negative before the meeting.

» Ask your primary contact, before the meeting, if there are any subjects, topics, or "land mines" that are to be avoided during the meeting. There could be sensitive areas in which there are hard feelings between the participants, and you do not want to exacerbate them.

» Internet connection problems can ruin the start of a meeting. Difficulty in accessing the internet causes meeting disruption, angst, and results in the loss of valuable presentation time with the buyer. I have also seen the sales pros lose their temper when it took an excessive amount of time to get connections working. The buyer will not forget this image. Assume that there will be a problem and be prepared with an alternative. It is essential to test the internet connections beforehand with the buyer to assure that this does not happen.

» Be on "Lombardi time." That means you should plan to arrive at least ten to fifteen minutes early. It is not their fault if you encounter bad traffic, or your flight is late. But do not arrive more than twenty minutes before the appointment. If you are going out of town and the meeting is in the morning, fly in the night before, as opposed to taking an early morning flight. There can be delays, and it is always better for you to be fresh and ready for the meeting.

» Be sure to book a flight *several hours **after** your presentation* to allow time at the end of the meeting— or take Southwest Airlines, which allows you to rebook without change fees (it just costs the difference in fares, if any.) One of the practices that has most hurt sales pros is the imposition of change fees by airlines for flight reservations. Sometimes sales pros rush out of a productive meeting to go to the airport in time for their departing flight. This tells your prospect that it is more important to you to save a few hundred dollars than it is to complete what could be the most important part of the meeting.

» There are no "do-overs" in presentations. You only get one chance. This is not like a "mulligan" in golf. So you must be ready, relaxed, and well-prepared. Sometimes things happen that cannot be anticipated., Make every effort to do the best that you can.

In the Meeting:

» Be sensitive to the customer's business, environment, and competition and consider those when you prepare for your visit. For example, if you are calling on Coca Cola do not mention Pepsi products, nor bring along a Mountain Dew. It is insulting to them.

» Be sure that if you are sitting down at a conference table, you do not have the people from your company sit on one side of the table and the prospects sit on the other side. That sets up an "us-versus-you" dynamic that is undesirable and certainly avoidable. Normally the sales team is escorted to the conference before the buyers arrive, so it is easy to split the sides of the table that you sit at. It is optimal for the sales manager to sit as close as possible to the decision-maker or in a place where you can make good eye contact. The sales pro should sit in the most visible position in the room, where they can direct conversations and observe all participants.

» When presenting in person or via videoconference it is best to stand rather than sit because this sets you apart from the audience and normally will increase attention to what you are saying and gains you respect. When you sit with the audience you are viewed more as a participant.

» Sincerely thank your attendees for providing you with their time—at the *beginning* of the meeting. Do not wait until the end. It is basic courtesy. Then do it again at the end.

» Discuss the time expectations for the meeting. If they gave you one hour—state "This meeting will last about one hour. Is that right?" If not, adjust. If the Economic Buyer says she must leave in twenty minutes, then go to the value proposition as quickly as possible and get her attention. You can go back and cover the introductory items that were skipped afterward.

» Validate the agenda at the beginning of the meeting. Even though you have already done this with your contact before the meeting, it is a good idea to ask the attendees if the agenda meets their objectives for today, and if not, what changes they would like to make to it. Then incorporate the suggested changes. I would estimate that more than 50 percent of the time members of the audience will add items to the agenda and identify additional needs. Expect this to occur and allow some time on the agenda to include any new items.

» I like to inform the audience that I prefer the meeting to be informal, interactive, and that I welcome their interruptions and questions.

» I welcome their questions and do not hold them to the end. This sets the tone that the meeting should be less formal and more friendly. And if a question is not answered promptly, the questioner either shuts down and is not attentive until the question is answered, or the question may be forgotten. Another tactic is to create a "parking lot" on a whiteboard or flip chart, where you can write down questions that are answered later.

» Communication is key. Some of you may remember the scene in the 1967 movie *Cool Hand Luke* when the Captain, (actor Strother Martin), said to Luke Jackson (Paul Newman) "What we've got here . . . is a failure to communicate."[72] If the seller and the buyer do not properly communicate during the meeting it is unlikely that a subsequent sale will occur.

» Deliver your brief explanation of why the buyer should do business with your company in a simple and well-rehearsed statement. I have been very successful at reference selling; telling the group about other similar companies (name dropping is fine) where we deployed similar solutions and the customer was satisfied, became more operationally

---

72 Strother Martin, "Cool Hand Luke - Failure to Communicate," Genius, accessed April 18, 2022, https://genius.com/strother-martin-cool-hand-luke-failure-to-communicate-annotated.

efficient, or either increased revenue or reduced costs. Hopefully, the audience will be impressed and think that if that company is happy with the product or solution, they should be as well.

» State your understanding of their problem or circumstance at the beginning of the meeting. Welcome any corrections. For example. "It is my understanding that the delivery times of your tires from the six U.S. warehouses have increased by more than 20 percent due to perceived inefficiencies in the selection and scheduling of carriers. Is that valid?" Do not offer your solution at this time.

» It is important to be nimble. Sometimes you prepare for one meeting, and after the meeting begins the discussion pivots into something unexpected. Do not resist the change in direction, but you can question if that is where they want to go, as it is an alteration to the agenda. If you are not prepared to make that change, inform the buyer that you must regroup to prepare the information that they are now requesting. Do not try to provide answers that are educated guesses, as they could be incorrect, and it is always difficult to correct that later. On the other hand, if you have strong product knowledge and sales skills, this situation could result in your enhanced credibility.

» Clarity is essential in presentations. Avoid acronyms or jargon, unless you are 100 percent sure the audience understands their meanings. It may be helpful to offer a contrasting example to help visualize your explanations.

» Focus on the core and keep your presentation simple—Remember the Albert Einstein quote: "Everything should be made as simple as possible, but not simpler."[73] Less is more.

» Be economical with your words during a meeting and not try to talk over the buyer. It is counterproductive.

» Understand the purpose of the demonstration; it is not product training. It is to show the prospect how your solution is the best fit for their needs.

» Any insights or best practices that you can offer to the audience are more important than your features and functions. They want to learn how others may have dealt with the same issue or problems, especially well-known leading companies, or those in their vertical markets.

» It is fine to refer to any notes that you prepared in advance during the meeting to remind yourself to cover certain topics or for more information. Some people view using notes negatively, like it's a crutch. It is not. Also ask permission to take notes during any meeting, whether one-on-one or with a large group. It is just a courtesy. I have never had an occasion when this request was denied.

» Vary your speech volume and cadence. Think about a classical symphony being performed by an orchestra—is it always at the same volume level? Never. There are always a lot of variations. Also, some portions are faster or slower in cadence than others. Think of your favorite song by your favorite artist. Was it performed in a monotone? Probably not.

73 "Albert Einstein Quotes," BrainyQuote, accessed April 18, 2022, https://www.brainyquote.com/quotes/albert_einstein_103652.

Neither should your presentation. Raise and lower your voice to emphasize points.

» The goal is not to get through the entire PowerPoint deck. The goal is to stimulate interest and conversation. Many of my best presentations resulted in active discussions on the third or fourth PowerPoint slide and the audience never viewed the remaining slides. I would then send them the whole deck to review on their own after the meeting with answers to any unanswered questions that came up during the meeting (there was always at least one).

» Reinforce the important takeaways that were presented or obtained through questioning and conversation at the conclusion of the meeting. Repetition increases retention. What five things do you want them to remember?

» It is important that you solicit verbal assurances from the attendees that they understand your value proposition, especially in a web meeting. It's hard to track facial expressions and body language in virtual meetings, so making sure people verbally tell you that they are following you is important.

» Get a commitment from the buyer to go to the next step and define what the next few steps in their buying cycle are—at the meeting, not afterward.

After the Meeting

» Conduct an internal debrief immediately after the sales call when everything is fresh in your mind. What went well? What did not go well? What were the problem areas? What was the group's reaction to the presentation? What were each person's reactions and body language during the meeting? What could you have done differently if you could have done this over? What more have we learned about what needs to be done to sell the solution to the buyer? What is your next step? The debrief will not only increase your chances of closing this sale it will also improve the way you approach succeeding presentations. Always keep formal notes of the debrief for later reference.

» Always send a follow-up letter or email the day after a meeting that summarizes the key points in the meeting and reminds the buyer of the next steps. It is a good practice to reinforce what was covered and to answer any questions not answered during the meeting. It is also a good courtesy. Did I say always? *Always.*

Let Your Prospect Do the Talking

Takeaway 40: The Prospect Should Speak More than 50 Percent of the Time.

Steve's *presentation word meter* is a fictitious invention that counts spoken words. Its purpose is to count the words spoken by each person during a meeting. If at the conclusion of the meeting, the word meter indicated that the buyer's attendees spoke more than 50 percent of all words during the meeting, it was likely successful. If the buyers spoke less than 20 percent, then it was probably sub-optimal. If it was under 10 percent, then it was probably a disaster. The attendees were just letting you speak, and they were not participating in the meeting. They were being polite, but their minds were elsewhere. Getting the attendees to participate in the meeting has greater importance in a web meeting than an in-person meeting.

Steve's Presentation Word-Meter

How do you increase the number of words spoken by the prospect during the meeting? In addition to building a stimulating agenda that addresses the topics they are most interested in discussing, and trying to solution with them, the sales pro needs to encourage the buyer to participate more in the meeting by stopping the presentation and by asking thought-provoking, open-ended questions. These could be about their current state, their desired solution, learning more about the company, and whether the proposed solution makes sense to them. If they still do not speak, keep asking them questions, but do not act like an interrogator. The attention needs to be on them, not on your sales pitch if you want to get them to talk.

Be quiet and wait for questions and then move to the next agenda item. If it appears that the team seems tired, or bored, or distracted, then call for a coffee break. The goal it to engage your audience in an authentic way. You should also always remember that the noisiest, or most vocal person in the room is rarely the decision-maker. They may command the most attention but are mostly "show ponies." People who are silent during your presentation will not be quiet after you leave. Try to get everybody engaged in the meeting on some level.

There also may come a time when your prospect asks a question that you do not know the answer to immediately. It is best to respond "I don't know" as an answer to a question than to try to improvise an answer. The audience will respect that you have admitted it. If you falsify your answer, or if it is incorrect, the buyers will often find out and it will destroy your credibility. I admit that I have answered "I don't know" to questions that I know the answer to but wanted to take the opportunity to acknowledge a good question and provide a well-thought-out response. It could also provide an opportunity for discussion with your prospect or the chance to ask more questions.

Takeaway 41: Advantages of Leaving Some of the Prospect's Questions Unanswered.

Letting the buyer know that you will get back to them after researching to find the answers has three benefits:

1. it compliments the question asker who stumped you (especially potent when in front of their peers)

2. it buys time if you do not know the answer

3. it provides you with a legitimate excuse to follow up with them after the meeting.

Meeting Don'ts

Finally, here are some "meeting don'ts." These are a couple pitfalls to avoid throughout the presentation process.

» Do not ever say that your solution is superior to other *named* competitors. This is unprofessional, not to mention that it may point out competitors they have not been considering. Every supplier will tell them what you said. Instead, provide them with the knowledge and reasons why your solution is superior; Paint the picture and let them come to their own conclusions.

» Do not try to improvise or "wing it." Not only will there be a greater likelihood of not achieving the meeting objective, but you are probably wasting the buyer's time and that can be considered insulting. It could cause them to exclude you from further consideration.

» Do not try to show the prospect everything you have or impress them with everything you know. It is judicious to leave some information for your next demonstration or conversation.

» Do not try to fill the silence with chatter.

» Do not make or take telephone calls, check for emails, or write emails during the meeting. Turn off your cellphone and leave it in your bag. I have disqualified sales pros who have done that to me.

» Do not ask "Does everybody understand what I am explaining?" Few people, if any, will say "No, I do not." That could make them feel stupid and they would not want to stand out as the only person in their group that did not understand you. Instead, put it on yourself and say, "Is there anything I can explain in greater detail." Then, if they do not understand what you have explained, they will readily answer "yes," and you can try harder to provide a better explanation.

» Do not negotiate during a presentation meeting. And if they ask you to "cut to the chase" and give them a price, be sure to resist the temptation to do so by telling them that you must gather more information before you can provide it. It would be premature to negotiate at that point. If somebody in the audience mentions that your price is too high, resist the urge to ask why they believe that. Instead, defer answering until a time when you can prepare a proper response.

The ultimate success of the meeting is your responsibility. Your job is comparable to that of the conductor of an orchestra who must know everybody's roles and make sure that they are performed, at the proper time, flawlessly. It is on you to make sure you are fully prepared and that the attendees have a positive experience. Do not blame others for the meeting or presentation failures. You will cash the commission check—or not.

NINETEEN
Make Your Sales Presentations More Memorable

Here is a sad and shocking fact: Studies have shown that buyers remember very little from your sales presentation—or the presentations of your competitors. They will likely not remember all that important material that your team worked on to put together an outstanding presentation. Even more disturbing is that "only 15 percent of sales conversations are considered valuable by customer executives", according to Forrester Research.[74] The tips below are intended to place you in the 15 percent.

According to presentation coach Jack Malcom "Researchers once ran a test to measure how much of a presenter's message sticks in the minds of their audience. They found that immediately after a ten-minute presentation, listeners only remembered 50 percent of what was said. By the next day that had dropped to 25 percent, and a week later it was 10 percent."[75] Sometimes the audience remembers something that was said, but not which presenter said it.

74   Dave Irwin, "Curiosity Saves the Sales Executive," Daily Herald, March 19, 2022, https://www.dailyherald.com/business/20220320/curiosity-saves-the-sales-executive.
75   Jack Malcolm, "How Much of Your Presentation Will They Remember?," Jackmalcolm.com, accessed April 18, 2022, http://jackmalcolm.com/2012/08/how-much-of-your-presentation-will-they-remember/.

Your goal is to make your presentation the primary topic of discussion when the project team meets afterward to consider their next steps. Your first step is to reimagine your presentation so that it is completely oriented toward the prospect's viewpoint—how will they receive it?—not your marketing department's viewpoint. If you were sitting in the presentation as the prospect, not the presenter, how would it resonate (or not) with you?

Takeaway 42: Avoid "Death by PowerPoint" Presentations.

Here are some additional tips to make your presentation more memorable:

» Do not try to show too many PowerPoint or Google Doc slides, (more than twenty, for example), unless it is for an all-day meeting. That will bore them (and you) to death. Also, there should be no more than fifteen words on each PowerPoint slide. "Death by PowerPoint" is defined as a "Phenomenon caused by the poor use of presentation software. Key contributors to death by PowerPoint include confusing graphics, slides with too much text, and presenters whose idea of a good presentation is to read slides, word for word, out loud. Death by PowerPoint is easily recognized by observing the audience members' glazed eyes, furtive use of smartphones, and trips to the bathroom."[76]

» Never have more than three takeaways or reasons to

---

[76] "What Is Death by Powerpoint?," WhatIs.com (TechTarget, August 28, 2013), https://www.techtarget.com/whatis/definition/death-by-PowerPoint.

buy on any single slide to keep it memorable. Less is more.

» Do not read every word on the PowerPoint slide to the audience. They can read it. That is why it is on the PowerPoint. It is best to paraphrase each point in your own way, with emphasis on what each item means to the buyer. Remember, *"So what?"*

» Keep your presentation "short and sweet." The longer your presentation the less likely the attendees will recall individual points that you wanted to emphasize. But they will remember if you were long and boring.

» The meeting must be compelling and should move the buyer to action. The action can be to research the new information you provided or even to schedule the next meeting to discuss items that were not covered or to go deeper into those that were introduced.

Takeaway 43: Your presentation should "Excite or Disturb."

» Jay Ryan, the Head of the Americas operation at my former employer, wanted to either "excite or disturb" the prospect in interactions. This should be an objective of your meeting—either get them interested in speaking further by sharing information that engages them intellectually or in some cases, disturb them from the current status quo to get their attention. An example of an "excite" message is, "Are you interested in reducing your order processing turnaround time by 33 percent, as many of our other customers have done?" An example of a "disturb" message is "Are you performing proper due diligence when you add vendors or suppliers to your vendor master file, as some may be sanctioned entities— which could result in significant fines from the Treasury Department?"

» Increase the curiosity of the audience by being less predictable. Do not utilize a scripted presentation. Your audience will appreciate it more.

Takeaway 44: Your Presentation Needs a "Hook" to Stand Out.

» Many of the vendors' or suppliers' presentations will sound similar to the buyer. This is to be expected as all trying to sell comparable solutions. And everybody will present a professional presentation that was likely prepared by their marketing department. Therefore, your presentation needs a "hook" to be memorable. Examples of hooks are statements that will resonate with the viewer such as: "XYZ Company, similar to yours, saved 65 percent in expenses by deploying this solution," or "ABC Imports improved their renewal rate by 15 percent by offering a two-year plan." Another hook could be "We will guarantee a successful implementation by June 1 or there is no cost to you." Or, "Your current HVAC is obsolete and is costing you at least $100,000 per year more than an updated system."

» Many people are more visual learners and remember

pictures better than words. If you are using PowerPoint, brochures, or other marketing materials, be sure to find and use impactful illustrations or photographs in your slide deck. Ordinary is sub-optimal. I remember a poster that I saw many years ago that showed a herd of wild horses running through a prairie. The caption said, "Unless you are the lead horse the view is the same." It left an impact on me that remains in my mind.

» Another tip is to make the audience think. A good example is the famous song "American Pie" by Don McLean. He used metaphors, imagery, and disguised names of famous people to make the audience try to decipher the words of the song into his story of famous rock and roll people. This was very effective, and the captivating tune resulted in people remembering much of the song. The song is still popular since its release in 1971.

» The facts and assumptions you use must be accurate. If not, your entire presentation becomes suspect to the viewer—and you will lose credibility. For example, if somebody stated in their presentation that the current capital of the United States was New York City, not Washington, D.C., would you believe the other facts in the presentation? Probably not. However, an abundance of facts and data in your presentation, as previously noted, can be boring and forgettable.

» Viewers will often lose interest in presentations after a certain amount of time; often this can happen in as quickly as ten minutes. If this happens in your presentation, try to get them more engaged in the conversation by listening more than talking, and place your most impactful facts or information earlier in the presentation. Or you can simply call for a short break.

» The repetition of a theme will make a presentation more memorable. If you continue to repeat the theme many people will believe it. Think of McDonald's "You deserve a break today," Nationwide Insurance's "Nationwide is on your side." and Miller Lite's "Tastes great, less filling."

» I competed with a smaller boutique software company that had basic features and functions and a primitive user interface that did not compare with our functionally rich offering. Throughout the competitor's sales presentation they kept repeating "Our system is simple and very easy to use." When I later asked the prospect what they thought of the competitor's offering they often restated, "We think it is simple and very easy to use." When I asked why they could not provide a specific reason.

» Understand that many companies' procurement practices have migrated to digital buying processes. This means that they may want you to provide an electronic proposal, as well as digital responses to their questions, diagrams, and charts, implementation plans, and marketing collateral—and they even may request a digital web presentation. This has the benefit for the buyer of assembling all the data, in one standardized format, in one folder or place for review. It also creates a physical distance between the buyer from the seller. It is not as beneficial for you as the seller, but if you refuse you may be deemed to be uncooperative or behind in technology. Regardless, always try to schedule a face-to-face meeting.

» It is on us, as sales pros, to ease any anxieties that unfamiliar buyers may have over the evaluation process by assisting them in understanding the typical steps in the buying cycle. Perhaps that is best done one-on-one, but it can be addressed in a presentation or follow-up meeting if it becomes apparent to you that the buyers seem uncomfortable with the process. That could also provide an opportunity for you to deliver a list of typical requirements that might provide a "jump-start" for them.

» Rehearse your presentation. Record it and play it back to yourself . . . Are you bored listening to it? If so, your audience will be, too.

Utilizing Storytelling

Takeaway 45: Stories Are Always More Memorable than Reciting Facts.

Stories help people remember your content. "Researchers Dan and Chip Heath found that after a presentation only 63 percent of attendees remember stories, while a small group totaling only 5 percent remember statistics."[77] Tell stories when you present. This seems to be a contradiction of the above instruction to be economical with your words, but it is not.

---

77 Dan Mack, "19-In-20 People Don't Remember Your Presentation," Drug Store News, January 6, 2022, https://drugstorenews.com/news/1-0-people-dont-remember-your-presentation.

When you tell stories, you invite your prospect to tell their own. People like to talk about themselves and their company, and this should not be discouraged in the interest of time. There is a Hopi proverb: "The one who tells the stories rules the world."[78] Frank Dodge, the co-founder of the very successful software company McCormack & Dodge, used to tell me, "Steve, paint word pictures for the audience so that they can visualize what you are explaining better."

Telling stories and using imagery also has the added benefit of making it easier for people to understand what you are presenting, and stories are more memorable than any PowerPoint or hand-out. The audience is also more likely to pay closer attention because they can relate to them. Your stories should include how similar other companies benefitted from the solution but the most interesting are customer success stories: the company, the history of the product or a solution—how it was invented or what problem it was intended to solve and how you have helped other companies. But the most interesting, and most productive for the sales pro, are personal customer success stories. The stories should be specifically chosen for each meeting so that you do not present any that do not apply to the buyer that you are meeting with. They must be relevant to the buyer, as a bad story is worse than no story.

Here is an example of a good word story:

"In our previous meetings, you indicated to me that your inventory is out of control and the records are inaccurate. It was determined that last year the cost of excess inventory and searches cost over half a million. Imagine a future situation in which you have complete knowledge of the inventory levels of all automotive parts, including where they are stored, so that

---

78 "American Indian Proverb, Hopi Quotes," Quotation.io, accessed April 18, 2022, https://quotation.io/page/quote/one-tells-stories-rules-world.

you never have a situation where production is halted for a product search, and you never have too many overstocks sitting around either. This is the benefit that company XYZ currently has using our solution. Does this sound attractive to you?"

In another example, if I told you all the facts about the temperatures in Chicago in January for the past ten years or a story about how I was stuck in my home for five days due to a record blizzard, which would you most likely remember? The blizzard story. You can make your presentation more memorable by telling the audience a brief story that illustrates your point, idea, or solution. How did another customer use your product to achieve success? Try to incorporate your value proposition into the story, perhaps how a similar company wrestled with the decision. What was their problem? What did they do? How did it help them solve the problem? What was the measurable result? Perhaps you can also discuss how other customers decided to go with your solution, which resulted in a successful introduction of a new product line within the budgeted time frame and amount. The story should be something that relates to them or their problem.

One final example: "One of our customers is the Brooklyn Baseball Cap Company. They had a critical supply chain challenge. They were unable to fill their customers' orders on time, and they lost some key customers as a result. The problem grew worse when the company expanded its geographical coverage. We worked with them on a solution to solve this issue by quicker identification of the location of their finished goods inventory, improving packaging options, and changing delivery companies. As a result, over eighteen months, they increased their speed of goods to customers by 25 percent." Perhaps show a photograph of their operation or warehouse. Or include a chart that showed the average delivery time before and after implementing the solution.

The above tips can truly help you make a compelling presentation, but there are always other ways you can incorporate your own personal flair into your presentation as well. Professor and author Art Markman suggests that the best way to make the presentation memorable is to "change the audience in some way."[79] Connect with them using a personal story, such as why you went into sales, or something unique about you or your family. Secondly, he suggests that you make connections between key points to improve retention. Thirdly, he suggests that you make the audience work. Ask for questions or their reaction to the presentation or poll them for their thoughts and ideas. Markman also suggests that you encourage the audience to explain the presentation back to you to reinforce their retention of it. I advise asking them to explain only the most important areas—in their own words—at the conclusion of the presentation so you can assess whether they understood and retained your message. I have also listed the (most important but less than ten) bullet points of the presentation on a whiteboard or flipchart at the beginning of the presentation and asked the audience what some points meant to them at the conclusion. That reinforces the presentation and brings them into the conversation.

Markman's advice would seem to imply that it is better to craft your presentations away from presenting facts and toward feelings. In sales, feelings are what you experience when you receive external stimuli, or due to emotions such as sadness, happiness, joy, or fear when you listen to a speaker or watch a

---

79 Art Markman, "Getting an Audience to Remember Your Presentation," Harvard Business Review, September 21, 2015, https://hbr.org/2015/09/getting-an-audience-to-remember-your-presentation.

presentation. Those that give us feelings of happiness or delight might be due to seeing content, ideas, or solutions that we judge to be creative, aesthetically pleasing, favorable to our careers, solves a critical problem, raises our levels of interest, provides us with greater personal respect, or inspires us.

Similarly, the poet and author Maya Angelou wrote: "I've learned that people will forget what you said, the things you did, but people will never forget how you made them feel."[80] People should feel better, not worse after they have spoken with you. It is on you, the sales pro, to make that happen. You will be more memorable if you are friendly, respectful, and do not waste time, all of which should make the audience feel better.

The lesson is to try to raise the level of the emotional response to your presentation by focusing on areas that might cause that to happen. Some ideas include focusing on what you have determined to be the "hot buttons" of the CEO or Economic Buyer:

» entering a new market or reducing expenses
» addressing the personal objectives (MBOs) of people on the evaluation team (what they are measured on in their annual review)
» introducing the fear of loss if they do not act quickly (people prefer avoiding loss to acquiring gains)
» calming the emotions of uncertainty
» utilizing doubt or greed (the window of opportunity to register for our next training class is closing quickly so you need to act now)
» proving a highly compelling value proposition

This does not include overwhelming the buyers with facts

---

80 "Carl W. Buehner Quotes," BrainyQuote (Xplore), accessed April 18, 2022, https://www.brainyquote.com/quotes/carl_w_buehner_392897.

and features on why you are better than your competition, or photographs of your new company offices, which will usually bore the audience. Steve Jobs, the co-founder of Apple, once said "We don't stand a chance of advertising with features and benefits and with RAMs and with charts and comparisons. The only chance you have of communicating is with a feeling."[81]

In summary, it is on you to make your presentation memorable by presenting thought-provoking, interesting, and unique content to the prospect. Since you are likely not a professional actor or performer, your personality will not be enough to draw their interest. A routine, solely facts-based presentation will not stand out from your competition and may relegate you to the group of companies that the prospect looked at but decided not to consider further. I have found it to be helpful to review my presentation and ask myself the question, "Would I buy from somebody if they approached me with this message?" When the answer was "no," I reworked and perfected the presentation.

---

81   Rufat Rassulov, "These Steve Jobs' Principles Will Change Your Approach to Marketing," Publicist Marketing and Communications Network, accessed April 24, 2022, https://www.publicist.co/the-spin/the-inside-scoop/these-steve-jobs-principles-will-change-your-approach-to-marketing#:~:text=%E2%80%9CWe%20don't%20stand%20a,to%20sell%20emotions%2C%20not%20features.

TWENTY
Avoid Competing on Price

In my early years in sales, I was convinced that my company's solution was far superior in features to others in the market-place, and I approached every sales situation as a challenge for me to explain what was obvious to me to the prospects I met. I assumed that the "best" product would be chosen by rational buyers who properly compared them. This was a time where most technology sales were sold by demonstrating features and benefits. I tried to "wow" the audience by showing them how much easier I could make their jobs with this new application software. I was very successful, especially early on in my career. Then something happened—the competition caught up with our company and in some cases had products that were more feature-rich—or easier to use. It was also about that time that I realized that being successful in sales was much more than having the "best" competitive product or solution to sell.

I also learned that the buyer often could not differentiate between the merits of the offerings, or if they did so, sometimes did not place as much value on some of the cool features as I did. That frustrated me until I realized that what was important to me (perhaps the features that were emphasized to me by our product managers) was often not as important to the buyer. I needed to adapt. So I became more of a consultative sales pro and tried to work with the buyer to help them determine the best solution for their needs. I also tried to educate them about alternative solutions that were available to them. That is when I went from being a very good product demonstrator to a sales pro.

It is more important to find out what the prospect's needs and wants are or what has the greatest value to them than to lead with product features. It is then your job to link their needs to your solutions. When you are surveying to try to determine the prospect's needs, doing a pre-call, or conducting a demonstration, you must probe whether the prospect needs specific features or functions that you offer, especially those that are unique to your company, the "real why" that I described in Chapter 8. If the specific solution or feature does not seem to have any benefit, financial or otherwise, note it and move along to something else. The prospect may have questions on how your solution works, or how it might operate in their environment. If so, be sure to take the time to answer and explore the possibilities with them. I call that "solutioning" and it is a key to closing a sale.

Discovering their specific needs or "hot buttons" and preparing your specific examples should be done before your presentation. There may be differing opinions within the company about specific needs as well. For example, Sally may want faster delivery, but Henry may want higher quality or perhaps other features. Do not dismiss one person because you think he or she is not as important as another, or higher or lower on the corporate hierarchy. Address each person's concerns, as you may not know what the real driver is at this point, or who has the greatest influence. Do not argue with them, even if it is something that your solution excels at and move on to the next topic. And remember their needs or priorities can, and usually, change throughout the sales cycle.

Sometimes the buyer will "parrot" information about a competitor's key feature to you that the competitor may have shown or discussed with them, but that feature may not be that important to the buyer. As you compete in the marketplace you will recognize when it does. So if you can identify this possible trap, please be sure to (not aggressively) question the buyer as to why they need that feature or function and if it is necessary, or just something that sounded nice to them when the competitor presented it. Sometimes they are just testing you, or they want to appear to be smart to their peers.

Takeaway 46: Price Is Only Important If You Do Not Differentiate Your Solution.

If you fail to differentiate your proposed solution relative to others in the marketplace, and especially to the status quo choice, the buyer will likely either do nothing or resort to using price as the differentiator. Price is always the default because it is the easiest path for the buyer. They then do not need to do the work necessary to differentiate the various offerings—such as researching the differences between the companies and the products, and the value proposition becomes irrelevant.

If the buyer resorts to using price, then the sales opportunity will probably become a *commodity* sale, in which the features, benefits, and values that each solution provides are ignored and the price is all that matters. The value proposition that you have worked so hard to develop becomes less important. When price matters most in the decision it often results in greater pressure on the proposed price from the buyer and often the low-cost provider is then chosen.

Furthermore, if the differences between the offerings are difficult for them to discern, or are esoteric, they will not do the necessary research and do not care about the consequence of going to the solution with the lowest price. Think of buying computer paper, corrugated boxes, gasoline, chicken wings, bananas, store-brand aspirin, or paper clips. Those are commodities and price is the most important determining factor when a choice is made. If the buyer primarily considers price as the most important factor in their decision criteria, they are saying that all the value adds that you explained did not matter to them. So even though you may be selling them a million-dollar solution it is being treated as a commodity sale.

I prefer not to participate in a commodity sale situation and recommend that you avoid competing by price unless that is your primary market. If the decision is based on price, why does your employer need you as a sales pro? All they need is a published price sheet or they can refer to the company's website. If you reach the point in a sales cycle where the buyer tells you that they are going to go with the best/lowest price *that means that you have not done a good job.*

When this happens, I advise trying to change the decision dynamic, by saying something like this to the Economic Buyer: "If your decision is going to be based on the lowest price it is obvious to me that I have not done a good job (always take ownership of this—do not blame them) of explaining the value of our solution to you. I suggest that we take another twenty minutes to review the value that our proposed solution brings to your organization (for example: increasing your ability to bring products to market quicker than you can do now). We previously discussed that this solution will result in increased sales of your new products." If they decline to let you do this, you have already lost. There is no point in playing the price game. I would tell them we are not lowering our price, as we feel it is a fair representation of the value we bring to their company. If procurement is driving this conversation, then your only chance is to get the decision back in the hands of the businesspeople. That is easier said than done because if procurement is in control, it often means that there is a corporate directive (reduce all existing contracts by 10 percent), or the businesspeople have indicated that they do not have the time, the interest, or the expertise to conduct the evaluation and negotiation.

Some buyers have told me that any of the alternative solutions they have looked at will do the job for them, so why not go with the lowest price? They have sometimes followed up with "We like yours, but you do not have the lowest price." I have told them that is intentional, and our company never wants to be the lowest price in the market because we provide greater value and have made investments to market a superior product with excellent service. This also indicates, in many cases, that the buyer has not done much research into the differences and cannot remember what each supplier or vendor proposed to them. In response to the "any will do" statement, I have often asked people if they understand why some products are priced higher than others, such as their own, as most of the companies I have sold to do not sell the lowest priced product, (think Apple, Microsoft, or Harley Davidson. This message doesn't work with Costco, BestBuy, or Amazon.)

What about reliability and quality? What about the support our company provides and the investments that we make in continually updating our products, services, and solutions that the others do not? We also have a first-class customer support department, as evidenced by the many satisfied customers that are using our solutions. There is a saying attributed to Aldo Gucci, the former chairman of the famous Gucci fashion company, that says, "The bitterness of poor quality is remembered long after the sweetness of low price has faded from memory."[82]

If you find the buyer cannot discern differences, it may be helpful to provide them with advice on how other organizations have approached the buying process. For example, explain what steps they took to make their decision. If they are making their decision mostly based on the price, they are most likely leaving out the phases of the evaluation where you review the value of the solution to the organization and validate whether or not it provides the necessary return on investment, whether it provides greater or lesser value than those of its competitors, whether it is compatible with the company's IT current and future architecture, whether its usability has been examined, and whether they've visited with other customers who are using the solution. A possible aid for this would be a hand-out of best-buying practices.

It is also important that there is an "apples to apples" comparison of alternatives by the buyer. I have been faced with situations where the buyer informed me that our price was much higher than our competitors, but when I did more research, I found that often certain costs were left off our competitors' price, such as training, services, on-site or 24x7 support or optional features that were included in our proposal. Each of those has a value that must be included. Or they were

---

82 "Aldo Gucci Quote," Quotefancy, accessed April 18, 2022, https://quotefancy.com/quote/1574585/Aldo-Gucci-The-bitterness-of-poor-quality-is-remembered-long-after-the-sweetness-of-low.

comparing a competitor's lower-cost product line, which naturally costs less, against our high-valued solution. The comparison must be on comparable solutions. And the decision should consider the total cost of ownership of each. The buyer needs to have a complete understanding of the feature and functions that each seller provides. If they do not understand the differences, it is your job to educate them.

If you sell to a company based on price, there is a greater likelihood the buyer will leave you in the future when another company offers an even lower price. Where they do not see value there is also no loyalty to you as a supplier. Why would there be? They have indicated that price is their priority. And sometime down the road, a lower-priced solution will emerge, perhaps just to initially win their business.

Price may also become an issue if a sales pro tries to close the opportunity too soon (sometimes because of prodding or questioning by the sales manager.) In that case, the buyer has not had a chance to understand the real value of the solution or product to them, or to present it to executive management. Since they are unaware of the possible ROI, they are apt to respond to a premature close by asking for the lowest price.

During the sales cycle, do not "trash talk" or mention your competitor's company names and products for several reasons. For one, it is unprofessional to do so. Other reasons include:

- » Sometimes the buyer will have a strong negative reaction to naming them.
- » Some buyers may react to your comments by defending the competitor's solutions.
- » It will probably not change their mind about the competitor's offerings.

» I prefer a positive, not a negative, message to buyers.
» Your knowledge of the competitor and its products and solutions may be outdated, which will hurt your credibility.
» They may not even be considering your competitor, but once you mention their name, they might check them out.
» It is more effective to focus on our solutions, not our opponents.
> It is permissible to state something like this "Our (specify) features, which provide you with unparalleled protection against fraud are unique in the marketplace" or "We do not believe any other company offers the protection that our company offers against fraud." That may be puffery, but it can be effective. And, again, we should not mention the competition by name.

I have often complimented our competitors to buyers. "Competitor X is an excellent company, and they have very good products; however, I will explain to you why ours is a better fit for your company (or problem)." This sets a better tone for discussions of the values and benefits of our solutions and is seen by the prospect as being nobler.

Avoid Providing Multiple Solutions

Takeaway 47: Do Not Offer Multiple Solutions and Expect the Prospect to Choose.

Be careful not to offer multiple solutions to the buyer for the same problem at one time as it will confuse them. You are also not being consultative, which builds trust, and it appears that you are shifting your job to them. For example, the company I worked for recently offered three different sanction compliance software solutions, each developed by separate companies. All have been successful in the marketplace. Each solution can handle most needs and have their strengths and weaknesses. But I do not recommend telling a buyer "We offer three solutions: A, B, and C. Each will result in improvements in your current processes. Why don't you look at all three and tell me which one you like better?" Instead, decide which is the best fit for them and recommend it.

Many companies have several product lines that are oriented to different needs and price points. The more options you offer to the buyer the more likely that it will cause confusion and decision paralysis, or further analysis and a longer sales cycle. It is also your job to recommend the (single) best solution to the buyer after learning what their needs and goals are. Try to match up the best (not best few) solution to solve their problem or improve their current processes. The simpler, more understandable, and less complex you make your offer to understand, and the more they agree that they will derive value from it, the greater the probability of closing the sale. If you do not make your solution simple and easy to understand there is a likelihood that your competitor will do so, and they will close the sale instead of you. If you cannot provide the best solution for their needs, it is your ethical obligation to inform the buyer of that and either withdraw or work on an alternative solution for them.

One Last Thought

The opposite of selling based on the lowest price is the pricing strategy employed by companies such as Starbucks, which has established itself in the marketplace as a premium brand. They deliberately price their coffee at the high end of the market and are proud of it. Starbucks would say they deliver an enriched coffee experience, which also includes the ambiance, the ability to surf the internet, work on your laptop or tablet while drinking coffee, a good place to meet friends, and have positive interactions between the customers and the employees, not just a cup of coffee.

Is Starbucks coffee worth the large price premium when compared to Dunkin Donuts, McDonalds, or your local restaurant? Why do people pay more for Starbucks? I suggest that it is because their customers place a higher value on their coffee than on others. So it is also an example of Value Based Pricing. The value may be due to brand loyalty, but also convenience is important, a relaxing and pleasurable atmosphere, the Starbucks ordering experience, market dominance, standardization across North America, bakery goods sales, mobile payments, and easy gifting. Perhaps there is also a certain amount of status or "snob" appeal. Its premium prices have not dissuaded customers or impaired its growth. An economist would say that the Starbucks demand curve is very "inelastic," meaning that increases in prices do not affect the demand very much. The lesson is that you do not have to lower your price to meet the low-cost provider—if it can be differentiated and the buyers perceive the extra value.

Is traveling in first-class worth up to five times more than a coach or economy class on a commercial airplane? First-class seats are wider and much more comfortable and first-class passengers are provided with meals, liquor, extra room for their carry-on luggage, better access to a lavatory, and much better service from the flight attendants. The fliers arrive at the same time, although first-class passengers always board and deboard first. Yet, many customers are willing to pay the difference for the superior experience because they either find the value worthwhile, or they are wealthy and do not care about the cost.

What about products or services that are not luxury goods? People will pay more for an item if they perceive that it provides greater value, whether it is a luxury good or not. They will even pay extra for a commodity product like bottled water. Consumers are willing to spend more on bottled water because of the perceived greater value from successful brand marketing that the bottled water companies have used.

It is your job to encourage your buyers to adopt the same mindset for your products. You must differentiate your solutions from the other alternatives and refute the commoditization argument. I try to end the price argument by asking the buyer *if they want to bet their job on the low-cost solution.* Most people, but not all, will say they do not.

TWENTY-ONE

When Is the Greatest Amount of Interest in Buying?

You have worked on the sale for possibly a long time, growing it from a lead that you may have developed, perhaps through a cold call. You had several meetings with your primary contact and others and have convinced them that your value proposition is superior to the alternatives, including the status-quo (doing nothing.) You have answered their questions and perhaps arranged a visit to one of your customers. You have worked to develop a return-on-investment business case with your contact, and you have shared it with the Economic Buyer, who has agreed with your ROI calculations. There has been increasing interest on the part of the buyer, which is manifested by calls to you for additional information, an on-site workshop, a request for a contract, or questions about training and deployment. Perhaps a procurement person has entered the sales cycle. Now your contact has informed you that they have met and have selected your solution as the one that they want to move forward with. There still needs to be a final negotiation to close the sale. What is the buyer's interest in closing the sale and when is it the greatest?

I have determined that the greatest amount of interest the buyer will have in concluding the sale is the day they decide which product or solution to buy. Each day afterward the level of interest drops by an increasing percent. Graphically this looks like:

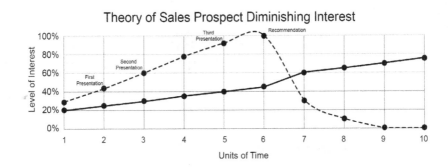

The y-axis represents the prospect's interest in concluding the sale. The x-axis represents time. The dashed horizontal line represents this specific opportunity. Observe that interest in concluding a purchase increases at a steady rate up until the point the recommendation is made, at the sixth point. The solid line represents the prospect's interest in remaining with the current situation. Once the recommendation is made the interest declines at an increasing rate. The dashed line moves downward from almost 100 percent to near 0 percent. At some point, in this example between periods six and seven, the interest in doing nothing is higher than the interest in concluding the sale with you.

So what does this mean to you? At first glance, it does not seem to be profound information. But it is not as obvious as it seems. You must dig deeper to gain an understanding of what this means to you as a sales pro.

Peak Interest

Takeaway 48: The Greatest Interest in Purchasing Is the Day They Decide to Buy.

According to my research, the buyers' interest in concluding the sale is greatest the day they make their decision to buy from you. Each day that goes by, the interest level in procuring your solution decreases, and staying with the status quo increases. At some point the interest level decreases at an increasing rate, eventually resulting in a stalemate situation.

This theorem came about when I tried to understand why a few of my competitive win decisions had not closed. My solution has been selected over my competitors, but they had stalled. The lack of inertia had won over a long thought-out plan to fix a problem. It was determined that staying with the status quo was preferable. I tried to understand how and why this could happen. I determined that the buyer's interest in fixing the problem and concluding a sale declined drastically each month, to the point where the fall was unrecoverable. What happened? It is hard to generalize, but in many cases, it was a combination of 1) the prospect determined that they could live with what they had; 2) a known problem is preferable to an unknown problem *("the devil you know"),* even if there is a possibility of a fix to the problem, and 3) other priorities overtook this specific one. Sometimes a competitor that becomes aware they are losing a sale will contact a buyer executive and gets a delay in the decision. The lesson here is that, as hard as you worked to win a decision, you must continue to work even harder once the decision is reached in your favor to close the sale before the interest fades. You must increase your level of urgency—it is not the time to take it easy. As President Abraham Lincoln noted after many of his generals prematurely reported successes that never happened, "The hen is the wisest of all the animal creation, because she never cackles until the egg is laid."[83]

Takeaway 49: Elapsed Time Is Your Enemy if You Are Winning, Your Ally if You Are Losing.

The more time that elapses after the decision, the more likely you will not close the sale, even if it is non-competitive. I suggest building a timeline with your contact or the project leader and define all the steps that need to take place to achieve a signed contract. Monitor the progress against this timeline in the same manner that a project manager would monitor the progress of an IT project. Where are you versus the agreed-upon timeline? What needs to be done today, this week, and next week? If a critical person, such as one in the legal department, is not available, find out who can take their place to keep the process moving. If you think that your work is complete when your buyer selected your solution, you have overestimated the process. Do not overlook the tasks that need to be completed.

As the famous New York Yankee baseball player, Yogi Berra said, "It ain't over until it's over."[84]

---

83 "Abraham Lincoln Quote," QuoteNova.net, accessed April 18, 2022, https://www.quotenova.net/authors/abraham-lincoln/dxvaaq.
84 "Yogi Berra Quotes," BrainyQuote (Xplore), accessed April 18, 2022, https://www.brainyquote.com/quotes/yogi_berra_110034.

TWENTY-TWO
Responding to Requests for Proposals

One of the struggles that many sales pros face today is whether to participate in a Request for Proposal (RFP) process. RFPs are a mixed blessing. Completing them can be a tedious, unpleasant task. And they can be timewasters. They cannot be completely ignored because some may lead to significant sales revenue. And many are issued by consulting firms with which you want to establish positive relationships. The key is to determine which has the greatest probability of your solution being chosen and respond only to those.

The purpose of an RFP is to solicit detailed information through a controlled competitive process. Included in the RFP are specifications for the goods or services that are to be purchased. The goal is to gather information from potential suppliers that will be analyzed to determine the best fit for the purchasing organization. It places much of the burden for analyzing product functionality questions on the seller, rather than the buyer.

RFPs are often required by governments and non-profit companies to ensure that purchases are not subject to corruption or bias. Governments sometimes call it a request for tender

(RFT.) Outside consultants are often hired to help prepare RFPs. They normally include a price quote that must be honored for a specified time. There is usually a period in which all vendors are allowed to submit questions for additional information, and the answers are then sent to all vendors or suppliers.

Sometimes a request for information (RFI) precedes the RFP and is less detailed and specific. RFIs are used to determine which suppliers the RFP should be sent to in the next step. The RFI will normally include questions such as the company's history, current and future product or service offerings, functional capabilities, and sometimes prices.

Many companies have procurement policies that stipulate that a certain minimum quantity of suppliers must be considered for purchases over a certain dollar amount. RFPs help companies achieve reductions in their spending level through competition for their business. They also reduce any influence or advantage that any supplier has over others by making the process more transparent. Control over the process is usually assigned to the procurement department.

Gather Additional Information

Takeaway 50: You Need Additional Information to Decide Whether to Respond to the RFP.

You can make a more informed decision with the answers to these nine questions:

1. Is the RFP from an existing customer?

2. Did you know the RFP was going to be issued, and have you been in contact and discussed it with the customer?

3. Do you understand the scope of what they are looking for? (If not, can you obtain this information before you respond?)

4. Do you think your product is an excellent fit for their needs? Will it help them solve their stated business problem?

5. Have you provided the product to other similar companies and have references?

6. Do you have the time and resources to prepare a superb response?

7. Will the issuer allow you access to the decision-makers and key staff?

8. Do you believe your price will be in the range they are expecting?

9. Can you meet the stated conditions of the RFP, including the deadline to submit the response?

If you answered "no" to any of the above, it may not be worth responding to the RFP, unless it is from a company that you have never done business with, and it might be an opportunity to gain a foothold into the company.

There is normally an enforced due date, usually two to four weeks from when it is received. If the stated deadline is unreasonable for you to prepare a first-rate response, then you must decide whether to participate. I advise calling or emailing the designated contact and ask for more time to respond. If they refuse to grant the extra time, ask if others received the RFP before you did or whether all were under the same unreasonable time restrictions. You may find that they included you at the last minute, which could be very good or very bad: good, if somebody referred them to you as a solution they should look at; bad, if you were included to fill a requirement. I discourage the practice of submitting a "quick and dirty" response, as it represents the quality of your company and may degrade your reputation.

Red Flag Warning

Takeaway 51: Not Knowing the RFP Is Being Issued Is a "Red Flag."

If you did not know the RFP was being sent out, another supplier likely did. And they may have helped write the RFP. (I have done so.) Or your company may have been included to meet the required minimum quantity of suppliers. As a result, there is a high probability that your product or service will not be selected, and your time and efforts will be wasted. Or perhaps you were not paying enough attention to that prospect. In either case, I recommend you consider the cost of completing the RFP. If it will take seven workdays to complete the RFP, for example, would you be better off investing your time elsewhere? If not, then complete the RFP.

Why do you think you have a chance of being selected? If you are aware that other suppliers or vendors may have a solution that better fits the company's needs, it is probably not worthwhile completing it. You also need to be able to differentiate your response from the others, because it is likely that all suppliers will answer "yes" to almost all questions and the responses will be very similar, usually differing only in price.

Sometimes you will receive an RFP from one of your customers and you may feel obligated to complete it to maintain a good business relationship. In that case, invest the time to provide a quality response because even if does not result in current business, it will help you gain business down the road by being included in the next RFP.

RFP Dealbreakers

The RFP often specifies that *all contact* is to go to a designated person during the process. The purpose is to centralize control of all contacts so that one supplier does not gain an advantage over the others by receiving information that the others did not have. This presents sales pros with a difficult circumstance. Failure to follow this rule can lead to your company being excluded from consideration. If you have built a long-standing relationship with several members of the executive and staff team, are you to cease conversations with them during this time? The answer is "yes," unless you receive permission from the procurement person to have the conversation, or your proposal may be disqualified. I have sometimes sent emails to both my primary contact and the procurement person requesting a conversation so that I can gather more information. If you find that your access is too limiting, then it is best to not submit a response. This restriction eliminates the discovery/solutioning steps from the sales process as conversations are forbidden unless you are selected.

I would also be reluctant to participate in a non-RFP sales cycle if they enforced a similar restriction on conversing or meeting with other stakeholders. This gives them complete control and takes away any advantage you might have by learning more about their needs and building a compelling value proposition.

Some RFPs also ask you to commit to agreeing to their contract terms and conditions in advance. This is a "deal-breaker" in every company I have worked for and would normally result in declining to participate unless it was for a lucrative multi-million-dollar federal government contract, and you are already comfortable with the terms. Or you could agree and try to "walk it back" later, which is not easy to do.

Whether the decision is made to proceed or decline participation in the RFP process, it is important that you notify the company of your intentions. If you decline to participate in this RFP there may be occasions in the future where you want to be included. If you decline participation, a one-sentence reply is adequate.

Proper Preparation Is Essential

Once an RFP is received and the decision is made to proceed with participation in the process you must assure that the response is professionally and thoroughly completed. So you are either "all in" or "all out." All team members must understand what their role is in the process, which sections or questions they are to answer, when their answers are due, and what is being proposed, as there is sometimes a decision as to which products or services are being included. A mistake that some companies make is that each product expert or a functional person provides responses for their respective area of expertise, and the answers are not similar in context or in style and could even be even contradictory. Extra care must be taken to assure that there is one voice presented back to the buyer.

Takeaway 52: The Wording in Your Response Must Be Carefully Prepared.

Your responses to their requirements need to be worded so it is clear what you are proposing and how your solution, or value proposition, will best fit their needs without relying on sales puffery. The usage of non-industry standard acronyms not in general usage (CIA, TSA, FBI) is not advised. Not everybody in the receiving organization may know what a 3DWQM is, or even what DoD is, for example. Your response should be informative enough so that a person unfamiliar with your solution, such as a procurement or financial analyst, would understand it. Also, be aware that your response may be shared with your competitors, so be careful not to reveal any information that you do not want them to know.

When preparing your response, be sure to explain where you have offered similar solutions to comparable organizations or customers in their geographical area or vertical industry and emphasize the value and benefits they have derived from it. If you are providing services, it is important to list the qualifications of the staff that will be assigned to the project.

Some companies assign the completion of RFPs to junior sales or support persons as a training exercise. While this is a good method to introduce newer people to the process and to the products or solutions, their unfamiliarity will almost always result in a sub-optimal RFP response. If it is decided to have these people begin the process, or do the first draft, it is important that all work is reviewed and corrected before it is submitted. Remember the advice your parents may have told you: "Anything worth doing is worth doing well." Otherwise, the time and effort invested are wasted.

Be sure to include your marketing department in the RFP preparation process and ask them to review the final document to ensure that proper spelling, grammar, and company marketing standards are being followed. I have been on the receiving side of RFPs and was amazed at the poor quality of some RFP responses submitted. Those were excluded immediately, without regard to the solution or the price. I concluded that the RFP demonstrated that the submitter was not serious about its preparation, and I felt that if they did not want to invest the time to prepare the document, they were unlikely to do a good job for my company.

So should you answer the RFP? Yes, if it meets the criteria I have discussed. No, if it does not. If you decide to respond to the RFP assure that it is so well prepared that you would be proud to show it to your CEO as an example of your best work.

It has been said that there are at least two winners when an RFP is issued: The supplier that is chosen and those that declined to participate in the process.

I am a huge fan of Scott Adams' Dilbert cartoons. Adams worked for a large organization, Pacific Bell Telephone, and he often satirizes bureaucratic corporate culture. The cartoon below reflects Dilbert's humor when this policy is abused.

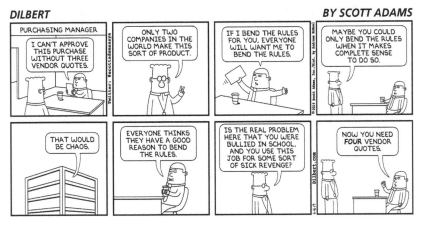

Dilbert © 2019, Andrews McMeel

TWENTY-THREE
It's About Time

Often the difference between a sales pro that meets their goals and another that exceeds them is simply a matter of optimizing one's own time. Some find time optimization to be difficult and spend valuable time and resources on opportunities that are not likely to close, chasing down "rabbit holes," or working on non-sales-related tasks during working hours. A high-performing sales pro focuses on sales activities, which include meeting with prospects, making telephone calls, preparing material for presentations, researching buyers' issues, and discussing sales strategies for each opportunity with their manager. According to an Accenture CSO Insights report in 2013, sales representatives were spending only 35.7 percent of their time selling (face-to-face or on the telephone) and 29.3 percent on administrative tasks and travel and training.[85] Akansha Sidhwani, a Senior Product Manager at Sales Cloud noted in a Salesforce.com 360 blog in 2020 that "Sales reps spend 66 percent of time on non-selling activities," such as service, internal

---

85 https://www.accenture.com/t20150523t052741__w__/us-en/_acnmedia/accenture/
conversion-assets/dotcom/documents/global/pdf/strategy_4/accenture-top-five-
improvements-sales-effectiveness.pdf

282 | *Above Quota Performance*

meetings, and administrative tasks.[86] Your success in sales will be enhanced by increasing the time spent on selling activities and decreasing the non-selling activities, which is often difficult. But many of these can be handled outside of prime business time (before 9:00 a.m. and after 5:00 p.m.)

Time Is Money

Takeaway 53: Time Optimization Is Essential to Your Success in Sales.

Appreciate your limited time resources. You must be able to reach and exceed your sales quota within the approximately 260 working days in a year. That means that it is essential to maximize your *available selling time* (AST). Tasks such as preparing expense reports and sales forecasts can be done before 9:00 a.m. and after 5:00 p.m. leaving the available working time for contacting prospects and customers.

It is important to respect one's own time. Time is far too valuable to waste. It is also important that others understand that your time is an asset of yours that must be respected, the same as your property, whether it is your home, your car, or your watch. You own it and you should control it. If they take it without your consent, they are stealing an asset of yours. Sounds harsh, but it is not.

In my most recent sales position, I estimated that many sales pros spent at least 25 percent of their time handling customer issues—from correcting invoices and accounts receivable issues to updating delivery records. This is not unusual. These

---

86 _Akansha Sidhwani, "4 Cornerstones of Sales Productivity Every Leader Should Know," The 360 Blog from Salesforce, May 13, 2020, https://www.salesforce.com/blog/four-cornerstones-sales-productivity/.

tasks must be completed accurately to ensure client satisfaction, but who should be doing them? You, as a sales pro, or someone else who can manage existing accounts?

15 Tips

You can gain greater control of your time and become more productive with these fifteen ideas:

1. "To-Do" Lists – I prepare a to-do list at the end of each day or the beginning of the next. I then number the items in priority and attack the highest priority first. The list should also contain telephone numbers and email addresses, so that time is not wasted looking for them. The next day's to-do list should include incomplete items carried over from the previous day but should be re-prioritized daily.

2. Keep your socializing time to coffee breaks and lunch. I know that many of us like to socialize and discuss sports or politics with co-workers. This should be kept to a minimum during AST. Also, stay away from the office gossips. They can waste a lot of your time.

Takeaway 54: Dedicate Time for New Business Development Every Day.

3. Dedicate specific times each day or each week for prospecting new business, then prepare goals and measure your actual performance against them. Many sales pros will do almost anything to avoid making cold calls, so the only way to ensure that this is a priority is to set aside a specific time. Unless there is

an emergency, this time should be blocked off on your calendar and it should not be interrupted. This practice requires great self-discipline but is often the difference between a person that does not achieve their quota and another that exceeds it.

4. Do not waste time on non-sales-related, or non-urgent, client matters during AST. Try to offload as many of these as you can on the customer or sales support staff, or even on your manager. Billing problem? Have finance or accounting fix it. Your time is valuable, and you and your company want you to close sales. Postpone reading e-mails or calling friends, instant messaging, checking Facebook, and surfing the web until after hours. If you do any of these activities, you are stealing from your AST.

5. Keep good written notes, whether on a computer or in a manila folder. I am a habitual note-taker. It helps me save time when I need to go back and research contracts or meeting discussions.

6. Shorten internal meetings. Meetings are necessary in today's collaborative world. You often need to speak with several people about a certain topic or plan a client meeting. Establish rules that attendees cannot use their smart telephone to check emails or websites during internal meetings. Try to shorten each meeting by fifteen minutes.

7. Track your own time. Do this for one week and you will be amazed at the amount of AST that you waste. This will be a revelation and will help you work on prioritizing your tasks. Do this again about three months later—have you improved? Inspirational speaker Michael Altschuler has noted "The bad news is time flies. The good news is you're the pilot."[87]

8. Allocate most of your time to the highest probability revenue prospects, those in your Sweet Spot. It may be difficult to disengage from a buyer that is not likely to buy your product, but it is likely a waste of your valuable time. Constantly assess where you allocate your time, at least daily, if not throughout the day, and track how much time you invest in each prospect. Be the pilot of your time.

9. The first prospects that should be called are those in the "best few" of the funnel, as these can soon be closed.

10. Alacrity, or your promptness of response, is essential. Why wait when you can quickly respond today?

11. Measure your progress against the goals you have set—for the year, month, or day. Keep a log of the calls and the results. Did you make the fifteen cold calls that were your goal for today? How many people did you reach live? Did you leave messages? Which type of message did you leave so you can measure the effectiveness of each? Did you close the amount of business you said you would close this month or quarter? Has your pipeline reached the dollar amount that is necessary to reach your sales goal?

12. Keep a "clean" desk. This will force you to become better organized, or you will be spending a lot of time

---

87 "Michael Altshuler Quote," Quotation Celebration, March 23, 2019, https://quotationcelebration.wordpress.com/2019/03/22/the-bad-news-is-time-flies-the-good-news-is-youre-the-pilot-michael-altshuler-2/.

looking for items formerly left on top of your desk or workspace.

13. Learn to say no to people who interrupt you while you are working, especially those that want to waste your time with idle chit-chat during normal work hours. There is a line between being seen as a grouch for not engaging in these activities and letting people know that you are more than willing to speak with them during a coffee break, lunch, or before or after work.

14. Approach each day as if it were the first day (not the last day) of the last month of the sales year. It is that precious and requires you to treat it as such.

15. Do not spend time surfing on the internet during prime sales times. I know it is important to check your work and personal emails, including LinkedIn, Facebook, and others throughout the day, but limit the time spent doing this. It can be absorbing, and if you are not careful before you know it thirty to forty-five valuable minutes are gone. Perhaps set two or three times per day to check the personal items, and then verify your time spent by looking at the apps that track how you spend online and which apps you are utilizing.

"Time isn't the main thing. It's the only thing."[88]

—Jazz Artist Miles Davis

---

88 Karac Avalron, "'Time Isn't the Main Thing. It's the Only Thing." Miles Davis," A Gen X Point of View, July 15, 2019, https://thegenxpointofview.home.blog/2019/07/15/time-isnt-the-main-thing-its-the-only-thing-miles-davis/.

TWENTY-FOUR
Characteristics of High Performers

Identifying, hiring, training, and coaching the best sales pros can be the difference between being a successful sales manager and achieving revenue targets—or not. And it is difficult to find high performers. Indeed, it can be the most challenging role of the sales manager. The underperformers seem to move from company to company in search of a place where they can be successful. High-performing sales pros, always a minority in the company, close a disproportionate amount of business at their companies, sometimes over 50 percent of the total new business.

This example pie chart shows that the great majority (90 percent) of high performers (20 percent of the total), or 18 out of 100, are from the group of natural sales pros, versus only 8 percent (10 percent of the 80 percent), come from the trained group.

Performance

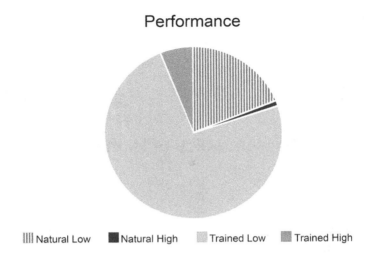

|||| Natural Low   ■ Natural High   Trained Low   Trained High

The sales pros who were not born with natural talent (80 percent of the total) have had to acquire many of the skills through hard work and training. These people are harder to identify in the hiring and interviewing process. They can also be successful because many are malleable. However, because they do not have the natural talent, they require a greater investment of time and resources from the sales manager. I have spent much of my time as a sales manager with this group and with the underperformers, trying to assist them to become successful sales pros.

Takeaway 55: Not Many Sales Caterpillars Become Sales Butterflies.

As previously noted, I have hired and trained over 1,000 sales pros throughout my career as a sales manager. Many were successes and many who I thought would succeed failed. A few of the highly successful sales pros who I hired, nurtured, or coached went on to become Vice Presidents of Sales or CEOs, and I am proud of any contribution that I made to their careers. I keep in contact with many of these people and cherish our friendships and the short amounts of time I can spend with them when I visit.

My colleague, Bill Hoffman, believes that most highly successful sales pros are structured and disciplined. They have a process and are disciplined to follow it consistently, and that leads to their success. Success is not an accident; it is the result of doing the right things most of the time. Bill notes that it does not come from "having a smile on your face" or "shine on your shoes."

High-Performance Traits

When I analyzed high-performing sales pros to determine common traits that would assist me in hiring, I found that they are different from each other, especially in selling styles but have some common personality traits, which I list below.

> ## Takeaway 56: High Performers Are Highly Focused, Have Specific Earnings Goals, and Understand What They Need to Do to Achieve Them.

In many cases, I just needed to stay out of the way of top-performers or do damage control for some of the issues they caused internally and externally by working outside some of the norms of the company—I called that "breaking glass."

Here is a more detailed explanation of thirty traits that are predictors of success that I look for when I hire sales pros:

1. High character and integrity: I do not want to have to worry about how they conduct themselves with potential clients or customers, on the telephone, in person, or meetings. Investor Warren Buffet cites intelligence, initiative, and integrity as the three traits he looks for when hiring new employees, with integrity being the most important. He defines integrity as being honest and having strong moral principles.[89]

2. Passion about their work and self-motivated: I want a person who loves their job, the product, and the company they are representing—a person with "fire in the belly." Or, as it was noted about Warren Buffet, "The reason he [Buffet] believes people are lucky when they find their passion, is because people who love what they do, end up doing that activity they love quite well."[90] He said that people should "take the job that he/she would take if they were independently wealthy."[91] I want people who enjoy getting up and going to work every day and not those that cannot wait until Friday afternoon or the next holiday. They need not be exuberant, but they should be generally happy people. These people are very determined and are self-motivated. I do not want malcontents or complainers.

3. Intelligent: All the high-performing sales pros I

89 Jon Miltimore, "The 3 Traits Warren Buffett Says He Looks for in an Employee," FEE Freeman Article (Foundation for Economic Education, March 14, 2022), https://fee.org/articles/the-3-traits-warren-buffett-says-he-looks-for-in-an-employee/?utm_source=email&utm_medium=email&utm_campaign=2020_FEEDaily.
90 The Strive Team, "Warren Buffett Advice on Success and Life," The STRIVE, November 22, 2021, https://thestrive.co/warren-buffett-advice-on-success/.
91 Ibid.

have hired have been intelligent individuals with exceptional cognitive abilities. They are naturally curious people who want to learn as much as they can. As a result, they ask a lot of questions. They discern and comprehend the buyer's needs and can "bridge the gap between the company and the customer, linking the product (or service) and its functions to the client's particular business environment and needs."[92] They provide *valuable* current insights on what is happening in the industry and how it may affect the buyer, both positively and negatively. This person can sort out the important from the unimportant and can offer options. The intelligent sales pro perceives the dynamics of what is happening throughout the sales process, especially when they sense changes in sales situations—and will react appropriately. They think quickly on their feet and have exceptional reasoning, planning, and problem-solving skills. They have excellent business acumen. An intelligent person is often self-aware.

4. Achievement: The high performer is driven to exceed his quota and earn President's Club recognition every year. It is a challenge that must be met consistently as a badge to show others that he is amongst the best in their company. It is how the company measures him versus the others and, more importantly, how he measures himself. He is embarrassed if he does not make this distinction of exceptionalism. He always knows how many more sales or dollars he needs to

---

92 Tom Sant, *The Giants of Sales: What Dale Carnegie, John Patterson, Elmer Wheeler, and Joe Girard Can Teach You About Real Sales Success* (New York, NY: AMACOM, 2006), 33.

close to achieve this goal, which remains his focus all year long.

High performers have a vision of what they want to accomplish, both short-term and long-term, and how to get there. Many write down their goals and post them on their wall. They "dream big" and are looking forward to their next big accomplishment, whether that is being the top sales pro in the company, a luxury vacation, or a new sports car.

Initial failure does not disqualify one for later success. Many top sales performers may have failed at some point but were able to recognize that they needed to make changes and corrected the behaviors that were causing them to fail.

5. Sales acumen or "sales intuition:" High performers have a complete understanding of the sales cycle. They read the sales situation, understand verbal and non-verbal communications, anticipate the prospect's actions, understand the company's politics, and react accordingly. They are instinctive "super-qualifiers" and determine the best prospects on which to focus and do not try to sell to low-probability prospects. They know how to add value to their solution to better position it against the competition. They sense whether they are winning the sale. They orchestrate the opportunity and know when they need to bring in other resources. Everything is under control and there are rarely surprises. They understand the art of closing the deal. They are adept at negotiations, which also may occur internally with sales and product management, legal, finance, and marketing staff, as

well as externally with the prospect. And importantly, they know when to walk away from a low probability or bad-fit opportunity.

6. Empathy: The best sales pros try to understand the customer's situation and relate to them. They empathize with their prospects and customers and want to provide value and help them resolve their problems. They will be an advocate for their customers to their company.

7. Emotional I.Q. (EQ): High-performing sales pros are attuned to their emotions and know how and when to express them both positively and negatively. They have an optimistic attitude, know how to harness their emotions positively, and they work well with others. They are humble and are not braggarts. They can take positive criticism from the sales manager or a peer and can explain to a pre-sales pro or consultant how they can do a better job next time they work together. I also believe that EQ includes having a positive, rather than negative, outlook on life. "Good talent with bad attitude equals bad talent."[93]

8. Self-Confidence: These sales pros believe they will close every opportunity. They are not self-conscious and do not worry about what others think about them. Many have large egos (yes, this "negative" can be positive, if they are not excessive.) Having a high ego also helps the sales pro deal with the normal rejection that is encountered from prospects without having it destroy their determination.

---

93 "Bill Walsh Quotes," Inspiring Quotes, accessed April 18, 2022, https://www.inspiringquotes.us/author/4152-bill-walsh.

9. Communication: I have found that success in selling is mostly about listening and responding accordingly. The best sales pros have outstanding verbal and listening skills that enable them to build rapport with their prospects throughout the sales cycle. They are articulate and can easily express their thoughts. It is impossible to be a poor communicator and an above-average sales pro. Good communication includes conveying your message or value proposition effectively, and listening skills, such as being adept at picking up on non-verbal communication. Some people do not listen because they are waiting for their turn to speak. Good communicators listen so that they can understand.

10. Persuasion: Outstanding sales pros can influence decision-makers and teams of people, though not in a negative manner, as I mentioned earlier. Persuasion includes communication and presentation skills, but also the ability to logically present the reasons or value propositions why the prospective customer should choose your solution to achieve positive outcomes. They can move others from their current ideas or to take action.

11. High energy: The late basketball star Kobe Bryant, known to begin practicing at 4:30 a.m. each day said "I can't relate to lazy people. We don't speak the same language. I don't understand you. I don't want to understand you."[94] Successful sales pros are hungry sales pros: They work nights, weekends, are

---

94 "Kobe Bryant Quotes," BrainyQuote (Xplore), accessed April 18, 2022, https://www.brainyquote.com/quotes/kobe_bryant_574691.

available while on vacation, and will do whatever it takes timewise to be successful. That is certainly how I conducted myself. But high energy and activity without results are meaningless.

12. Sense of urgency: Successful sales pros have a sense of urgency and will always want to get things done today rather than tomorrow or the next day. They are impatient, but not careless, and. understand that it is important to close the sale today rather than later, even though it may be for a lesser amount or lesser commission.

13. Trust builder: The successful sales pro must be able to build trust with several people at the buyers' company. Helping the buyer achieve their personal goals and providing solutions to the company shows that the sales pro puts their interests first. Building trust also requires integrity, credibility, and truthfulness. It takes time to build trust; it does not happen overnight, often taking several months or more. If the buyer does not trust a sales pro, it is unlikely they will purchase from them.

14. Problem identifiers and solvers: The best sales pros are solution oriented. They are perceptive and can identify and solve problems. Often that means thinking "outside of the box," or beyond what is normal. Mark Cuban, the billionaire entrepreneur, told Fox television's Chris Wallace in an interview that "Selling is not convincing. It is helping. Once you learn the value to customers, it is not convincing."[95]

---

95   Catherine Clifford, "Mark Cuban Reveals 3 Secrets for Growing a Successful Business," CNBC, February 9, 2018, https://www.cnbc.com/2018/02/09/mark-cuban-reveals-3-secrets-for-growing-a-successful-business.html.

15. Agile and adaptive: I look for sales pros who are agile, adaptive, and can "think on their feet." They can react and make astute decisions on the spot, especially when something changes, without panicking. These people have situational awareness—they are "tuned in," can go off the script, are highly adaptive, will not become flustered, and can "roll with the punches." They do not freeze when faced with adversity.

16. Creative: The best sales pros are resourceful and will find new and different uses of their product or application, often something that was not intended by the developer. They also find new ways to sell solutions. They will also find areas that are not currently addressed by the product or solution set and will propose new products, applications, or services. They will "push the envelope" and sometimes annoy the product development people because they want to invent new ways to use the solution. These often will lead to greater sales, even non-competitive sales, in the future. And happier customers.

17. Competitive: Do you love to win or hate to lose? Some sales managers want to hire sales pros who hate to lose. That seems negative to me. I think those people are looking through the wrong end of the telescope. It reminds me of coaches that try to tie a game rather than win it. I want the person that goes for the two points after a touchdown to win the game, or that shoots a three-pointer when down by two in the last second of a basketball game. My attitude is that "either I win, or they win." I want sales pros who are similar.

18. Coachable: Greek philosopher Epictetus said: "It is impossible to begin to learn that which one thinks one already knows."[96] I have found that the best sales pros are always coachable, and even when they are at the top, they welcome feedback, and they continually want to know what they could have done to be even better and do not feel threatened by positive criticism. The top performers have often had and keep mentors. I have found that some sales pros, even if they have been over-quota in the past, think they know everything and are unwilling to adapt when joining a new company or faced with new competition. Sadly, many of them fail at the new jobs.

19. Self-confidence: A person who has self-confidence, self-respect, and belief in their company and products will perform better than those that do not. High performers have pride in themselves but are not overconfident or arrogant. Since they have self-confidence, they are also humble. They are not burdened with doubts about their abilities but are not overly cocky. They are not braggarts and do not believe that others are beneath them. I do not want what some people call "gunslingers" who tend not to plan, are often careless, and over-confident to a fault.

20. Perseverance: I want somebody who does not give up, not unless it becomes a waste of time to continue. I am looking for a person that balances optimism with realism. Outstanding sales pros do not have much quit in them. They also have a healthy dose of impatience.

96 "Top 25 Quotes by Epictetus," AZ Quotes, accessed April 18, 2022, https://www. azquotes.com/author/4528-Epictetus.

I have often been accused, not without merit, of being too impatient. I also rarely give up on an opportunity, sometimes to a fault.

21. Enthusiasm: I want sales pros who are enthusiastic about themselves, their family, and the company they work for and its products or solutions. These people do not wake up every morning with a "dark cloud over their head," nor have a never-ending list of how the world is out to get them. Their enthusiasm does not have to be "over the top," but I want somebody who wants to go to work in the morning selling solutions for their employer. True enthusiasm will be noticed by the buyers. One of the greatest of all twentieth-century leaders was British Prime Minister Winston Churchill who noted that "Success consists of going from failure to failure without loss of enthusiasm."[97] This certainly applies to the vocation of sales.

22. Accountability: As a sales manager, I want sales pros who are accountable—to themselves, their spouse, the company that pays them a salary in addition to commissions, and especially to me. Accountable sales pros understand the commitments they make and follow through on them to the best of their ability. Top performers are responsible and reliable.

23. Desire to learn: The best sales pros always want to learn more. They are naturally curious. They are not "know-it-alls." They are inquisitive and want to learn more about their industry, their customers, the latest technology trends, even more about non-job-related

---

97 "Winston Churchill Quotes," BrainyQuote (Xplore), accessed April 18, 2022, https://www.brainyquote.com/quotes/winston_churchill_131188.

areas such as politics, history, culture, arts, and sciences. They are always asking questions and listening to the answers.

24. Domain expertise: The top sales pros have mastered their chosen market. They speak with credibility. They know the appropriate vernacular and technical language. They keep current on the latest developments, and they know a lot of key people in the industry. Understanding how the product features and functions will solve buyers' problems is essential. If the prospect does not sense that you know something that she does not, she will dismiss you as just another sales pro that does not bring any value.

25. Courage: I am looking for somebody who dares to ask the tough, hard questions, not just the easy ones. When qualifying a buyer, a successful sales pro asks the tough questions before moving on with the sales cycle. Courage also means that the high performer knows when an opportunity is not worth pursuing and can walk away from it. It also means asking for the prospect's business, at the appropriate time, rather than avoiding this conversation. This sales pro has the courage to say no when a buyer asks if your solution has a feature that is not included in the offering yet will explore reasons for the request and offer other solutions. It also shows courage when a sales pro says no to a request for something to be included in the contract that you know your legal department will never approve. It brings a big smile to my face when I see a sales pro say, "No, we cannot do that," and then explain why or seek an alternative solution. The sales

pro with courage can also handle a "fight or flight" situation and respond accordingly. I want the sales pro to be one that when confronted with a threatening situation decides to fight, rather than leave. They are adaptive to stress, perhaps even thrive with it.

26. Authentic: High performing sales pros are authentic. They are not like anybody else. They have their style and nuances that work for them, just like professional actors, singers, or musicians. Many flaunt their individuality, perhaps in the way they dress, wear makeup, walk, or which cars they choose to own. An authentic person is true to themselves; they do not try to be anybody else. They are comfortable with themselves and exude confidence. Authentic people have no problem building relationships because they are never trying to impress or be somebody they are not.

27. Exceptional basic sales skills: High performers demonstrate mastery of most of the sales attributes, such as prospecting/cold calling, questioning, presentation, building solutions that bring value to the prospect, follow-up and closing skills, as well as the intangibles. In many cases, these skills come naturally.

28. Navigates well through corporate politics: The highly competent sales pro understands that all corporations have different cultures, strategies, priorities, and rules of operation. This sales pro will know how to navigate the office politics, identify the sales roles, and act accordingly with each, in both the buyer's company and their own. They will also be adaptive to different

circumstances, such as the absence of a key person at a meeting or a change in decision criteria.

29. Consistency: Sales pros must understand that they must perform at a high level consistently, not once every three months or at year-end to achieve quota. They always try to close something each month, even if it is a small amount. Success also brings success. It changes your attitude and helps keep you focused on activities and results.

30. Independent: They like to work independently (like eagles), are sometimes iconoclasts, and often are not "team-players."

Takeaway 57: High Performers Have Dissimilar Selling Styles.

High performers do not have a singular, remarkable selling style that works for everybody. I have seen all kinds of styles work (and not work) and no two high-performing sales pros have the same style. Some are hard closers; some, like me, are not. I am more collaborative and rely on establishing strong relationships. Some people are very demonstrative; they like to use the whiteboard or flipchart a lot. Others are very consultative and are motivated by helping customers. Some like tell/sell. Others rely on strong persuasion skills and the ability to overcome every objection. Most people now sell solutions, not product features. Some people are all about technology and love to engage early adopters where they can chat for one half-hour using acronyms and discuss all the latest "bells and whistles." Others are more introverted, but still very effective.

The fact that different selling styles can work equally well is a realization that did not come easily to me. Early on I tried to "cookie-stamp" new hire sales pros to be like those that were most successful. It did not work, and it was frustrating both to the new sales pros and me. What works well for one person does not normally work well for another. The sales pros must be comfortable and will not be if they need to adopt a style not their own. It is on the sales manager to allow these differences.

Although some people consider sales pros to be "coin-operated," which can be viewed as a derogatory description, I do not consider W-2 earnings or commissions to be the primary motivator I am looking for, as that will happen naturally due to above-quota performance. It is more important that they have a record of sustained success and are not willing to lower their earnings expectations. Status, such as being "number one" or achieving President's Club (above-quota performance), is more important than actual earnings.

EPILOGUE
The Future for the Sales Profession

The days of sales pros getting by with "a smile and a shoeshine"[98] are long gone. And that is a good thing. Selling has become a highly valued skill. The future looks great.

In the movie "Rushmore," Bill Murray's character, Herman Blume, asks Jason Schwartzman's character, Max Fischer, what is the secret to life? Fischer responds, "The secret, I don't know—I guess you've just gotta find something you love to do and then—do it for the rest of your life."[99] For me, that was sales. Since you are reading this, perhaps it is yours. Welcome to an interesting and challenging career!

Fortunately, most enterprise sales organizations have come a long way from just providing new hires with a territory, a sales target or quota, a sales compensation plan, price list, laptop, sometimes a desk or workstation, and perhaps a few days of product training. Many companies did not offer formal sales training until the semi-annual or annual sales meeting. The mentality was "sink or swim." But this was costly to companies in turnover and lost sales opportunities, as well as destructive

---

98 Arthur Miller, *Death of a Salesman* (New York, NY: Penguin Books, 1949), 138.
99 "Rushmore (Film) Quotes," Poem of Quotes: Read, Write, Learn, accessed April 18, 2022, https://www.poemofquotes.com/quotes/film-tv/rushmore-film-quotes.

to the underperforming sales pros. Since the mid-2000s companies have devoted more resources to onboarding and training sales pros, which results in greater success for new hires.

Takeaway 58: Sales Enablement Tools Are Game Changers.

Many companies have recently started focusing on sales enablement to increase the productivity of their salesforces. This includes software, data, and processes that provide support to sales activities and training. The sales-enablement platforms were created to focus on helping sales pros become more productive, decrease the amount of elapsed time it takes a new sales pro to become effective, and increase the success rate of reaching their quarterly or annual quota, thus decreasing turnover. Each provides advanced content management, as well as tools for sales training, coaching, and communication. They are also easily accessible utilizing smartphones, tablets, and laptops.

Perhaps with the exceptions of the adoption of personal computers for business purposes and the implementation of SAP enterprise resource planning packages by manufacturers and pharmaceuticals, I have not seen such a strong movement toward a single solution in my lifetime.

There is no doubt that technology has had a significant impact on sales pros during the past twenty-five years. The old days of door-to-door Fuller brush, Avon goods, insurance sales pros, and characters like Willy Loman are gone. We should assume that technological changes will continue, or even accelerate, into the future, and that sales pros must continue to be adaptive, while also taking advantage of the productivity gains those new technologies bring. If the standard workweek shrinks to under twenty hours due to artificial intelligence and telecommuting as forecasted by Alibaba founder Jack Ma,[100] sales pros will need to adapt and meet their sales goals within that shorter workweek. This will make it more difficult to book meetings with buyers, as they will be at the office less than half of the time as is the case today.

As with most advances in technology, there are some downsides and unintended negative consequences, such as increased security steps necessary to prevent hacking, phishing, and viruses. Some social media applications have resulted in increased bullying. The unintended negative consequences of the increase in spending by corporations on sales enablement are the increased complexities that sales pros must deal with now. Sales pros need to become more proficient in additional applications and must continually utilize and update the data. Remember, automating a bad process just means that you will just be doing something bad faster than before the automation.

Gartner, Inc. has recommended that organizations decrease the burden on sales pros by driving "ruthless simplicity" to achieve a "world-class" sales organization. Gartner further recommends decreasing the "friction" on the sales pro and increasing the focus on finding tools that will aid the sales process. In other words, strip the requirements down to solve the essential objectives and endeavor to make it easier for sales pros to sell, rather than more difficult by adding complexity.[101] I believe simplicity is one key to achieving sales success.

During the past several years there has been an increase

---

100 "Jack Ma Says Forget Long Days, AI Could Bring 12-Hour Work Weeks," Bloomberg.com (Bloomberg, August 29, 2019), https://www.bloomberg.com/news/articles/2019-08-29/jack-ma-says-forget-long-days-ai-could-bring-12-hour-work-weeks.
101 Brent Adamson, "Traditional B2B Sales and Marketing Are Becoming Obsolete," Harvard Business Review, February 1, 2022, https://hbr.org/2022/02/traditional-b2b-sales-and-marketing-are-becoming-obsolete.

in the knowledge and sophistication of buyers, in which their access to more digital information from the internet has resulted in less interaction with the sellers, thus making the job of selling more difficult.

Takeaway 59: The COVID-19 Pandemic Has Changed B2B Selling Forever.

The coronavirus in 2020 – 2022 caused sales pros to sell virtually, at least for the first couple of contact meetings, and this is likely to be a permanent process in most cases. Sales pros are becoming more accustomed to holding meetings via Zoom or Skype. Prospects will still not want to let too many people in their offices. Sales pros now have less or no "face time" with the buyers. You must maximize your opportunity to speak via video rather than in-person, making selling more difficult. It is more important than ever to be highly organized, ensure that the proper attendees are included, prepare mutually agreed-upon agendas before all meetings with the prospect to assure that you cover all important concerns, and close all meetings with defined follow-ups and a commitment to the next meeting.

Supplier's CFOs have been looking at their P&L reports, and they like the huge reduction in selling and travel expenses. So accept that the B2B selling model has changed. It is not going back to how it was before the pandemic.

Another change is the buyer is much better informed and has more power in the sales process than before, as I described in Chapters 6 and 7. More people are now involved in the sales process on the buyer's side and determining who the person or persons are that make the buying decision is more difficult for the seller. At the same time, buyers seem to be less patient and often have difficulty determining which offer is the best fit for their needs and, as a result, along with the increased influence of the procurement function, are making more decisions based on price and not on value. As a result, sales pros are more challenged now to become more adept at shifting the buyer's inclination to purchase the lowest price without considering the value that each alternative can bring to their company. This tension will only become greater in the future. If sales pros cannot sway the buyer to do a more detailed evaluation, then more and more decisions will be made according to price reviews, thus decreasing the value of sales pros to organizations.

Takeaway 60: The Future Is Very Bright for the Career of Sales.

Nevertheless, I am very excited about the future for sales pros. In addition to being financially rewarding if you are successful, more and more small, medium, and large companies are recognizing the value of selling and are promoting sales pros to executive positions. Chief executive officers recognize the critical role that sales plays and, as a result, some line executives, such as vice presidents of operations and plant managers, as well as staff executives, such as controllers and customer support executives, have moved into sales to prepare themselves for higher-level positions.

I have been fortunate to work with diverse sales teams. Companies will benefit from having more and more women and minorities hired into sales positions because, in addition to their individual sales performances, salesforces will continue to be calling on more diverse buyers. My research indicates that businesses across the board, including accounting, finance, treasury, information technology, medical and legal areas, and others, are increasing the number of women and minorities in management positions, especially in technology companies.

I am convinced that there will continue to be significant breakthroughs in technology that will result in companies incorporating them in their products, or in developing new products, which leads to an expansion of markets—and an organic increase in sales opportunities. For example, the addition of smartphones has resulted in the incorporation of wireless and Bluetooth features into home heating and air conditioning, kitchen and laundry room appliances, and home security systems. You can now access the home thermostat remotely and adjust the temperature, and access the washer, dryer, and refrigerator (even the coffee maker and toaster) to turn them on and off. I recently installed a home security system that is completely wireless. I can see who is at my front door at my home by looking at my smartphone. I can also view a camera inside my home to see if an unauthorized person has entered my home. People can observe their children or pets throughout the day on their smartphones. With the imminent release of 5G wireless technology the possibilities are endless.

Perhaps the most disruptive and impactful technological changes will come as the result of ubiquitous artificial intelligence applications. Many of the easiest applications of artificial intelligence will be in machine learning, which will result in computers making decisions. One that is now being introduced to baseball is the electronic strike zone, which will reduce the number of errors by umpires. This is an example of how artificial intelligence will continue to transform the relationship between people and technology, requiring new skill sets in the future, from programming to monitoring computers.

Another emerging change that is likely to continue to have positive ramifications for sales shortly is blockchain technology. This technology of tracking time-stamped transactions on a shared, open ledger with complete transparency and authenticity, is revolutionary and has thousands of potential applications which can expect to be rolled out in the 2020s, from banking to medical to retail to insurance applications, including cryptocurrency, claims processing, medical records, passport validation, and real estate property records. The possibilities are endless. This will provide even greater potential value adds for sales pros to sell to corporations.

Albert Einstein, the famous scientist, once said "I never worry about the future. It comes soon enough."[102]

I have had a more than thirty-year, highly-rewarding, love affair with sales and hope that, as a result of reading this book and following my advice, you will, too.

---

102 "Memorable Albert Einstein Quotes," ASL Associates, accessed April 18, 2022, http://www.asl-associates.com/einsteinquotes.htm.

APPENDIX A
Takeaways

Takeaway 1: Closing Should Be a Natural Progression—If You Have Prepared For It

Takeaway 2: If You Are Winning You Should Be Receiving Continuous Feedback

Takeaway 3: Some Sales Advice Is Obsolete and May Be Harmful

Takeaway 4: Formal Sales Training Is Still Worthwhile

Takeaway 5: Objections Should Be Welcomed

Takeaway 6: Solutioning Should Never Be Interrupted!

Takeaway 7: People Buy From Sellers They Trust, Not Just the Ones They Like

Takeaway 8: The Economic Buyer Gives Final Approval to Purchase

Takeaway 9: User Buyers Cannot Approve the Purchase

Takeaway 10: Don't Challenge a Technical Buyer

Takeaway 11: Technical Buyers Cannot Approve a Purchase, But Can Impair It

Takeaway 12: The Coach Is the Key to Closing Your Sale

Takeaway 13: The Corporate Purchasing Process Is Not Linear

Takeaway 14: Educate or Be Educated

Takeaway 15: Sales Pros Need to Be Proactive

Takeaway 16: Discover the Real "Why" That Drives the Purchase Decision

Takeaway 17: Know the Difference Between Want and Need

Takeaway 18: The Real Competitor Is Not Who You Think It Is

Takeaway 19: Know Your Products Before Worrying About Your Competitors' Weaknesses

Takeaway 20: Deals Stall for Many Reasons, Mostly Because They Were Not Qualified or Lacked Executive Sponsorship

Takeaway 21: Your Value Proposition Must be Strong and Quantifiable.

Takeaway 22: The Validity of the Value Proposition Is Determined By the Buyer, Not the Seller.

Takeaway 23: There Is No Standard Price List With Value-Based Selling

Takeaway 24: Sum of Your Pipeline Goal = At least Three Times Your Annual Target

Takeaway 25: Five Ways to Increase Sales Revenue: Develop More Leads, Increase the Average Sales Price, Change the Quality of Leads; Improve the Win Percent; Hire More Sales Pros.

Takeaway 26: The Sweet Spot is the Best Place to Prospect

Takeaway 27: The Prospect's Annual Report Contains Strategic Information

Takeaway 28: Your Prospecting Objective Is to Get the NEXT Call, Not a Sale!

Takeaway 29: There Is a Reverse Relationship Between Authority and Accessibility

Takeaway 30: LinkedIn.com is the "Secret Sauce" That Will Help You Develop Leads

Takeaway 31: Join and Participate in LinkedIn.com Groups

Takeaway 32: Do Not Make Sales Pitches on LinkedIn.com

Takeaway 33: LinkedIn.com Is a Terrific, Easily Utilized Networking Tool for Business Development.

Takeaway 34: When Asking Questions Be Sure to Listen to—and Understand—the Answers

Takeaway 35: The Objective of the Meeting Is Simply to Secure the Next Meeting.

Takeaway 36: Never Pitch to a Prospect in Your First Meeting.

Takeaway 37: An Interesting Agenda Is Key to the Success of the Meeting.

Takeaway 38: Use the "So what?" Test When Evaluating PowerPoint Slides.

Takeaway 39: Avoid Multiple Presentations by Different Vendors on the Same Day.

Takeaway 40: The Prospect Should Speak More than 50 Percent of the Time.

Takeaway 41: Advantages of Leaving Some of the Prospect's Questions Unanswered.

Takeaway 42: Avoid "Death by PowerPoint" Presentations.

Takeaway 43: Your presentation should "Excite or Disturb."

Takeaway 44: Your Presentation Needs a "Hook" to Stand Out.

Takeaway 45: Stories Are Always More Memorable than Reciting Facts.

Takeaway 46: Price Is Only Important If You Do Not Differentiate Your Solution.

Takeaway 47: Do Not Offer Multiple Solutions and Expect the Prospect to Choose.

Takeaway 48: The Greatest Interest in Purchasing Is the Day They Decide to Buy.

Takeaway 49: Elapsed Time Is Your Enemy if You Are Winning, Your Ally if You Are Losing.

Takeaway 50: You Need Additional Information to Decide Whether to Respond to the RFP.

Takeaway 51: Not Knowing the RFP Is Being Issued Is a "Red Flag."

Takeaway 52: The Wording in Your Response Must Be Carefully Prepared.

Takeaway 53: Time Optimization Is Essential to Your Success in Sales.

Takeaway 54: Dedicate Time for New Business Development Every Day.

Takeaway 55: Not Many Sales Caterpillars Become Sales Butterflies.

Takeaway 56: High Performers Are Highly Focused, Have Specific Earnings Goals, and Understand What They Need to Do to Achieve Them.

Takeaway 57: High Performers Have Dissimilar Selling Styles.

Takeaway 58: Sales Enablement Tools Are Game Changers.

Takeaway 59: The COVID-19 Pandemic Has Changed B2B Selling Forever.

Takeaway 60: The Future Is Very Bright for the Career of Sales.

APPENDIX B
Bonus Tips

In Chapter 4, I advised that a lot of what your sales trainer told you was incorrect or out of date. The well-meaning, but outdated, advice often resulted in lost or stalled competitive sales. Below are additional tips and techniques that helped me become a highly successful sales pro. Most are not normally taught by sales trainers or sales managers. I guarantee that many of these valuable tips will help you increase your sales success this year.

1. Think of your sales territory as a "franchise." In other words, it's your business to manage. In a typical franchise arrangement, the franchisor supplies the brand, products, training, operations manual, geographical territory, advertising, commercial standards, and support. The franchisee must procure their customers, staffing, facilities, and equipment. You sell products developed or sourced by a company that provides similar supplemental support as a franchise, including marketing, territory, pricing, salaries, commissions, benefits, and legal assistance. By treating

your territory as a franchise, you will naturally try to optimize your time, revenue, and minimize expenses.

2. Sales is not about the "bells and whistles." Emphasize simplicity in presenting your product or solution, making it less complex and more understandable. Do not try to dazzle your prospect with superfluous facts and statistics. Think about the last time you made a large purchase, such as a refrigerator or a washer and dryer. Did you prefer the sales pro to bring out a lengthy list of all the product specifications and features and have her recite them to you for ten minutes, or did you want the sales pro to listen to your needs and then recommend one or two alternative solutions and explain why it was the best fit?

3. Always clarify terminology that could be misinterpreted with the buyer. Minimize the usage of non-industry acronyms. The meaning of a term to you and to the buyer is often completely different and could result in your removal from consideration.

4. Try the "The Trojan horse" approach to penetrate a new account—or one that is currently working with a competitor. It can also be referred to as "land and expand." If you are having difficulty selling a larger solution to the prospect, propose an easier, smaller solution, and then after the customer becomes satisfied with your company, upsell them with a more costly solution. Or offer a proof of concept (PofC) to demonstrate the viability of your solution.

5. Try to provide a "total solution" to the buyer, even beyond the solutions that your company may provide. That increases your company's value to the prospect—and also may help keep out competition. If your company cannot provide the solution, I suggest that you find other companies that may be willing to work on providing the total solution. For example, let's assume that your buyer is looking for a total solution that includes an inventory control application. But your company does not provide one (or perhaps maybe yours is not a good fit for the customer). Then do the research and find a reputable one that is technically compatible with your offerings. Even if the other company is unwilling to work with you, it may still be wise to recommend them, as an alternative, to your buyer.

6. Build relationships with non-competitive business and integration partners. Partnerships work well when both sides benefit economically and by expanding their markets. There needs to be a synergistic relationship where both sides' benefit is greater than if there were no cooperation. If not, there will be little incentive to increase business with the other. Some of these companies, such as SAP, Microsoft, and Oracle have built ecosystems of cooperating partners that have greatly benefited all parties. They have also recognized that they cannot provide all the solutions to their customers, but if they manage a franchise-type arrangement with partners, they can increase their

value to buyers. During my career I closed hundreds of thousands of dollars of sales because our company was recommended by an integration partner.

7. The use of handwritten, cursive, personalized thank-you notes is not out of style and will never go out of style. Who does not enjoy receiving one? Emails are acceptable, but not the best choice.

8. A mistake that some sales pros make is to not show interest in the buyer's products, processes, or production facilities. Often the buyer will invite you to go on a tour of their plant. I have never declined this opportunity and have learned a lot about the company's business and processes by doing so. Be proactive: When visiting a company, ask for a tour of their facilities. You will learn a lot about the company, which will always be helpful as you build your sales strategy. Indeed, I have often observed some areas that might help me in working on the value proposition. For example, there might be opportunities to reduce inventories or decrease production hours.

If you decline to go on the tour, you are sending the message "I am only here to make a sales presentation or attend a meeting. I am not interested in learning more about your company or your processes, and I do not want to waste time on a tour of your plant." Does that sound like the best way to impress the buyer that you are interested in them and want to help them solve problems? Many sales pros are in a hurry to return to the airport and sit and wait for their flight, or to go to Starbucks or lunch. If you have prepared well for the meeting, you have invested hours of your time.

The time for the meeting has come and either before or after the meeting the customer has invited you to tour their plant, of which they are proud, and some sales pros stupidly decline this opportunity.

9. I make it a practice to visit with other customers when I am in the area to meet with a prospect. For example, if I am traveling to Atlanta, I will contact my customers in the area, such as Coca-Cola, and invite my contacts out to lunch and dinner (or even baseball, hockey, or basketball games) the day before or after my scheduled sales meeting. The purpose is to reinforce the message that our company values them as customers and to listen to any concerns or ideas that they might have. I recommend that you take advantage of meeting with customers face to face whenever possible.

10. Sometimes it is necessary to give bad news, such as that we cannot meet the delivery date that was previously quoted, that we cannot honor last year's price, or that the feature that we thought was going to be in the next release has not been included. Sales pros need to be forthright and deliver these messages to prospects. Some sales pros ruin relationships with prospects because they were reluctant to discuss negative news with the buyer. They avoided the difficult conversation. Eventually, the customer found out and was upset. I believe that this news needs to be delivered as quickly as practicable and preferably in person with an apology. Always be honest and forthright.

11. Be aware of corporate internal, intercompany, or interdivisional politics and how they may affect your sale opportunity. When I called on the Coca-Cola Foods Division, I assumed that our existing business with Coca-Cola corporate would give us an advantage. It was exactly the opposite. I was told by the project leader that they would not select any supplier that corporate chose just because they wanted to assert their independence and their dislike of corporate.

APPENDIX C
Acronyms

A.I. = Artificial Intelligence

AST = Available Selling Time

BANT = (IBM term) Budget, Authority, Need, Timeline

Block Chain Technology = an unchangeable digital ledger which is managed by a decentralized network and the entire transaction history is recorded.

Breaking Glass = working outside some of the company's norms

B2B = Business to Business

CEO = Chief Executive Officer

CFO = Chief Financial Officer

CRM = Customer Relationship Management System

CSR = Company's Social Responsibility

Enterprise Sales = selling to medium to large companies

EPA = Environmental Protection Agency

EQ = Emotional Quotient (attuned to their emotions and expresses them appropriately)

FOMO = Fear of Missing Out

FUD = Fear, Uncertainty, Doubt

GSA = Government Services Administration

Hard Dollars = easier to quantify relative to profitability & goals

HQD = High Quality Deal

KPI = Key Performance Indicators

LI = LinkedIn.com

MBOs = Management By Objectives

OEM = Original Equipment Manufacturer

P & L = Profit and Loss

POC = Proof of Concept (or PoC): when solution performs to buyer's expectations

RFP = Request for Proposals (sometimes called RFT)

RFT = Request for Tender (sometimes used by governments instead of RFP)

ROI = Return on Investment (also known as VBP)

SaaS = Software as a Service

SEO = Search Engine Optimization

SMART (lead campaign) = Specific, Measurable, Achievable, Realistic, & Time Bound

Soft Dollars = indirect costs that are difficult to measure. They are usually tied to efficiencies.

VBP = Value Based Pricing (also known as ROI)

White Horse Charger = person(s) in company most enthusiastic about your product

YE = Year End

APPENDIX D
Sales/Discovery Checklist
©STEVEWEINBERGSALES

Prospect Name _____

Date _____

Sales Pro _____

I. Pre-call Preparation

a. Thoroughly research the prospect (internet, annual report, SEC 10-K report, D&B, Hoovers, LinkedIn.com).

b. Prepare your list of questions (*customize* for each prospect).

c. If videoconference, be sure to test ahead of time.

d. This assumes you have already qualified the prospect.

e. Reminder: The objective of the call is to gather information to be used later, not to provide a sales pitch—no matter how tempting.

II. Call Opening

a. Thank them for attending the meeting and taking their time today.

    b. Mention your common interests, links, and any prior experience with the company.

    c. Your introduction (your background and role).

    d. Ask them to introduce themselves and state their functions/role in eval.

    e. Explain why you are doing this—what are the benefits to them?

    f. Why have you invited me in today? What is the urgency, if any?

    g. Reach agreement on time expectations for the meeting today.

III. Basic Questions/Probes (examples)

    a. What do you expect to get out of today's meeting?

    b. Tell me about your company (what business are you in? your products, how is it organized? Are there divisions, subsidiaries, centralized versus decentralized? Which organization are you under?)

    c. What are some of your company's key core strategies this year? (Ex. Green energy, entering new markets, diversity, lowering costs, acquisitions, etc.)

    d. What are some of the most important business issues your company is currently facing? (Competition, new markets, unprofitable divisions, merger)

    e. What is your company's target or vertical market? How many customers do you have? Who are some of your most important customers?

    f. Who are your primary competitors? What is your competitive advantage?

    g. Is there anything else that you would like me to know about your company?

    h. Can you tell me about your roles and responsibilities?

IV. **Advanced Questions/Probes** (move from broad to specific areas, examples)

    a. What are the biggest challenges your company or team is currently facing? (1-3)

    b. How are you addressing those challenges now?

    c. What is your current process for_____? (One area you are probing.)

    d. How is the current process working?

    e. What problems does it cause? How severe is it? What are the costs? Who resolves these problems? Why hasn't it already been resolved?

    f. What other areas does it affect or complicate?

    g. When did you first decide to look at alternatives? Which are you currently considering? Where are you in your decision process?

    h. What do you see as the pros and cons of each alternative? (Or What do you like or dislike about each?) What do you see as the ideal solution?

    i. If you made a change, what would be the first thing that you would do?

    j. What do you see as "roadblocks," "bottlenecks" or obstacles in the current process? What are your obstacles to change?

    k. When do you hope to have a solution in place?

    l. Who is the executive responsible for this area?

    m. Do you have any customer satisfaction issues that would be helpful for me to know about? Do you have any supply-chain issues?

    n. Could you give me some background on the decision-making process?

    o. What happened the last time you/your company made a major change? Was it successful or unsuccessful?

    p. What is the consequence if you do not make a change now or sometime this year?

    q. How do you think we might be able to help you?

V. Sum Up Your Learnings/Takeaways (brief)

    – (example)

    a. "As a result of the call today I have learned that your company is interested in exploring global markets, improving the efficiency of your supply chain, and improving diversity hiring in 2022. Also, I have learned that you are researching solutions that will help you speed-up your monthly accounting closing and financial statements cycle."

VI. Close/Define the Next Steps

    a. Thank them for their confidence in you and your company.

    b. What is the next step?

    c. Schedule it—get their agreement and select date and time.

    d. Should we have a "signing ceremony"?

    e. Can we compose a joint press release?

LEAD QUALIFICATION CHECKLIST
©STEVEWEINBERGSALES

Prospect Name _____

Date _____

Sales Pro _____

RATE EACH ON A SCALE OF 1-5, WITH 5 BEING THE HIGHEST

Pre-call Preparation

a. Thoroughly research the prospect (internet, annual report, SEC 10-K report, D&B, Hoovers, LinkedIn.com).

b. Prepare your list of questions (*customize* for each prospect).

c. If for a videoconference, be sure to test ahead of time.

d. This assumes you have already qualified the prospect.

e. Reminder: The objective of the call is to gather information to be used later, not to provide a sales pitch. (No matter how tempting).

Call Opening

a. Thank them for taking the meeting and their time today.

b. Mention your common interests, links, any prior experience with the company.

c. Your introduction (your background and role).

d. Ask them to introduce themselves and state their functions/role in eval.

e. Explain why you are doing this—what are the benefits to them?

f. Why have you invited me in today? What is the urgency, if any?

g. Reach agreement on time expectations for the meeting today.

Basic Questions/Probes (examples)

a. What do you expect to get out of today's meeting?

b. Tell me about your company (what business are you in? your products, how is it organized? Are there divisions, subsidiaries, centralized versus decentralized? Which organization are you under?)

c. What are some of your company's key core strategies this year? (Ex. Green energy, entering new markets, diversity, lowering costs, acquisitions, etc.)

d. What are some of the most important business issues your company is currently facing? (Competition, new markets, unprofitable divisions, merger.)

e. What is your company's target or vertical market? How many customers do you have? Who are some of your most important customers?

   f. Who are your primary competitors? What is your competitive advantage?

   g. Is there anything else that you would like me to know about your company?

   h. Can you tell me about your roles and responsibilities?

Advanced Questions/Probes (move from broad to specific areas, examples)

   a. What are the biggest challenges your company or team is currently facing? (1-3)

   b. How are you addressing those challenges now?

   c. What is your current process for_____? (One area you are probing.)

   d. How is the current process working?

   e. What problems does it cause? How severe is it? What are the costs? Who resolves these problems? Why hasn't it already been resolved?

   f. What other areas does it affect or complicate?

   g. When did you first decide to look at alternatives? Which are you currently considering? Where are you in your decision process?

   h. What do you see as the pros and cons of each alternative? (Or What do you like or dislike about each?) What do you see as the ideal solution?

   i. If you made a change, what would be the first thing that you would do?

   j. What do you see as "roadblocks," "bottlenecks" or obstacles in the current process? What are the obstacles to change?

   k. When do you hope to have a solution in place?

   l. Who is the executive responsible for this area?

m. Do you have any customer satisfaction issues that would be helpful for me to know about? Supply-chain issues?

n. Could you give me some background on the decision-making process?

o. What happened the last time you/your company made a major change? Was it successful or unsuccessful?

p. What is the consequence if you do not make a change now or sometime this year?

q. How do you think we might be able to help you?

Sum Up Your Learnings/Takeaways (brief) – (example)

a. "As a result of the call today I have learned that your company is interested in exploring global markets, improving the efficiency of your supply chain, and improving diversity hiring in 2022. Also, I have learned that you are researching solutions that will help you speed-up your monthly accounting closing and financial statements cycle."

Close/Define the Next Steps

a. Thank again for their time.

b. What is the next step?

c. Schedule it: get their agreement and select date and time.

Works Cited

"37 LinkedIn Statistics You Need to Know In 2021." Social Media Marketing & Management Dashboard. Accessed April 18, 2022. https://blog. hootsuite.com/linkedin-statistics-business/.

"55+ Linkedin Statistics." 99firms, May 27, 2021. https://99firms.com/blog/ linkedin-statistics/.

"Abraham Lincoln Quote." QuoteNova.net. Accessed April 18, 2022. https:// www.quotenova.net/authors/abraham-lincoln/dxvaaq.

Adams, Susan. "Why Public Speaking Scares You and How to Overcome Your Fear." Forbes. Forbes Magazine, May 7, 2012. https://www. forbes.com/sites/susanadams/2012/03/07/why-public-speaking-scares-you-and-how-to-overcome-your-fears/#3a5854792c86.

Adamson, Brent. "Traditional B2B Sales and Marketing Are Becoming Obsolete." Harvard Business Review, February 1, 2022. https://hbr. org/2022/02/traditional-b2b-sales-and-marketing-are-becoming-obsolete.

"Albert Einstein Quotes." BrainyQuote. Accessed April 18, 2022. https:// www.brainyquote.com/quotes/albert_einstein_103652.

"Aldo Gucci Quote." Quotefancy. Accessed April 18, 2022. https://quotefancy. com/quote/1574585/Aldo-Gucci-The-bitterness-of-poor-quality-is-remembered-long-after-the-sweetness-of-low.

"American Indian Proverb, Hopi Quotes." Quotation.io. Accessed April 18, 2022. https://quotation.io/page/quote/one-tells-stories-rules-world.

"Apple Watch Series 6." Apple.com. Accessed April 18, 2022. https://www. apple.com/apple-watch-series-6/.

Aslam, Salman. "81 LinkedIn Statistics You Need to Know in 2022." Omnicore, April 15, 2022. https://www.omnicoreagency.com/linkedin-statistics/.

Avalron, Karac. "'Time Isn't the Main Thing. It's the Only Thing." Miles Davis." A Gen X Point of View, July 15, 2019. https://thegenxpointofview.home.blog/2019/07/15/time-isnt-the-main-thing-its-the-only-thing-miles-davis/.

"Bant Opportunity Identification Criteria." IBM. Accessed April 18, 2022. https://www-2000.ibm.com/partnerworld/flashmovies/html_bp_013113/html_bp_013113/bant_opportunity_identification_criteria.html.

Barnes, Hank. "94% = Enterprise Buying Teams That Have Abandoned a Buying Effort With No Decision (in the Past 2 Years)." Gartner, September 20, 2016. https://blogs.gartner.com/hank-barnes/2016/09/20/94-enterprise-buying-teams-that-have-abandoned-a-buying-effort-with-no-decision-in-the-past-2-years/.

Barnes, Hank. "The Cost of No Decisions May Be Greater Than We Think." Gartner, July 30, 2019. https://blogs.gartner.com/hank-barnes/2019/07/30/cost-no-decisions-may-greater-think/.

Belosic, Jim. "21 Insightful Quotes About the Power of Good Customer Service." Inc.com. Inc., June 26, 2015. https://www.inc.com/jim-belosic/21-insightful-quotes-that-link-customer-service-to-profit.html.

Bettger, Frank. *How I Raised Myself from Failure To Success In Selling*. New York, NY: Fireside, 1992.

"Bill Walsh Quotes." Inspiring Quotes. Accessed April 18, 2022. https://www.inspiringquotes.us/author/4152-bill-walsh.

Blount, Jeb. *Sales EQ: How Ultra High Performers Leverage Sales-Specific Emotional Intelligence to Close the Complex Deal*. Hoboken, NJ: Wiley, 2017.

Bova, Tiffani. "26 Sales Statistics That Prove Selling Is Changing." The 360 Blog from Salesforce, January 25, 2019. https://www.salesforce.com/blog/2017/11/15-sales-statistics.html.

Callahan, Sean. "22 Sales Quotes to Inspire You to Make 2022 Your Best Year Yet." LinkedIn, January 3, 2022. https://www.linkedin.com/business/sales/blog/modern-selling/sales-quotes-to-inspire-you-2022.

Cameron, Cody. "Closing Technique of the Week: The Ben Franklin Close." Medium. The Startup, September 19, 2018. https://medium.com/swlh/closing-technique-of-the-week-the-ben-franklin-close-2bda69c87b6.

"Carl W. Buehner Quotes." BrainyQuote. Xplore. Accessed April 18, 2022. https://www.brainyquote.com/quotes/carl_w_buehner_392897.

Carnegie, Dale. *How to Win Friends and Influence People*. Reviseded. New York, NY: Simon & Schuster, 1981.

Cespedes, Frank V. *Sales Management That Works: How to Sell in a World That Never Stops Changing*. Boston, MA: Harvard Business Review Press, 2021.

"Cherokee Proverb." Education Project Management, March 9, 2005. https://educationprojects.blogs.it.umich.edu/post/79068639172/listen-to-the-whispers-and-you-wont-have-to-hear.

Clifford, Catherine. "Mark Cuban Reveals 3 Secrets for Growing a Successful Business." CNBC, February 9, 2018. https://www.cnbc.com/2018/02/09/mark-cuban-reveals-3-secrets-for-growing-a-successful-business.html.

CSO Insights. "2016 Sales Performance Optimization Study." MHI Global, 2016. http://www.critical-moments.com/wp-content/uploads/2016/05/2016-Sales-Performance-Optimization-Study-Key.pdf.

Daly, Donal. "Why Understanding the '57%' Buying Process Will Help You Sell Better." Business 2 Community, July 5, 2014. https://www.business2community.com/sales-management/understanding-57-buying-process-will-help-sell-better-0935491.

Dudek, Matt. Lecture. *Gartner Research Webinar*. Presented at the Gartner Research Webinar, November 13, 2019.

Freese, Thomas A. *Secrets of Question-Based Selling: How the Most Powerful Tool in Business Can Double Your Sales Results*. Naperville, IL: Sourcebooks, 2013.

Gallo, Carmine. "Warren Buffett Was 'Terrified' of Public Speaking and Took 3 Steps to Conquer His Fear." Inc.com. Inc., February 27, 2018. https://www.inc.com/carmine-gallo/3-steps-to-overcome-stage-fright-that-worked-for-warren-buffett.html.

Gartner, Inc. "The Who, What, How and Why of Sales Enablement." Gartner, Inc., August 28, 2018. https://www.gartner.com/en/articles/the-who-what-how-and-why-of-sales-enablement.

Glenn Croston. "The Thing We Fear More Than Death." Psychology Today. Sussex Publishers, November 29, 2012. https://www.psychologytoday.com/us/blog/the-real-story-risk/201211/the-thing-we-fear-more-death.

Halabi, Sami. "Dear Salesperson: It's Not Me, It's You." Blogs.oracle.com, January 14, 2019. https://blogs.oracle.com/cx/post/dear-salesperson-its-not-me-its-you.

Hallquist, Chris. "According to Dale Carnegie, You Can't Win an Argument— and He Has a Point." LessWrong, November 29, 2013. https://www. lesswrong.com/posts/HxWdXMqoQtjDhhNGA/according-to-dale- carnegie-you-can-t-win-an-argument-and-he.

Hatami, Homayoun, Isabel Huber, Vinay Murthy, and Candace Lun Plotkin. "Sales Incentives That Boost Growth." McKinsey & Company. McKinsey & Company, October 19, 2018. https://www.mckinsey.com/ business-functions/marketing-and-sales/our-insights/sales-incentives- that-boost-growth#.

Irwin, Dave. "Curiosity Saves the Sales Executive." Daily Herald, March 19, 2022. https://www.dailyherald.com/business/20220320/curiosity- saves-the-sales-executive.

"Jack Ma Says Forget Long Days, AI Could Bring 12-Hour Work Weeks." Bloomberg.com. Bloomberg, August 29, 2019. https://www. bloomberg.com/news/articles/2019-08-29/jack-ma-says-forget-long- days-ai-could-bring-12-hour-work-weeks.

"Job Openings and Labor Turnover." Bureau of Labor Statistics. US Department of Labor, March 29, 2022. https://www.bls.gov/news. release/pdf/jolts.pdf.

"Kobe Bryant Quotes." BrainyQuote. Xplore. Accessed April 18, 2022. https:// www.brainyquote.com/quotes/kobe_bryant_574691.

MacDonald, William. "What's the Number One Reason Salespeople Miss Quota?" Pleinaire Strategies. Accessed April 25, 2022. https:// pleinairestrategies.com/2016/01/whats-the-number-one-reason- salespe ople-miss-quota/#:~:text=A%20whopping%2045.4%20 percent%20of,enough%20revenue %20to%20meet%20quota.

Mack, Dan. "19-In-20 People Don't Remember Your Presentation." Drug Store News, January 6, 2022. https://drugstorenews.com/news/1-0- people-dont-remember-your-presentation.

Malcolm, Jack. "How Much of Your Presentation Will They Remember?" Jackmalcolm.com. Accessed April 18, 2022. http://jackmalcolm. com/2012/08/how-much-of-your-presentation-will-they-remember/.

Markman, Art. "Getting an Audience to Remember Your Presentation." Harvard Business Review, September 21, 2015. https://hbr. org/2015/09/getting-an-audience-to-remember-your-presentation.

Martin, Strother. "Cool Hand Luke - Failure to Communicate." Genius. Accessed April 18, 2022. https://genius.com/strother-martin-cool- hand-luke-failure-to-communicate-annotated.

McSpadden, Kevin. "Science: You Now Have a Shorter Attention Span Than a Goldfish." Time, May 14, 2015. https://time.com/3858309/attention-spans-goldfish.

"Memorable Albert Einstein Quotes." ASL Associates. Accessed April 18, 2022. http://www.asl-associates.com/einsteinquotes.htm.

"Michael Altshuler Quote." Quotation Celebration, March 23, 2019. https://quotationcelebration.wordpress.com/2019/03/22/the-bad-news-is-time-flies-the-good-news-is-youre-the-pilot-michael-altshuler-2/.

Miller, Arthur. Death of a Salesman. New York, NY: Penguin Books, 1949.

Miller, Robert B., Stephen E. Heiman, and Tad Tuleja. The New Strategic Selling: The Unique Sales System Proven Successful by the World's Best Companies. New York, NY: Grand Central Publishing, 2005.

Miltimore, Jon. "The 3 Traits Warren Buffett Says He Looks for in an Employee." FEE Freeman Article. Foundation for Economic Education, March 14, 2022. https://fee.org/articles/the-3-traits-warren-buffett-says-he-looks-for-in-an-employee/?utm_source=email&utm_medium=email&utm_campaign=2020_FEEDaily.

Musk, Elon. "Elon Musk Quotes." Goodreads. Goodreads. Accessed April 18, 2022. https://www.goodreads.com/author/quotes/7221234.Elon_Musk.

"The New B2B Buying Process." Gartner. Accessed April 18, 2022. https://www.gartner.com/en/sales/insights/b2b-buying-journey.

"No One Wants a Drill. What They Want Is the Hole." Quote Investigator, March 23, 2019. https://quoteinvestigator.com/2019/03/23/drill/.

Pink, Daniel H. To Sell Is Human: The Surprising Truth About Moving Others. New York, NY: Riverhead Books, 2012.

Protocol 80. "The Ultimate Buyer Persona Guide (for Beginners)." HubSpot. Accessed April 24, 2022. https://cdn2.hubspot.net/hubfs/1547213/ContentOfferFiles/Ultimate_Buyer_Persona_Guide_For_Beginners_by_protocol_80.pdf?t=1459517429021.

Rassulov, Rufat. "These Steve Jobs' Principles Will Change Your Approach to Marketing." Publicist Marketing and Communications Network. Accessed April 24, 2022. https://www.publicist.co/the-spin/the-inside-scoop/these-steve-jobs-principles-will-change-your-approach-to-marketing#:~:text=%E2%80%9CWe%20don't%20stand%20a,to%20sell%20emotions%2C%20not%20features.

"Remembering Names." Remembering Names | Dale Carnegie. Accessed April 18, 2022. https://www.dalecarnegie.com/en/courses-v2/3741.

"Robert Louis Stevenson Quote." Treasure Quotes. Accessed April 24, 2022. https://www.treasurequotes.com/quotes/everyone-lives-by-selling-something.

"Rushmore (Film) Quotes." Poem of Quotes: Read, Write, Learn. Accessed April 18, 2022. https://www.poemofquotes.com/quotes/film-tv/rushmore-film-quotes.

Sandler, David H., and John Hayes. *You Can't Teach a Kid to Ride a Bike at a Seminar: The Sandler Sales Institute's 7-Step System for Successful Selling.* Pegasus Media World, 1996.

Sant, Tom. *The Giants of Sales: What Dale Carnegie, John Patterson, Elmer Wheeler, and Joe Girard Can Teach You About Real Sales Success.* New York, NY: AMACOM, 2006.

Sidhwani, Akansha. "4 Cornerstones of Sales Productivity Every Leader Should Know." The 360 Blog from Salesforce, May 13, 2020. https://www.salesforce.com/blog/four-cornerstones-sales-productivity/.

Snyder, Benjamin. "7 Insights from Legendary Investor Warren Buffett." CNBC. CNBC, May 1, 2017. https://www.cnbc.com/2017/05/01/7-insights-from-legendary-investor-warren-buffett.html.

"Steve Jobs Quotes." Goodreads. Goodreads. Accessed April 18, 2022. https://www.goodreads.com/quotes/420161-details-matter-it-s-worth-waiting-to-get-it-right.

The Strive Team. "Warren Buffett Advice on Success and Life." The STRIVE, November 22, 2021. https://thestrive.co/warren-buffett-advice-on-success/.

Thomas, Patrick. "The Pay Is High and Jobs Are Plentiful, but Few Want to Go into Sales." The Wall Street Journal. Dow Jones & Company, July 14, 2021. https://www.wsj.com/articles/the-pay-is-high-and-jobs-are-plentiful-but-few-want-to-go-into-sales-11626255001.

"Top 25 Quotes by Epictetus." AZ Quotes. Accessed April 18, 2022. https://www.azquotes.com/author/4528-Epictetus.

van Camp, Brenda. "Lessons From Volkswagen: Branding Is Not Just A Marketing Tool, Trust Matters, And The Possibility Of Combining Profit And The Common Good." LinkedIn. LinkedIn, September 27, 2015. https://www.linkedin.com/pulse/lessons-from-volkswagen-branding-just-marketing-tool-trust-van-camp/.

"Viewing Your Profile Level Meter." Viewing Your Profile Level Meter | LinkedIn Help. LinkedIn. Accessed April 18, 2022. https://www.linkedin.com/help/linkedin/answer/391/viewing-your-profile-strength-meter?lang=en.

"Voltaire Quotes." Goodreads. Accessed April 18, 2022. https://www. goodreads.com/author/quotes/5754446.Voltaire.

Weinberg, Steve. B. Hoffman Personal Conversation. Personal, January 4, 2021.

"What Is Death by Powerpoint?" WhatIs.com. TechTarget, August 28, 2013. https://www.techtarget.com/whatis/definition/death-by-PowerPoint.

"Winston Churchill Quotes." BrainyQuote. Xplore. Accessed April 18, 2022. https://www.brainyquote.com/quotes/winston_churchill_131188.

"Yogi Berra Quotes." BrainyQuote. Xplore. Accessed April 18, 2022. https:// www.brainyquote.com/quotes/yogi_berra_110034.

Zigler, Zig. *Zigler on Selling*. Nashville, TN: Thomas Nelson, 1991.

"'Where's The Beef?' w/ Clara Peller - 1984 Wendy's Commercial #1." YouTube. Accessed April 19, 2022. https://www.youtube.com/ watch?v=eANcbFSPHyA.

ACKNOWLEDGMENTS

Many people have contributed to this manuscript, but most especially my wife, Phyllis. My children Genevieve and Joel encouraged me to move forward with my dream of transferring the knowledge gained from my years of experience to paper with the objective of helping more sales pros become successful.

Special mention also goes to my publisher Maryann Karinch of Armin Lear Press and Kimberly Peticolas, my amazing agent. I am also grateful to my online marketing and publicist Fauzia Burke of FSB Associates, Meredith Wisniewski and Monica Monroe who built my website and assisted in marketing, and Schuyler Michael and Jennifer Greene, who assisted with the graphics.

I also wish to thank many former colleagues with whom I consulted while writing this book: Bill Hoffman, Hugh Jones, Mark Cavendar of the Chasm Institute, Jay Ryan, Tom Markert, and Rick Nichols. I consulted with many subject matter experts, including Frank Cespedes, Anthony Iannarino, Warren Weiss, Tom Sant, Sarah Monroe, Joe Arrigo, Tony Alessandra, Lee Sundholm, and Chad Coe.

Thanks also to Frank Dodge, the late Jim McCormack, Tammy Davis Hammortree, James Pugh, Ralph Babusci, Laurie Rosen, Tom Potter, John Hunnicutt, Mike Dockery, Regina Brandys, and Tom Krawczyk for being there for me when I needed it most.

ABOUT THE AUTHOR

Steve Weinberg has spent most of his life selling and helping others sell better, sell faster, and sell more. He is an expert at building, guiding, and sustaining high performing sales teams, and creating exemplary standards in account management. He has over three decades of leadership experience in sales, including Vice Presidencies at Dun & Bradstreet Software, AC Nielsen, Solcorp (then part of EDS, now HP), McCormack & Dodge, Deloitte and Touche, and most recently as Director of Sales at Accuity (– now Lexis Nexis Risk Solutions.) Steve was also the President of Cyborg Systems, which was acquired by Hewitt Associates (now Aon) in 2003.

In his last assignment Steve had the difficult role of managing a team of salespeople as well as carrying his own quota. While in this role Steve led the salesforce in sales achievement and closed the largest sale in the company's history.

Steve earned a B.A. in Economics / Business Administration from North Park University, and an MBA from Loyola University of Chicago. He is also a CPA and has experience in accounting, consulting, and as a graduate-level Economics instructor. He is married and has two adult children.

CPSIA information can be obtained
at www.ICGtesting.com
Printed in the USA
LVHW110028011022
729705LV00001B/34

9 781956 450279